2016 SQA Past Papers With Answers

National 5
HISTORY

2014, 2015 & 2016 Exams

National 5 HISTORY

HODDER GIBSON
AN HACHETTE UK COMPANY

This book contains the official SQA 2014, 2015 and 2016 Exams for National 5 History, with associated SQA-approved answers modified from the official marking instructions that accompany the paper.

In addition the book contains study skills advice. This has been specially commissioned by Hodder Gibson, and has been written by experienced senior teachers and examiners in line with the new National 5 syllabus and assessment outlines. This is not SQA material but has been devised to provide further guidance for National 5 examinations.

Hodder Gibson is grateful to the copyright holders, as credited on the final page of the Answer Section, for permission to use their material. Every effort has been made to trace the copyright holders and to obtain their permission for the use of copyright material. Hodder Gibson will be happy to receive information allowing us to rectify any error or omission in future editions.

Hachette UK's policy is to use papers that are natural, renewable and recyclable products and made from wood grown in sustainable forests. The logging and manufacturing processes are expected to conform to the environmental regulations of the country of origin.

Orders: please contact Bookpoint Ltd, 130 Park Drive, Milton Park, Abingdon, Oxon OX14 4SE. Telephone: (44) 01235 827720. Fax: (44) 01235 400454. Lines are open 9.00–5.00, Monday to Saturday, with a 24-hour message answering service. Visit our website at www.hoddereducation.co.uk. Hodder Gibson can be contacted direct on: Tel: 0141 333 4650; Fax: 0141 404 8188; email: hoddergibson@hodder.co.uk

This collection first published in 2016 by
Hodder Gibson, an imprint of Hodder Education,
An Hachette UK Company
211 St Vincent Street
Glasgow G2 5QY

Typeset by Aptara, Inc.

Printed in the UK

A catalogue record for this title is available from the British Library

ISBN: 978-1-4718-9114-4

3 2 1

2017 2016

Introduction

Study Skills – what you need to know to pass exams!

Pause for thought

Many students might skip quickly through a page like this. After all, we all know how to revise. Do you really though?

Think about this:

"IF YOU ALWAYS DO WHAT YOU ALWAYS DO, YOU WILL ALWAYS GET WHAT YOU HAVE ALWAYS GOT."

Do you like the grades you get? Do you want to do better? If you get full marks in your assessment, then that's great! Change nothing! This section is just to help you get that little bit better than you already are.

There are two main parts to the advice on offer here. The first part highlights fairly obvious things but which are also very important. The second part makes suggestions about revision that you might not have thought about but which WILL help you.

Part 1

DOH! It's so obvious but …

Start revising in good time

Don't leave it until the last minute – this will make you panic.

Make a revision timetable that sets out work time AND play time.

Sleep and eat!

Obvious really, and very helpful. Avoid arguments or stressful things too – even games that wind you up. You need to be fit, awake and focused!

Know your place!

Make sure you know exactly **WHEN and WHERE** your exams are.

Know your enemy!

Make sure you know what to expect in the exam.

How is the paper structured?

How much time is there for each question?

What types of question are involved?

Which topics seem to come up time and time again?

Which topics are your strongest and which are your weakest?

Are all topics compulsory or are there choices?

Learn by DOING!

There is no substitute for past papers and practice papers – they are simply essential! Tackling this collection of papers and answers is exactly the right thing to be doing as your exams approach.

Part 2

People learn in different ways. Some like low light, some bright. Some like early morning, some like evening / night. Some prefer warm, some prefer cold. But everyone uses their BRAIN and the brain works when it is active. Passive learning – sitting gazing at notes – is the most INEFFICIENT way to learn anything. Below you will find tips and ideas for making your revision more effective and maybe even more enjoyable. What follows gets your brain active, and active learning works!

Activity 1 – Stop and review

Step 1

When you have done no more than 5 minutes of revision reading STOP!

Step 2

Write a heading in your own words which sums up the topic you have been revising.

Step 3

Write a summary of what you have revised in no more than two sentences. Don't fool yourself by saying, "I know it, but I cannot put it into words". That just means you don't know it well enough. If you cannot write your summary, revise that section again, knowing that you must write a summary at the end of it. Many of you will have notebooks full of blue/black ink writing. Many of the pages will not be especially attractive or memorable so try to liven them up a bit with colour as you are reviewing and rewriting. **This is a great memory aid, and memory is the most important thing.**

Activity 2 – Use technology!

Why should everything be written down? Have you thought about "mental" maps, diagrams, cartoons and colour to help you learn? And rather than write down notes, why not record your revision material?

What about having a text message revision session with friends? Keep in touch with them to find out how and what they are revising and share ideas and questions.

Why not make a video diary where you tell the camera what you are doing, what you think you have learned and what you still have to do? No one has to see or hear it, but the process of having to organise your thoughts in a formal way to explain something is a very important learning practice.

Be sure to make use of electronic files. You could begin to summarise your class notes. Your typing might be slow, but it will get faster and the typed notes will be easier to read than the scribbles in your class notes. Try to add different fonts and colours to make your work stand out. You can easily Google relevant pictures, cartoons and diagrams which you can copy and paste to make your work more attractive and **MEMORABLE**.

Activity 3 – This is it. Do this and you will know lots!

Step 1

In this task you must be very honest with yourself! Find the SQA syllabus for your subject (www.sqa.org.uk). Look at how it is broken down into main topics called MANDATORY knowledge. That means stuff you MUST know.

Step 2

BEFORE you do ANY revision on this topic, write a list of everything that you already know about the subject. It might be quite a long list but you only need to write it once. It shows you all the information that is already in your long-term memory so you know what parts you do not need to revise!

Step 3

Pick a chapter or section from your book or revision notes. Choose a fairly large section or a whole chapter to get the most out of this activity.

With a buddy, use Skype, Facetime, Twitter or any other communication you have, to play the game "If this is the answer, what is the question?". For example, if you are revising Geography and the answer you provide is "meander", your buddy would have to make up a question like "What is the word that describes a feature of a river where it flows slowly and bends often from side to side?".

Make up 10 "answers" based on the content of the chapter or section you are using. Give this to your buddy to solve while you solve theirs.

Step 4

Construct a wordsearch of at least 10 × 10 squares. You can make it as big as you like but keep it realistic. Work together with a group of friends. Many apps allow you to make wordsearch puzzles online. The words and phrases can go in any direction and phrases can be split. Your puzzle must only contain facts linked to the topic you are revising. Your task is to find 10 bits of information to hide in your puzzle, but you must not repeat information that you used in Step 3. DO NOT show where the words are. Fill up empty squares with random letters. Remember to keep a note of where your answers are hidden but do not show your friends. When you have a complete puzzle, exchange it with a friend to solve each other's puzzle.

Step 5

Now make up 10 questions (not "answers" this time) based on the same chapter used in the previous two tasks. Again, you must find NEW information that you have not yet used. Now it's getting hard to find that new information! Again, give your questions to a friend to answer.

Step 6

As you have been doing the puzzles, your brain has been actively searching for new information. Now write a NEW LIST that contains only the new information you have discovered when doing the puzzles. Your new list is the one to look at repeatedly for short bursts over the next few days. Try to remember more and more of it without looking at it. After a few days, you should be able to add words from your second list to your first list as you increase the information in your long-term memory.

FINALLY! Be inspired...

Make a list of different revision ideas and beside each one write **THINGS I HAVE** tried, **THINGS I WILL** try and **THINGS I MIGHT** try. Don't be scared of trying something new.

And remember – "FAIL TO PREPARE AND PREPARE TO FAIL!"

National 5 History

The course requirements

The Assignment – how to be successful

The Assignment is an essay written under exam conditions and then sent to the SQA to be marked.

The Assignment counts for 20 marks out of a total of 80 so doing well in it can provide you with a very useful launch pad for future success.

How long does my essay have to be?

There are NO word limits in the Assignment – it is whatever you can write in one hour!

What should I write about?

First, it makes sense to choose a question from the syllabus you are studying, which you can check at: www.sqa.org.uk/sqa/47447.html.

Second, your essay title should be based on a question that allows you to use your evidence to answer the question. You must avoid titles that are just statements such as "The Slave Trade" or "Appeasement". They do not allow you to use information to provide an overall answer to your title question.

Finally, try NOT to make up questions that are too complicated or that ask two questions within the same title.

What is the Resource Sheet?

Your Resource Sheet provides a framework and notes for your essay.

It shows the marker

- that you have researched, selected and organised your information
- that you have thought about your work and reached a decision about the question in your title
- which sources you have used and demonstrates how you have used them.

Your Resource Sheet MUST be sent to the SQA with your finished essay.

Your Resource Sheet should NOT be just a collection of facts, figures and quotes. It should outline the main parts of your essay and remind you what to write. Remember that this has a limit of 200 words.

The Exam Paper

The question paper is made up of three **sections**:

Section 1 – Historical Study: Scottish
Section 2 – Historical Study: British
Section 3 – Historical Study: European and World.

In each **section** you will select **one** part to answer questions on:

Section 1: Historical Study: Scottish

Part A: The Wars of Independence, 1286–1328 ✓
Part B: Mary Queen of Scots and the Scottish Reformation, 1542–1587 ✓
Part C: The Treaty of Union, 1689–1715 ✓
Part D: Migration and Empire, 1830–1939 ✓
Part E: The Era of the Great War, 1910–1928 ✓
      (NB - from 2016 exam onwards, 1900–1928)

Section 2: Historical Study: British

Part A: The Creation of the Medieval Kingdoms, 1066–1406
Part B: War of the Three Kingdoms, 1603–1651
Part C: The Atlantic Slave Trade, 1770–1807 ✓
Part D: Changing Britain, 1760–1914 ✓
Part E: The Making of Modern Britain, 1880–1951 ✓

Section 3: Historical Study: European and World

Part A: The Cross and the Crescent, the Crusades, 1071–1192
Part B: 'Tea and Freedom': the American Revolution, 1774–83 ✓
Part C: USA 1850–1880 ✓
Part D: Hitler and Nazi Germany, 1919–1939 ✓
Part E: Red Flag: Lenin and the Russian Revolution, 1894–1921 ✓
Part F: Mussolini and Fascist Italy, 1919–1939
Part G: Free at Last? Civil Rights in the USA, 1918–1968 ✓
Part H: Appeasement and the Road to War, 1918–1939 ✓
Part I: World War II, 1939–1945 ✓
Part J: The Cold War 1945–1989 ✓

The titles with the tick after them are all included in the model papers.

Answering the Exam Questions

The first rule is simple and is the most important thing that will get you marks:

Answer the question that you are asked, NOT what you would like it to ask.

The Exam paper has 6 types of questions.

TYPE 1 – the **"Describe"** question, worth **5 marks**.

In this type of question you must describe what happened by using five or six pieces of your own knowledge, known as **recall**. There is no source to help you with information so your answer will be based on your own recall.

TYPE 2 – the **"Explain"** question, worth **5 or 6 marks**.

To be successful with this type of question you must give 5 or 6 reasons why something happened. Once again, there is no source to help you. Use recall that is correct and accurate.

(**Note:** question types 3, 4 and 5 are very similar in nature, but remember to pay close attention to the wording of the question – and make sure you answer it!)

TYPE 3 – the **"To what extent…"** question, worth **8 marks**.

To be successful with this type of question you must write a balanced answer. That means you must decide how important a particular factor was in explaining why something happened. Include at least five pieces of relevant information and give a short conclusion which sums up your answer to the question, including a reason to support your conclusion.

TYPE 4 – the **"how successful"** question, worth **8 marks**.

To be successful with this type of question you must write a balanced answer. That means you must decide how successful a particular factor was in explaining why something happened. Include at least five pieces of relevant information and give a short conclusion which sums up your answer to the question, including a reason to support your conclusion.

TYPE 5 – the **"how important"** question, worth **8 marks**.

To be successful with this type of question you must write a balanced answer. That means you must decide how important a particular factor was in explaining why something happened. Include at least five pieces of relevant information and give a short conclusion which sums up your answer to the question, including a reason to support your conclusion.

TYPE 6 – the **"Evaluate the usefulness…"** question, worth **5 or 6 marks**. This question will ask "Evaluate the usefulness of a source as evidence of …."

Evaluate means **to judge** how good a source is as evidence for finding out about something. The short answer is that it will always be partly useful but it will never be entirely useful in giving all the information you need.

In this type of question it is never enough just to **describe** what is in a source. It might be helpful to base your answer around the following guide questions.

WHO produced the source? Why is the AUTHORSHIP of the source relevant and therefore useful in assessing the value of a source?

WHEN was the source produced and how might that help in the evaluation of the source?

WHAT'S NOT THERE? What important information is missing from the source that makes you think the source was not as useful as it could be?

TYPE 7 – the **"Compare"** question, worth **4 marks**

You will always get one question that asks you to compare two sources in your exam. To be successful with this type of question you must make clear connections between sources but do not just describe the two sources.

These questions are easy to spot because they are the only ones that will refer to TWO sources. For this type of question you must say whether you think the sources agree or not and then support your decision by making two comparisons using evidence from the sources.

TYPE 8 – the **"How fully…"** question, worth **5 or 6 marks**.

To be successful with this type of question you must select information from the source which is relevant to the question – usually there will be three points of information in the source for you to use. Use recall that is accurate and relevant to make your answer more balanced. You will never get a source that gives the full story so it is up to you to say that the source PARTLY explains or describes something but there is more information needed to give the full story. That's where you show off your recalled extra knowledge.

Good luck!

Remember that the rewards for passing National 5 History are well worth it! Your pass will help you get the future you want for yourself. In the exam, be confident in your own ability. If you're not sure how to answer a question, trust your instincts and just give it a go anyway. Keep calm and don't panic! GOOD LUCK!

NATIONAL 5

2014

National
Qualifications
2014

X737/75/01

History

WEDNESDAY, 7 MAY

9:00 AM – 10:30 AM

Total marks — 60

SECTION 1 — SCOTTISH CONTEXTS — 20 marks

Attempt ONE part.

SECTION 2 — BRITISH CONTEXTS — 20 marks

Attempt ONE part.

SECTION 3 — EUROPEAN AND WORLD CONTEXTS — 20 marks

Attempt ONE part.

Write your answers clearly in the answer booklet provided. In the answer booklet, you must clearly identify the question number you are attempting.

Use **blue** or **black** ink.

Before leaving the examination room you must give your answer booklet to the Invigilator; if you do not, you may lose all the marks for this paper.

SECTION 1 — SCOTTISH CONTEXTS

PARTS

SECTION 2 — BRITISH CONTEXTS

PARTS

SECTION 3 — EUROPEAN AND WORLD CONTEXTS

PARTS

SECTION 1 — SCOTTISH CONTEXTS — 20 marks

MARKS

Part A — The Wars of Independence, 1286–1328

Attempt the following questions using recalled knowledge and information from the sources where appropriate.

1. Explain the reasons why Edward I was able to become involved in Scottish affairs between 1286 and 1292.

5

2. Describe what happened at the Battle of Stirling Bridge in 1297.

5

Source A is from the chronicle of Walter of Guisborough, written in 1306.

Source A

> Robert the Bruce wanted to be king of Scotland but feared Lord John Comyn would stop him. He lured him to a meeting in Greyfriars Church in Dumfries to deal with business concerning them both. Comyn suspected nothing and they greeted each other in a friendly way. Suddenly Bruce accused Comyn of telling lies about him to the king of England. He struck him with his sword and marched out.

3. Evaluate the usefulness of **Source A** as evidence of Bruce's actions in 1306.

   (You may want to comment on who wrote it, when they wrote it, why they wrote it, what they say or what has been missed out.)

5

Source B describes how Bruce established himself as king of an independent Scotland.

Source B

> After Bannockburn, Bruce's parliament agreed that Scots nobles who had not made peace with him would lose their lands in Scotland. Bruce gave this forfeited land to his own supporters. The Douglases benefited greatly from this. Scots nobles would no longer be allowed to have English estates so their loyalties would not be divided. Bruce also backed his brother's campaign in Ireland to continue to challenge English rule. He continued to raid the north of England to put pressure on Edward to recognise him as king of an independent nation.

4. How fully does **Source B** describe how Bruce established himself as king of an independent Scotland after the Battle of Bannockburn? (Use **Source B** and recall.)

5

[Now go to SECTION 2 starting on *Page eight*]

SECTION 1 — SCOTTISH CONTEXTS — 20 marks

Part B — Mary Queen of Scots and the Scottish Reformation, 1542–1587

Attempt the following questions using recalled knowledge and information from the sources where appropriate.

1. Describe the events which led Mary, Queen of Scots, to move to France in 1548.

    5

Source A is about the growth of Protestantism in Scotland.

Source A

> The Protestant form of worship meant that people could participate much more in services. The Bible was available in English, not Latin; therefore people who could not read Latin could still understand it. Only churchmen and a few others could understand Latin. A conflict between Catholics and Protestants was developing in Scotland for various reasons. Some people began to criticise the Catholic Church because of its great wealth. Local priests were resented for charging people for christening their children. This was a ceremony people would not dare go without.

2. How fully does **Source A** explain the reasons for the growth in the Protestant religion in Scotland? (Use **Source A** and recall.)

    5

Source B is from a sermon written in the 1560s by John Knox.

Source B

> In 1563 there was a great famine in Scotland. But in the north of the country, where Mary had travelled before harvest time, the famine was hardest with great suffering. Many people died. Thus did God punish the many sins of our wicked Queen and her followers. The excessive celebrations and huge feasts in the palace and in the country provoked God into this action.

3. Evaluate the usefulness of **Source B** as evidence of Protestant attitudes towards Mary, Queen of Scots, during her reign in Scotland.

    5

    (You may want to comment on who wrote it, when they wrote it, why they wrote it, what they say or what has been missed out.)

4. Explain the reasons why Riccio became unpopular with Darnley and the Scottish nobles.

    5

[Now go to SECTION 2 starting on *Page eight*]

SECTION 1 — SCOTTISH CONTEXTS — 20 marks

MARKS

Part C — The Treaty of Union, 1689–1715

Attempt the following questions using recalled knowledge and information from the sources where appropriate.

1. Describe the worsening relations between Scotland and England between 1689 and 1705.

5

Source A is from a leaflet written by Andrew Fletcher in 1706.

Source A

> Let me explain my opposition to Union. Scotland needs to keep its own separate law and church. They cannot be governed and supported by a Parliament in London. If the Scots agree to these interests being controlled by a single Parliament they will surrender control to the English. The Scots deserve no pity if they surrender their interests to a Parliament where the English will have a vast majority.

2. Evaluate the usefulness of **Source A** as evidence of the arguments used by Scots against the Union.

   (You may want to comment on who wrote it, when they wrote it, why they wrote it, what they say or what has been missed out.)

5

Source B is about the Treaty of Union.

Source B

> I could give you some account of the many advantages we will obtain by a union with England. By this union we will all have access to all the advantages of trade that the English enjoy at the moment. We will be able to improve our wealth which will be for the benefit of the whole island. We will have our liberty, our property and our religion secured. Scotland will be under the protection of one sovereign and one Parliament of Great Britain.

3. How fully does **Source B** explain the arguments used by Scots in favour of the Union? (Use **Source B** and recall.)

5

4. Explain the reasons why many Scots participated in the Jacobite rebellion of 1715.

5

[Now go to SECTION 2 starting on *Page eight*]

SECTION 1 — SCOTTISH CONTEXTS — 20 marks

Part D — Migration and Empire, 1830–1939

Attempt the following questions using recalled knowledge and information from the sources where appropriate.

1. Explain the reasons why many Scots resented immigrants between 1830 and 1939.

    5

2. Describe the assistance given to Scots to help them to emigrate to the Empire.

    5

Source A describes the career of a Scots emigrant to Australia in the 19th century.

Source A

> Alexander Spark left Elgin for lack of local opportunities. With a good education and some inherited money he applied for a land grant in Australia. He settled in Sydney. Within three years he was a leading member of the business community, prominent in banking and by 1840 owned £40,000 of land. He became the local agent for a variety of companies including shipping, banks and the Australian Gas company. Scottish Agents in Australia handled the interests of many Scots who invested money in Australian businesses without ever leaving Scotland.

3. How fully does **Source A** describe the contribution of Scots to their new countries? (Use **Source A** and recall.)

    5

Source B is from a memoir by Mary Contini, about her Italian grandparents who emigrated to Scotland in the early 20th century.

Source B

> When my grandparents visited other Italian families, invariably the conversation turned to the price of potatoes. The price they paid was important because so many of them made their living selling fish and chips. The unfamiliar ideas of banks and debt worried them and made them work even harder. Their shops were open long hours and the whole family helped serve customers. This helped their shops become the focus of social life in many communities.

4. Evaluate the usefulness of **Source B** as evidence of the ways immigrants fitted in to Scottish society.

    5

    (You may want to comment on who wrote it, when they wrote it, why they wrote it, what they say or what has been missed out.)

[Now go to SECTION 2 starting on *Page eight*]

SECTION 1 — SCOTTISH CONTEXTS — 20 marks   MARKS

Part E — The Era of the Great War, 1910–1928

Attempt the following questions using recalled knowledge and information from the sources where appropriate.

1. Describe the use of new technology on the Western Front.   5

Source A is from the memoirs of David Lloyd George who was in charge of the Ministry of Munitions in 1915.

Source A

> The courage of the women engaged in these factories has never been sufficiently recognised. They had to work under conditions of real danger to life. What some of them probably dreaded more was horrible disfigurement — for one of the risks of the shell filling factories was toxic jaundice resulting from TNT poisoning. The poor girls were nicknamed "canaries". They were quite proud of this. They had earned it in the path of duty.

2. Evaluate the usefulness of Source A as evidence of the impact of the Great War on Scottish women.   5

   (You may want to comment on who wrote it, when they wrote it, why they wrote it, what they say or what has been missed out.)

Source B is about the treatment of conscientious objectors.

Source B

> Men who refused to enlist in the army had to face military discipline. Some were sentenced to death for refusing orders although the sentence was always reduced if the "conchie" still refused to give in. Many refused non-combatant duty on the grounds that it simply released another man to kill. Special prisons and work camps were opened up in addition to ordinary prisons to which many objectors were sent. Twenty-four objectors died while detained at these work camps.

3. How fully does Source B describe how conscientious objectors were treated during the Great War? (Use Source B and recall.)   5

4. Explain the reasons why heavy industry declined in Scotland after the Great War.   5

[Now go to SECTION 2 starting on Page eight]

SECTION 2 — BRITISH CONTEXTS — 20 marks

Part A — The Creation of the Medieval Kingdoms, 1066–1406

Attempt the following questions using recalled knowledge and information from the sources where appropriate.

1. To what extent was William I's leadership the main reason why the Normans won the Battle of Hastings?

    8

    (You must use recalled knowledge to present a **balanced account** of the influence of different factors and come to a **reasoned conclusion**.)

Source A is from a chronicle written by a royal clerk in 1174.

Source A

> Whilst Henry was dealing with problems elsewhere in his kingdom, the king of Scotland, William the Lion, rebelled and attacked Northumberland. William's army committed terrible crimes wherever they went. Women and children were slaughtered and priests murdered inside their own churches. Next William travelled to Carlisle. His army besieged the castle and, by cutting off their supplies, forced the English to make a treaty with the Scots.

2. Evaluate the usefulness of **Source A** as evidence of the rebellions faced by Henry II during his reign.

    6

    (You may want to comment on who wrote it, when they wrote it, why they wrote it, what they say or what has been missed out.)

3. Explain the reasons why there was a Peasants Revolt in 1381.

    6

[Now go to SECTION 3 starting on *Page thirteen*]

SECTION 2 — BRITISH CONTEXTS — 20 marks

Part B — War of the Three Kingdoms, 1603–1651

Attempt the following questions using recalled knowledge and information from the sources where appropriate.

1. To what extent were arguments between King James VI and I and Parliament the result of religious differences?

    (You must use recalled knowledge to present a **balanced account** of the influence of different factors and come to a **reasoned conclusion**.)

    8

2. Explain the reasons why Charles I was an unpopular monarch by 1640.

    6

Source A is from a letter dated 17 September 1649, written by Oliver Cromwell to the House of Commons.

Source A

> Our army came to Drogheda on 3rd September. On Monday 9th the battering guns began. I sent Sir Arthur Aston a request to surrender the town but received no satisfactory answer. Our guns then beat down the corner tower, and made gaps in the east and south walls. On the following day, after some fierce fighting, we entered the town. Several of the enemy, including Sir Arthur Aston, retreated into Mill Mount, a place very difficult to attack.

3. Evaluate the usefulness of **Source A** as evidence of what happened at Drogheda in Ireland during the Civil War.

    (You may want to comment on who wrote it, when they wrote it, why they wrote it, what they say or what has been missed out.)

    6

[Now go to SECTION 3 starting on *Page thirteen*]

SECTION 2 — BRITISH CONTEXTS — 20 marks

MARKS

Part C — The Atlantic Slave Trade, 1770–1807

Attempt the following questions using recalled knowledge and information from the sources where appropriate.

1. To what extent was the success of the abolitionist campaigns due to the work of campaigners such as Thomas Clarkson?

   (You must use recalled knowledge to present a **balanced account** of the influence of different factors and come to a **reasoned conclusion**.)

   8

2. Explain the reasons why many people in Britain continued to support the slave trade.

   6

Source A is from *Black Peoples of the Americas*, a book written by an historian in 1995.

Source A

> The planters in the Caribbean were afraid of a rebellion and they followed a policy of control through fear. Slaves had no rights. They were seen as possessions rather than human beings. Owners could deal with slaves exactly as they pleased and there was no punishment for owners who worked their slaves to death. Until the nineteenth century, no-one questioned owners burning or torturing their slaves.

3. Evaluate the usefulness of **Source A** as evidence of the treatment of slaves on the plantations.

   6

   (You may want to comment on who wrote it, when they wrote it, why they wrote it, what they say or what has been missed out.)

[Now go to SECTION 3 starting on *Page thirteen*]

SECTION 2 — BRITISH CONTEXTS — 20 marks

MARKS

Part D — Changing Britain, 1760–1900

Attempt the following questions using recalled knowledge and information from the sources where appropriate.

Source A is from a report on housing in Manchester, written by a doctor in 1832.

Source A

> The houses that the mill workers live in are poorly ventilated and do not have toilets. The streets are narrow, unpaved and worn into deep ruts. These ruts become the common resting place of mud, refuse and disgusting rubbish. In Parliament Street there is only one toilet for 380 inhabitants. The flow of muck from this toilet infests close-by houses and must be a source of disease.

1. Evaluate the usefulness of **Source A** as evidence of housing conditions in British cities in the nineteenth century.

   (You may want to comment on who wrote it, when they wrote it, why they wrote it, what they say or what has been missed out.)

   6

2. To what extent was new technology the main reason for improvements in coal mining by 1900?

   (You must use recalled knowledge to present a **balanced account** of the influence of different factors and come to a **reasoned conclusion**.)

   8

3. Explain the reasons why there was a decline in the use of canals after the 1840s.

   6

[Now go to SECTION 3 starting on *Page thirteen*]

SECTION 2 — BRITISH CONTEXTS — 20 marks

MARKS

Part E — The Making of Modern Britain, 1880–1951

Attempt the following questions using recalled knowledge and information from the sources where appropriate.

1. To what extent was poor health the main cause of poverty by 1900?

   (You must use recalled knowledge to present a **balanced account** of the influence of different factors and come to a **reasoned conclusion**.)

   8

Source A is from the book *From the Cradle to the Grave: Social Welfare in Britain 1890s–1951* by historians and published in 2002.

Source A

> One of the groups of "deserving poor" that the Liberals aimed to help in Britain was the young. The Boer War and the condition of many recruits led politicians to act. The Liberal government knew that poorer children would be the soldiers of the future. Healthy children would grow up to be healthy soldiers and workers, and the British Empire would be stronger as a result.

2. Evaluate the usefulness of **Source A** as evidence of the reasons why the Liberals introduced reforms to help the young.

   (You may want to comment on who wrote it, when they wrote it, why they wrote it, what they say or what has been missed out.)

   6

3. Explain the reasons why the Second World War changed attitudes to welfare reform in Britain.

   6

[Now go to SECTION 3 starting on *Page thirteen*]

SECTION 3 — EUROPEAN AND WORLD CONTEXTS — 20 marks

MARKS

Part A—The Cross and the Crescent: the Crusades, 1071–1192

Attempt the following questions using recalled knowledge and information from the sources where appropriate.

1. Describe the use of castles in medieval times.

5

2. Explain the reasons why people joined the First Crusade.

5

Source A describes the relationship between Emperor Alexius and the Crusaders.

Source A

> Emperor Alexius was horrified when the Crusader knights arrived at Constantinople. Fearing they would attack his city, Alexius made the Crusaders camp outside and only allowed them to enter in small groups. In a desperate attempt to take charge of the army, Alexius offered treasure and supplies to the Crusaders who agreed to fight for him. Any Crusader who refused was attacked and forced to surrender. Although Alexius had asked the Pope for knights he did not trust them and made plans to remove them from Constantinople.

3. How fully does **Source A** describe the relationship between Emperor Alexius and the Crusaders? (Use **Source A** and recall.)

6

Sources B and **C** are about the character of Richard I.

Source B

> When the king of France left the Crusade, Richard vowed to fulfil his Christian duty and continue to Jerusalem. An excellent military commander, Richard used clever tactics to win key battles and drive the Muslims back. Richard had such a fearsome reputation that the Muslims dreaded facing him on the battlefield. Despite the danger involved Richard always fought alongside his men, courageously attacking the enemy.

Source C

> The Crusaders had been besieging Acre for two years before Richard arrived with his army. Richard immediately took charge of the attack and using his experience and leadership forced the city to surrender. Throughout the fighting Richard showed great bravery by defending his men and killing the enemy. When some Crusaders returned home, Richard refused to leave promising he would keep his oath to God and recapture Jerusalem.

4. Compare the views of **Sources B** and **C** as evidence of the character of Richard I. (Compare the sources overall and/or in detail.)

4

SECTION 3 — EUROPEAN AND WORLD CONTEXTS — 20 marks

MARKS

Part B — "Tea and Freedom": the American Revolution, 1774–1783

Attempt the following questions using recalled knowledge and information from the sources where appropriate.

Source A explains why there was growing tension between Britain and the colonists.

Source A

> The war with France had ended in 1763. Although victory was widely celebrated, there were already voices being raised against British rule in the thirteen colonies. The decision to increase taxes on the colonists was very unpopular. Britain had gone to great expense to protect the colonies and wanted the colonies to pay some of this money back. The decision to maintain a standing army in the colonies also alarmed the colonists. The Stamp Act of 1765 provoked a furious reaction. Colonists responded by organising a boycott of British goods.

1. How fully does **Source A** explain why there was growing tension between Britain and the colonists by 1774? (Use **Source A** and recall.)   **6**

2. Describe the events of the Boston Tea Party and the British government's reaction to it.   **5**

3. Explain the reasons why Britain lost the war against the colonists.   **5**

Sources B and C are about the events that led to the British defeat at Saratoga.

Source B

> In June 1777 General Burgoyne set out from Canada with nearly 8,000 men but his progress was then slowed by mountains and dense forest. The British fought off American forces in September. However, unlike the Americans, Burgoyne had no reinforcements. In October, Burgoyne tangled with the Americans once again. He was forced to retreat and his army was trapped against the Hudson River. On 17 October, Burgoyne was forced to surrender almost 6,000 men and 30 cannons.

Source C

> General Burgoyne was eager to win fame for himself. He planned to march south to Albany. Another British army was due to join up with Burgoyne's forces. However, they were stopped by heavy resistance and Burgoyne's army was left on its own. Burgoyne decided to carry on but his progress was slowed by the difficult terrain and lack of supplies. The British were trapped at the little community of Saratoga and had no option but to surrender.

4. Compare the views of **Sources B** and **C** about the British defeat at Saratoga. (Compare the sources overall and/or in detail.)   **4**

SECTION 3 — EUROPEAN AND WORLD CONTEXTS — 20 marks

MARKS

Part C — The USA, 1850–1880

Attempt the following questions using recalled knowledge and information from the sources where appropriate.

1. Describe slave life on Southern plantations before the outbreak of the civil war.

   5

2. Explain why there was a growth in tension between the Northern and Southern States by 1860.

   5

Source A describes the reasons why some settlers and prospectors headed west after 1850.

Source A

> After 1850 large numbers of settlers and prospectors were heading west. They were attracted by the promise of a better life. Some were fed up with the cold winters in the east and were attracted by the warmer weather in California. Many farmers went west because they thought the land would be more fertile. Ranch owners, such as Charles Goodnight, quickly realised that the plains could be used to feed their huge herds of cattle. However, it was hard going. One person in ten died before they reached their destination.

3. How fully does **Source A** describe the reasons why large numbers of settlers and prospectors were attracted west after 1850? (Use **Source A** and recall.)

   6

Sources B and **C** are about the Sand Creek Massacre in 1864.

Source B

> Black Kettle and other chiefs of the Cheyennes were opposed to hostilities with the whites. Yet their village was still attacked by Colonel Chivington, who commanded 900 to 1,000 men. There were 500 people in the village, two-thirds of whom were women and children. I rode over the field after the slaughter was over, and counted from 60 to 70 dead bodies. A large majority of the dead were women and children.

Source C

> In the Cheyenne camp there were about 1,200 people in the village and about 700 were warriors. My reason for making the attack was that I believed they were hostile to the whites. I estimate that there were 500 or 600 people killed. I saw only one woman who had been killed and I saw no dead children. We found the scalps of 19 white people in the camp.

4. Compare the views of **Sources B** and **C** about the events which took place during the Sand Creek Massacre of 1864. (Compare the sources overall and/or in detail.)

   4

SECTION 3 — EUROPEAN AND WORLD CONTEXTS — 20 marks

MARKS

Part D — Hitler and Nazi Germany, 1919–1939

Attempt the following questions using recalled knowledge and information from the sources where appropriate.

1. Describe the rights all Germans had in the Weimar Republic.

5

Sources A and **B** are about hyperinflation in Germany.

Source A

> Workers were paid twice a day and when they were given their wages, they threw bundles of banknotes out of factory windows to waiting members of their families who would then rush to the shops to buy food or coal or clothes before the prices went up. Millions of people faced starvation due to hyperinflation. People such as pensioners who were living on fixed incomes found that prices rose much faster than their earnings.

Source B

> Almost overnight the life savings of many Germans became worthless. Some workers were paid twice a day and could spend their wages instantly. People who were paid monthly or depended on savings suffered because these could not keep up with price rises. Pensioners lived on fixed incomes. They always received the same amount of money each week. These incomes were now worth nothing. They faced homelessness and starvation.

2. Compare the views of **Sources A** and **B** on the effects of hyperinflation on the people of Germany. (Compare the sources overall and/or in detail.)

4

3. Explain the reasons why Hitler and the Nazi Party attracted so much support by January 1933.

5

Source C is about Nazi control of people's lives.

Source C

> Hitler and the Nazi Party aimed to control every part of people's lives, and that included their free time. The KDF (Strength through Joy Organisation) controlled most forms of entertainment. Each year around seven million people took part in KDF sports matches. Mass outings to the theatre and the opera were arranged. The KDF had its own symphony orchestra which toured the country. Workers were also provided with affordable holidays including cruises and walking or skiing holidays.

4. How fully does **Source C** describe how the Nazis controlled people's lives? (Use **Source C** and recall.)

6

SECTION 3 — EUROPEAN AND WORLD CONTEXTS — 20 marks

MARKS

Part E — Red Flag: Lenin and the Russian Revolution, 1894–1921

Attempt the following questions using recalled knowledge and information from the sources where appropriate.

1. Describe the methods used by the Tsar to control Russia before 1905.   5

2. Explain the reasons why the Tsar's control of Russia was threatened in 1905.   5

Source A describes some of the effects of the First World War on Russia.

Source A

> The outbreak of the First World War in August 1914 was to have a terrible impact on Russians. Russia went to war to support its friends and allies. Russian armies were in action against Germany and Austria-Hungary within only six days. Heart-breaking losses were suffered by the Tsar's armies during the early years of the war. Thousands of wounded soldiers were left lying untreated on the ground for days. Nurses and doctors lacked enough bandages to treat even a quarter of the wounds.

3. How fully does **Source A** describe the effects of the First World War on Russia? (Use **Source A** and recall.)   6

Sources B and **C** describe the events in Petrograd during February 1917.

Source B

> The disturbances which have begun in Petrograd are becoming more serious. Shortages of bread and flour cause panic. The workers are without jobs, the unemployed take the path to riot and revolt. The capital is in a state of anarchy. The Government is paralysed. The transport system has broken down. The suppliers of fuel and food are completely disorganised. There is wild shooting on the streets and troops are firing at each other.

Source C

> The situation was already very serious. Some of the factories had to close down and there were several thousand workmen unemployed. They wanted bread, but after waiting for hours in the queues outside the bakers' shops, many had been unable to get any. On Thursday, March 8, there had been a stormy sitting in the Duma and it was the bread shortage that was the cause of the unrest.

4. Compare the views of **Sources B** and **C** on the events in Petrograd during February 1917. (Compare the sources overall and/or in detail.)   4

SECTION 3 — EUROPEAN AND WORLD CONTEXTS — 20 marks   MARKS

Part F — Mussolini and Fascist Italy, 1919–1939

Attempt the following questions using recalled knowledge and information from the sources where appropriate.

1. Describe Mussolini's foreign policy up to 1939.   5

2. Explain the reasons why many Italians were unhappy with Mussolini's economic policies.   5

Source A describes the use of propaganda in Fascist Italy.

Source A

> Mussolini had long experience in the newspaper business and so he knew a thing or two about how to make effective propaganda. Mussolini's press office issued official versions of events which all the newspapers were expected to publish without question. The radio and cinema were also used to broadcast Fascist propaganda. News bulletins broadcast a daily diet of Mussolini's speeches and praised him as the saviour of Italy. The media played a very crucial role in the cult of "Il Duce."

3. How fully does **Source A** describe the use of propaganda in Fascist Italy? (Use **Source A** and recall.)   6

Sources B and C are about opposition to Mussolini.

Source B

> The Fascists used terror and violence, but for the most part this was not necessary. Unpopular groups like the Communists and Socialists were treated brutally. Fascist policies benefited the rich to ensure their support. The signing of the Lateran agreement in 1929 was important in winning the support of Catholics. There was some opposition in the army but this was never carried out in a coordinated way.

Source C

> While there was opposition to the Fascists, this never really posed a threat to the government. While some army generals opposed Mussolini, others liked his aggressive attitude. Mussolini changed his policy towards the Roman Catholic Church. This new close relationship with the church reduced the threat of opposition from Catholics. Big businessmen and landowners supported a regime which always seemed to be on their side.

4. Compare the views of **Sources B** and **C** on opposition to Mussolini. (Compare the sources overall and/or in detail.)   4

SECTION 3 — EUROPEAN AND WORLD CONTEXTS — 20 marks

MARKS

Part G — Free at Last? Civil Rights in the USA, 1918–1968

Attempt the following questions using recalled knowledge and information from the sources where appropriate.

Sources A and B are about immigrants in American cities in the 1920s.

Source A

> The early twentieth century saw a massive growth in immigration from Southern and Eastern Europe. Immigrants from the same country usually lived in the same areas of the city. These areas contained tenement slums which were damp, dark and filthy with no water supply, toilets or drains. Immigrants had to take any work they could get, usually low paid jobs such as labourers or servants.

Source B

> Finding a well-paid, skilled job was a common problem for poorly educated immigrants. Immigrants tended to live in their own communities: in New York there was a Polish district, a Jewish district and an Italian district. Tenement buildings in these areas were often five or six storeys high with rooms which lacked light or sanitation. Many of the new immigrants found that life in America was not what they expected.

1. Compare the views of **Sources A** and **B** about the living and working conditions of immigrants in American cities.   **4**

2. Describe the non-violent protests of the Civil Rights Movement in the 1950s and 1960s.   **5**

Source C is about the actions taken by federal authorities to help black Americans.

Source C

> Federal authorities did take action. President Truman issued orders to desegregate the US military in 1948. He also set up a President's Committee on civil rights in 1946 to report to him on how progress towards black civil rights could be made. However no legislation followed. In 1960 Congress passed a Civil Rights Act which established penalties for obstructing black voting. The assassination of President Kennedy in November 1963 came at the time he was preparing a Civil Rights Bill.

3. How fully does **Source C** describe the actions taken by federal authorities to improve civil rights for black Americans between 1945 and 1964? (Use **Source C** and recall.)   **6**

4. Explain the reasons why the Black Panthers gained the support of many black Americans.   **5**

SECTION 3 — EUROPEAN AND WORLD CONTEXTS — 20 marks

MARKS

Part H — Appeasement and the Road to War, 1918–1939

Attempt the following questions using recalled knowledge and information from the sources where appropriate.

1. Describe the military terms of the Treaty of Versailles.

5

Source A is about the weaknesses of the League of Nations.

Source A

> The USA refused to join as they were not interested in getting involved in the problems of other countries. Initially Russia was not invited to join, so another great country of the world was absent. Therefore, right from the start the League of Nations was actually rather weak. Taking decisions was difficult as the Assembly had to be unanimous and member states often could not agree. A further problem was that the League did not have its own army to back up its decisions.

2. How fully does **Source A** explain the reasons why the League of Nations was weak? (Use **Source A** and recall.)

6

3. Explain the reasons why Britain did not take military action against Germany's reoccupation of the Rhineland.

5

Sources B and **C** are about the Anschluss.

Source B

> Germany and Austria are now one. It was a mistake of the peacemakers at Versailles to forbid the union of Austria and Germany. The population of Austria comprised ethnic Germans, the majority of whom are enthusiastic about the Anschluss. The Austrians will not only feel at home as part of Germany, they will benefit financially too from an increase in trade with their German brothers.

Source C

> That there has been no fighting is proof of the desire of the Austrian people to belong to Germany. Austrians will also benefit from greater markets for their raw materials and manufactured goods. The union of these two countries should never have been forbidden at Versailles. Winston Churchill has argued that Austria is a small country "brutally struck down". I do not see what there is to complain about.

4. Compare the views of **Sources B** and **C** about the Anschluss. (Compare the sources overall and/or in detail.)

4

SECTION 3 — EUROPEAN AND WORLD CONTEXTS — 20 marks

Part I — World War II, 1939–1945

Attempt the following questions using recalled knowledge and information from the sources where appropriate.

Sources **A** and **B** are about the German strategy of Blitzkrieg.

Source A

> Blitzkrieg was a tactic based on speed and surprise. It required the effective use of light tank units supported by planes and infantry. The tactic was developed by army officer Hans Guderian. He had written a military pamphlet called "Achtung Panzer" which got into the hands of Hitler. It was used effectively in the first years of the Second World War and resulted in the British and French armies being pushed back in just a few weeks to the beaches of Dunkirk.

Source B

> Hitler had spent four years in World War One fighting a static war with neither side moving far for months on end. He was enthralled by Guderian's plan that was based purely on speed and movement. When Guderian told Hitler that he could reach the French coast in weeks if an attack on France was ordered, fellow officers openly laughed at him. Once a strategic target had been selected, Stuka dive bombers were sent in to "soften" up the enemy, then the tanks approached, supported by infantry.

1. Compare the views of **Sources A** and **B** on the German strategy of Blitzkrieg. (Compare the sources overall and/or in detail.)   **4**

2. Describe what life was like for the ordinary citizens of Nazi occupied Europe.   **5**

Source **C** is about the activities of the French Resistance.

Source C

> The French Resistance movement developed in 1940. It helped Jews, and Allied airmen who had crash landed in France, to escape. Many resistance workers paid for their courage with their lives. Even school children were recruited to help smuggle people across the borders of northern and southern France. As well as this, the Resistance movement was crucial to undermining Nazi rule by producing publications of news and information. Nazi rule was further challenged by the Resistance who worked together to discover French collaboration.

3. How fully does **Source C** describe the activities of the French Resistance? (Use **Source C** and recall.)   **6**

4. Explain the reasons why the Russian army was able to take over Berlin in 1945.   **5**

SECTION 3 — EUROPEAN AND WORLD CONTEXTS — 20 marks

MARKS

Part J — The Cold War, 1945–1989

Attempt the following questions using recalled knowledge and information from the sources where appropriate.

1. Explain the reasons why a Cold War developed after 1945.

5

Source A is about American intervention in Vietnam.

Source A

> The Americans intervened in Vietnam for several reasons. In a speech in March 1947 President Truman explained that America would resist the spread of Communism. This became known as the Truman Doctrine. In the 1950s the Americans had responded to French requests for assistance in Vietnam by giving money to try to halt the Vietminh. By the early 1960s it was clear that South Vietnam could not resist Communism without the support of American troops. Many in America believed war was necessary to stop the spread of Soviet influence.

2. How fully does **Source A** explain the reasons why Americans intervened in Vietnam? (Use **Source A** and recall.)

6

Sources B and **C** are about the crisis in Berlin in 1961.

> There is peace in Berlin today. The source of world trouble and tension is Moscow, not Berlin. And if war begins, it will have begun in Moscow and not Berlin. For the choice of war or peace is largely theirs, not ours. It is the Soviets who have stirred up this crisis. It is they who are trying to force a change. They have rejected an all-German peace treaty and the rule of international law.

Source C

> We can now look back on the Berlin crisis and say with confidence that this crisis was caused by Moscow. It was the brutal Soviet-backed regime in East Germany which caused so many people to leave. The Soviet domination of East Germany was a clear breach of international law. The Soviets rejected an American proposal for a peace treaty which would have dealt with all of the issues in Germany.

3. Compare the views of **Sources B** and **C** on the crisis in Berlin in 1961. (Compare the sources overall and/or in detail.)

4

4. Describe the impact of the Cuban Missile Crisis on international relations.

5

[END OF QUESTION PAPER]

Page twenty-two

NATIONAL 5

2015

National Qualifications 2015

X737/75/11

History

FRIDAY, 01 MAY

09:00 AM — 10:45 AM

Total marks — 60

SECTION 1 — SCOTTISH CONTEXTS — 20 marks

Attempt ONE part.

SECTION 2 — BRITISH CONTEXTS — 20 marks

Attempt ONE part.

SECTION 3 — EUROPEAN AND WORLD CONTEXTS — 20 marks

Attempt ONE part.

Write your answers clearly in the answer booklet provided. In the answer booklet you must clearly identify the question number you are attempting.

Use **blue** or **black** ink.

Before leaving the examination room you must give your answer booklet to the Invigilator; if you do not, you may lose all the marks for this paper.

[BLANK PAGE]

DO NOT WRITE ON THIS PAGE

SECTION 1 — SCOTTISH CONTEXTS

PARTS

SECTION 2 — BRITISH CONTEXTS

PARTS

SECTION 3 — EUROPEAN AND WORLD CONTEXTS

PARTS

MARKS

SECTION 1 — SCOTTISH CONTEXTS — 20 marks

Part A — The Wars of Independence, 1286–1328

Answer the following questions using recalled knowledge and information from the sources where appropriate.

Sources A and **B** are about Edward I's plans for Scotland after the death of Alexander III.

Source A

> When Alexander III died, Edward I took steps to take control of Scotland. His aim was to unite the kingdoms of Scotland and England by a marriage treaty. Edward plotted to marry his son to Scotland's infant queen, Margaret, Maid of Norway. He secretly asked the Pope's permission for the marriage before any details had been discussed with the Scots. When Margaret's death ended this scheme, he looked for other ways to control Scotland.

Source B

> In 1289 Edward was in France attending to his lands there. Erik, King of Norway, father of Margaret Maid of Norway, sent messengers to him to discuss her safety. He suggested her possible marriage with Edward's son. Edward asked for Scottish representatives to be present before any negotiations began. The Maid would have Edward's protection and this would ensure peace in Scotland. This marriage would mean a union of the kingdoms.

1. Compare the views in **Sources A** and **B** about Edward I's intentions towards Scotland after the death of Alexander III. (Compare the sources overall and/or in detail.)   **4**

2. Describe what happened when Edward I attacked Berwick in 1296.   **5**

MARKS

Source C is about Bruce's campaign to capture the Scottish castles.

Source C

> In 1307, Bruce returned to Scotland. Although many of his leading supporters had been captured by Edward I he still had experienced commanders such as James Douglas. Bruce and his small army marched north and destroyed castles in Inverness and Nairn. He could not spare men to defend castles from attack. Meanwhile, Douglas recaptured his own castle in the south and burned it down. Edward I had taken Stirling castle by using the siege engine, *Warwolf*. Lack of such siege engines forced Bruce to use other methods.

3. How fully does **Source C** describe Bruce's campaign of capturing the Scottish castles? (Use **Source C** and recall.)   6

4. Explain the reasons why English mistakes led to their defeat at the Battle of Bannockburn in 1314.   5

[Now go to SECTION 2 starting on *Page fourteen*]

MARKS

SECTION 1 — SCOTTISH CONTEXTS — 20 marks

Part B — Mary Queen of Scots and the Scottish Reformation, 1542–1587

Answer the following questions using recalled knowledge and information from the sources where appropriate.

5. Describe the events of the "Rough Wooing". 5

Sources A and **B** are about the murder of Riccio.

Source A

> Mary was in her chamber enjoying a meal with Riccio and some other friends. Suddenly, Darnley forced his way into the chamber with a large group of followers. One of the intruders held Mary back and a pistol was pointed towards her pregnant belly. Ruthven and another man then attacked Riccio. He was then dragged from the room and stabbed many times. His lifeless body was discovered early next morning.

Source B

> Darnley unexpectedly appeared with a group of armed nobles, including Lord Ruthven, and burst into Mary's chamber. Ruthven shouted to Riccio to step forward away from Mary. Riccio was then pulled out of the room and stabbed over 50 times before his body was thrown downstairs. Mary, who was pregnant, could not do anything because she had been seized and had a gun pointed to her stomach.

6. Compare the views of **Sources A** and **B** about what happened to Riccio. (Compare the sources overall and/or in detail.) 4

7. Explain the reasons why Mary was forced to abdicate in 1567. 5

MARKS

Source C describes the events surrounding the trial of Mary, Queen of Scots in 1587.

Source C

> At first Mary thought that she would not attend her trial. However she learned that the trial would be held even in her absence. Mary defended herself but she was not allowed to call her own witnesses. The trial started on the 14th of October and lasted two days. During this time she was not even allowed to consult any documents. Mary told her servants that she knew she would be found guilty because it was too great a risk to let her live.

8.   How fully does **Source C** describe the events surrounding the trial of Mary, Queen of Scots in 1587? (Use **Source C** and recall.)   6

[Now go to SECTION 2 starting on *Page fourteen*]

MARKS

SECTION 1 — SCOTTISH CONTEXTS — 20 marks

Part C — The Treaty of Union, 1689–1715

Answer the following questions using recalled knowledge and information from the sources where appropriate.

9. Explain the reasons why there was tension between Scotland and England by 1705.   **5**

Source A is about Scottish attitudes towards the Union.

Source A

> Opponents of the Union warned of higher taxes. However supporters of the Union were clear that it would help Scotland to become richer in the future. Many Protestants argued that the main advantage of the Union would be securing the Protestant Succession. They also pointed out that the English had made it clear they would respect the independence of the Church of Scotland. It was also argued that if the Union was rejected England might simply invade and take over anyway.

10. How fully does **Source A** explain the arguments used by supporters of the Union? (Use **Source A** and recall.)   **6**

Sources B and **C** are about the Union debate.

Source B

> In 1706 the debate over the Union was in full flow. All of the leaflets produced for the public expressed opposition. Many feared that the proposed Union would lead to a rise in taxes. Some feared for the independence of the Church of Scotland. Many leaflets were produced on the subject. They argued that England was the far bigger country and so would control Scotland.

Source C

> Many powerful Scots argued for the Union, but their views did not represent the majority. Many Scots felt that the Union would not be a partnership but a takeover. Economic arguments were the most important ones and it was claimed that after Union higher taxes would hit all Scots in the pocket. Religion was very important to many Scots and they did not want the English to interfere in their Church.

11. Compare the views of **Sources B** and **C** on Scottish attitudes to the proposed Union. (Compare the sources overall and/or in detail.)   4

12. Describe the effects of the Treaty of Union on Scotland up to 1715.   5

[Now go to SECTION 2 starting on *Page fourteen*]

MARKS

SECTION 1 — SCOTTISH CONTEXTS — 20 marks

Part D — Migration and Empire, 1830–1939

Answer the following questions using recalled knowledge and information from the sources where appropriate.

Source **A** describes the impact of the Empire on Scotland.

Source A

> Many Scots invested money in the Empire and reinvested their profits in Scotland which added to Scotland's wealth. Scotland's large workforce and the large number of immigrant workers kept wages low. Profits were spent in other ways on luxury houses and impressive public buildings which changed the appearance of Scottish cities. However, profits from trade with the Empire were also used to develop chemical industries and textiles, creating even more jobs. The Empire provided markets for Scottish coal, employing thousands of miners.

13. How fully does **Source A** describe the impact of the Empire on Scotland? (Use **Source A** and recall.)   6

14. Explain the reasons why Lowland Scots emigrated from Scotland between 1830 and 1939.   5

15. Describe how Scots tried to keep their traditional Scottish way of life in their new countries.   5

MARKS

Sources **B** and **C** are about the contribution Scots made to the development of Australia.

Source B

> The links between Scotland and Australia stretch back to the landing of the *Endeavour*. Thomas Mitchell from Stirling was the first European to explore the rich lands of Victoria for new settlement. The Scottish Australia Company was formed in Aberdeen to encourage Scottish investment to businesses in Australia. Education was supported by successful Scots such as Fife-born Sir Peter Russell who gave £100,000 to the University of Sydney to develop the study of engineering.

Source C

> Scots made their mark in shaping modern Australia. Francis Ormond from Aberdeen gave large sums to set up the Working Men's Technical College in Melbourne to support education. Glasgow investors formed the influential New Zealand and Australian Land Company to encourage the wool export trade. The Scottish explorer John McDouall Stuart was the first European to cross Australia. Even "Waltzing Matilda" was written by the son of a Scot.

16. Compare the views in **Sources B** and **C** about the contribution of Scots to the development of Australia. (Compare the sources overall and/or in detail.)

4

[Now go to SECTION 2 starting on *Page fourteen*]

SECTION 1 — SCOTTISH CONTEXTS — 20 marks

Part E — The Era of the Great War, 1910–1928

Answer the following questions using recalled knowledge and information from the sources where appropriate.

Source A is about the use of tanks on the Western Front.

Source A

> Thirty-six tanks led the way in an attack at Flers. The sudden appearance of the new weapon stunned their German opponents. However, Sir Douglas Haig used them before they were truly battle ready in an attempt to break the trench stalemate. These early tanks were very slow moving. They often broke down. Tanks often became stuck in the heavy mud of no man's land. Conditions for the tank crews were awful. The heat generated inside the tank was tremendous and fumes often nearly choked the men inside.

17. How fully does **Source A** describe the impact tanks had on fighting on the Western Front during the Great War? (Use **Source A** and recall.) **6**

MARKS

Sources **B** and **C** are about conditions in the trenches.

Source **B**

> I sincerely hope it will not freeze. It is so hard on the poor men in trenches standing in very deep mud. Water is often up to their waists. A frost will mean so many frozen feet. I spent my New Year's Eve in a dugout lying on a stretcher on the floor with a wounded man over me. Rats were playing about all over. Shells burst all round and shook the place.

Source **C**

> If anyone had to go to the company on our right he had to walk through thirty yards of waterlogged trench, which was chest-deep in water in some places. The duckboard track was constantly shelled, and in places a hundred yards of it had been blown to smithereens. It was better to keep off the track when walking back and forth. Soldiers had to make their way sometimes through very heavy mud.

18. Compare the views of **Sources B** and **C** about conditions in the trenches. (Compare the sources overall and/or in detail.)   4

19. Explain the reasons why some people were unhappy with government restrictions like DORA.   5

20. Describe the economic difficulties faced by Scotland after the Great War.   5

[Now go to SECTION 2 starting on *Page fourteen*]

MARKS

SECTION 2 — BRITISH CONTEXTS — 20 marks

Part A — The Creation of the Medieval Kingdoms, 1066–1406

Answer the following questions using recalled knowledge and information from the sources where appropriate.

21. Describe the role of a baron in medieval times.   **5**

22. Explain the reasons why Henry II and Archbishop Becket quarrelled.   **5**

Source A describes the duties of a monk.

Source A

> Early in the morning all monks met in the chapter house. When not attending church services, monks were expected to carry out hard physical labour in the field or herb garden. Well-educated monks studied the Bible or spent hours copying and illuminating books. Although monks lived in isolation, they often supported their local community by collecting alms and caring for the poor. Monks also provided the only medical help available at the time, looking after the sick in the monastery's infirmary.

23. How fully does **Source A** describe the duties of a monk in medieval times?   (Use **Source A** and recall.)   **5**

Source B is from a book written by a doctor in 1350.

Source B

> The first sign of death was a swelling called a buboe, under the armpit or in the groin. Usually the swelling grew to the size of an egg or an apple and spread all over the body. Soon after, the victim began to vomit and developed a fever. This was followed by the appearance of black and purple spots on the arms or thighs. No doctor could cure this terrible disease and so thousands died.

24. Evaluate the usefulness of **Source B** as evidence of the symptoms of the Black Death.   **5**

(You may want to comment on who wrote it, when they wrote it, why they wrote it, what they say or what has been missed out.)

[Now go to SECTION 3 starting on *Page nineteen*]

MARKS

SECTION 2 — BRITISH CONTEXTS — 20 marks

Part B — War of the Three Kingdoms, 1603–1651

Answer the following questions using recalled knowledge and information from the sources where appropriate.

25. Describe the changes to the ways Scotland and England were governed after the Union of the Crowns.

5

Source A is from a book written by King James VI and I.

Source A

> The power of the monarchy is the supreme authority on Earth. To question what God may do is to show disrespect to God. Therefore it is treason for a King's subjects to challenge what a King may or may not do. A good King will make decisions according to the law, but he is not obliged to follow that law unless he sees fit to do so.

26. Evaluate the usefulness of **Source A** as evidence of James VI and I's belief in the Divine Right of Kings.

    (You may want to comment on who wrote it, when they wrote it, why they wrote it, what they say or what has been missed out.)

5

27. Explain the reasons why Charles I faced opposition to his rule in Scotland.

5

Source B describes the events that led to the outbreak of the Civil War in 1642.

Source B

> In June 1642 the Long Parliament passed a set of demands called the Nineteen Proposals. These demands called for the King's powers to be reduced and more control to be given to Parliament. This event divided Parliament between those who supported the Nineteen Proposals and those who thought Parliament had gone too far. Parliament and Charles then began to raise their own armies. People were then forced to choose sides and on 22nd August 1642 the King raised his standard at Nottingham.

28. How fully does **Source B** describe the events that led to the outbreak of the Civil War in 1642? (Use **Source B** and recall.)

5

[Now go to SECTION 3 starting on *Page nineteen*]

MARKS

SECTION 2 — BRITISH CONTEXTS — 20 marks

Part C — The Atlantic Slave Trade, 1770–1807

Answer the following questions using recalled knowledge and information from the sources where appropriate.

29. Describe the different stages of the triangular trade. **5**

Source A is about the importance of the slave trade to Britain's economy.

Source A

> The slave trade was considered essential to Britain's economy in the eighteenth century. For example, the slave trade had raised Liverpool from a struggling port to one of the richest and most prosperous trading centres in the world. The slave trade provided work in almost every industry in the town. Slave cotton provided work for the mills of Lancashire. However, little thought was given to the suffering of those involved in its production. Merchants made huge profits importing sugar from the Caribbean, a product which was in great demand.

30. How fully does **Source A** explain the importance of the slave trade to Britain's economy? (Use **Source A** and recall.) **5**

Source B is from a book written by a modern historian published in 1987.

Source B

> The island of Barbados was transformed by the slave trade. By the eighteenth century, small farms had been replaced by large plantations which grew sugar more profitably. The island had once been a beautiful wilderness. However, accounts tell of how the island was slowly but surely cleared of its native people and its vegetation. These were replaced by plantations. These became the work place, and final resting place, of armies of African slaves.

31. Evaluate the usefulness of **Source B** as evidence of the impact of the slave trade on the Caribbean islands. **5**

    (You may want to comment on who wrote it, when they wrote it, why they wrote it, what they say or what has been missed out.)

32. Explain the reasons why resistance was difficult for slaves on plantations. **5**

[Now go to SECTION 3 starting on *Page nineteen*]

SECTION 2 — BRITISH CONTEXTS — 20 marks

Part D — Changing Britain, 1760–1900

Answer the following questions using recalled knowledge and information from the sources where appropriate.

Source A is about the impact of new technology on textile factories.

Source A

> After 1760 there were many inventions that helped to speed up the production of textiles. Spinning was improved by the invention of the Spinning Jenny in 1763, which could spin eight threads at once. In 1769, Arkwright invented the Water Frame which used water power and made much better thread than the Spinning Jenny. A steam engine which was easy to use in factories was developed by Boulton and Watt in the 1780s. This meant that factories did not have to be built near fast-flowing water for a power supply.

33. How fully does **Source A** explain the impact of new technology on textile factories? (Use **Source A** and recall.)   **5**

34. Describe working conditions in coal mines before 1842.   **5**

Source B is from a book by a railway inspector, published in 1870.

Source B

> The comforts, or rather discomforts, of railway travelling about thirty years ago were very different from those of the present day. Third-class carriages were often little different from basic cattle trucks. For a considerable time they were completely open and had no seats. First and second class carriages were covered and had seating. The luggage of the passengers was packed on top of the carriages.

35. Evaluate the usefulness of **Source B** as evidence of railway travel in the nineteenth century.   **5**

    (You may want to comment on who wrote it, when they wrote it, why they wrote it, what they say or what has been missed out.)

36. Explain the reasons why people's health had improved by 1900.   **5**

[Now go to SECTION 3 starting on *Page nineteen*]

MARKS

SECTION 2 — BRITISH CONTEXTS — 20 marks

Part E — The Making of Modern Britain, 1880–1951

Answer the following questions using recalled knowledge and information from the sources where appropriate.

37. Describe the reforms introduced by the Liberal Government of 1906–1914 to help the sick.

5

Source A is from a book by Flora Thompson about her own life, published in 1939.

Source A

> When pensions began, life was transformed for the old. They were no longer anxious and were suddenly rich. When they went to the Post Office to collect it, tears of gratitude would run down their cheeks and they would say as they picked up their money "God bless that Lord George". They gave flowers from their gardens and apples from their trees to the girl who merely handed them the money.

38. Evaluate the usefulness of **Source A** as evidence of the benefits of the 1908 Old Age Pensions Act.

5

(You may want to comment on who wrote it, when they wrote it, why they wrote it, what they say or what has been missed out.)

Source B is about the Beveridge Report which was published in 1942.

Source B

> The Beveridge Report was published in 1942 and sold over 635,000 copies. The report identified the five "giant evils" facing Britain. Beveridge believed that tackling one of the five giants wouldn't do much good; the government would have to tackle them all. He recommended that there should be a welfare system that would look after people from the "cradle to the grave". He believed that there should be benefits for the unemployed, the sick, the elderly and widows. He also advised the government to adopt a policy of full employment.

39. How fully does **Source B** explain the recommendations of the 1942 Beveridge Report? (Use **Source B** and recall.)

5

40. Explain the reasons why the Labour Government reforms of 1945–1951 did not fully tackle the problem of squalor.

5

MARKS

SECTION 3 — EUROPEAN AND WORLD CONTEXTS — 20 marks

Part A — The Cross and the Crescent: the Crusades, 1071–1192

Answer the following questions using recalled knowledge and information from the sources where appropriate.

41. To what extent did Pope Urban II call for the First Crusade for religious reasons?   8

    (You must use recalled knowledge to present a **balanced assessment** of the influence of different factors and come to a **reasoned conclusion**.)

42. Explain the reasons why the Crusaders lost control of Jerusalem in 1187.   6

Source A is from a chronicle written by a Crusader in 1191.

> Despite his promises, Saladin did not pay the ransom agreed for the Muslim hostages and did not return the True Cross to the Crusaders. Instead, Saladin attempted to trick King Richard, sending him gifts and treasures. He hoped that Richard would release the Muslims for free. Eventually King Richard grew tired of Saladin. The next morning the king ordered the Muslims to be led out of the city and beheaded.

43. Evaluate the usefulness of **Source A** as evidence of the massacre at Acre.   6

    (You may want to comment on who wrote it, when they wrote it, why they wrote it, what they say or what has been missed out.)

MARKS

SECTION 3 — EUROPEAN AND WORLD CONTEXTS — 20 marks

Part B— "Tea and Freedom": the American Revolution, 1774–1783

Answer the following questions using recalled knowledge and information from the sources where appropriate.

44. Explain the reasons why a war broke out between Britain and the American colonists.

6

Source A is from the diary of an American army surgeon during the winter of 1777.

> December 14: The army now begins to grow tired of the continued difficulties they have faced in this winter campaign. Poor food, tough living conditions, cold weather, sickness, fatigue, nasty clothes, nasty cookery, the Devil's in it! I can't endure it! Why are we sent here to starve and freeze? Yet our men still show a great spirit and morale that is unexpected from such young soldiers.

45. Evaluate the usefulness of **Source A** as evidence of the experience of soldiers who fought in the Wars of Independence.

6

(You may want to comment on who wrote it, when they wrote it, why they wrote it, what they say or what has been missed out.)

46. To what extent did the intervention of foreign countries lead to Britain's defeat in the Wars of Independence?

8

(You must use recalled knowledge to present a **balanced assessment** of the influence of different factors and come to a **reasoned conclusion**.)

MARKS

SECTION 3 — EUROPEAN AND WORLD CONTEXTS — 20 marks

Part C — USA, 1850–1880

Answer the following questions using recalled knowledge and information from the sources where appropriate.

47. Explain the reasons why Native Americans opposed westward expansion.

6

48. To what extent did the election of Lincoln as President in 1860 lead to the outbreak of the Civil War?

8

(You must use recalled knowledge to present a **balanced assessment** of the influence of different factors and come to a **reasoned conclusion**.)

Source A is from a report written by an officer of the Freedmen's Bureau in 1866.

> The freed slaves in Texas have been terrorised by attacks from the desperate men of the local area. These freed men are scared to report any murder of a black man. The murderers dislike the fact that they no longer have control over their former slaves. Many of the former slaves are unhappy with their freedom and would prefer to still be slaves as it offered them some protection.

49. Evaluate the usefulness of **Source A** as evidence of the effects of Reconstruction on the Southern States after 1865.

6

(You may want to comment on who wrote it, when they wrote it, why they wrote it, what they say or what has been missed out.)

MARKS

SECTION 3 — EUROPEAN AND WORLD CONTEXTS — 20 marks

Part D — Hitler and Nazi Germany, 1919–1939

Answer the following questions using recalled knowledge and information from the sources where appropriate.

50. Explain the reasons why the Weimar Government was unpopular up to 1925.

6

51. To what extent were the social policies of the Nazi Government crucial to their maintenance of power between 1933 and 1939?

8

(You must use recalled knowledge to present a **balanced assessment** of the influence of different factors and come to a **reasoned conclusion**.)

Source A is from a textbook written by a modern historian, published in 2013.

> On buses and park benches, Jews had to sit on seats marked for them. Children at German schools were taught anti-Semitic ideas. Jewish children were ridiculed by teachers. Bullying of Jews in the playground by other pupils went unpunished. If Jewish children then chose not to go to school, the Nazis claimed this proved that Jewish children were lazy and could not be bothered to go to school.

52. Evaluate the usefulness of **Source A** as evidence of the treatment of Jews in Nazi Germany.

6

(You may want to comment on who wrote it, when they wrote it, why they wrote it, what they say or what has been missed out.)

MARKS

SECTION 3 — EUROPEAN AND WORLD CONTEXTS — 20 marks

Part E — Red Flag: Lenin and the Russian Revolution, 1894–1921

Answer the following questions using recalled knowledge and information from the sources where appropriate.

53. Explain the reasons why it was so difficult to oppose the Tsar before 1905.

    6

54. To what extent did problems caused by the First World War lead to the Tsar's downfall in February 1917?

    8

    (You must use recalled knowledge to present a **balanced assessment** of the influence of different factors and come to a **reasoned conclusion**.)

Source A is from the diary of the British Ambassador to Russia dated 24th October 1917.

> I heard this morning that the Bolsheviks would overthrow the Government in the course of the next few days because they had captured enough weapons. At one o'clock, three Government Ministers arrived. I was not convinced that the Government had enough force behind them to deal with the situation. I told them that I could not understand how the Government could allow Trotsky to go on encouraging the population to murder and steal.

55. Evaluate the usefulness of **Source A** as evidence of the reasons for the Bolshevik seizure of power in October 1917.

    6

    (You may want to comment on who wrote it, when they wrote it, why they wrote it, what they say or what has been missed out.)

MARKS

SECTION 3 — EUROPEAN AND WORLD CONTEXTS — 20 marks

Part F — Mussolini and Fascist Italy, 1919–1939

Answer the following questions using recalled knowledge and information from the sources where appropriate.

56. To what extent was the widespread appeal of Fascism the main reason why Mussolini was able to seize power by 1925?

    (You must use recalled knowledge to present a **balanced assessment** of the influence of different factors and come to a **reasoned conclusion**.)

8

Source A is from a book by a modern historian published in 2006.

> By 1925 Fascist control of Italy was secure. The Battle for Grain began in 1925 and was a major attempt to promote Fascist power and national self-sufficiency. The government tried to boost grain production by giving farmers grants so that they could buy tractors, fertiliser and any other machinery necessary for wheat production. Farmers were also guaranteed a high price for the grain they produced.

57. Evaluate the usefulness of **Source A** as evidence of Mussolini's economic policies.

    (You may want to comment on who wrote it, when they wrote it, why they wrote it, what they say or what has been missed out.)

6

58. Explain the reasons why Mussolini was able to crush opposition in Fascist Italy.

6

MARKS

SECTION 3 — EUROPEAN AND WORLD CONTEXTS — 20 marks

Part G — Free at Last? Civil Rights in the USA, 1918–1968

Answer the following questions using recalled knowledge and information from the sources where appropriate.

59. To what extent was the fear of white violence the main reason for the migration of black Americans to the North?

    (You must use recalled knowledge to present a **balanced assessment** of the influence of different factors and come to a **reasoned conclusion**.)

    8

60. Explain the reasons why the Montgomery Bus Boycott was an important step forward in the campaign for civil rights.

    6

Source A is from a speech made by Malcolm X in December 1962.

> The teaching of the Honourable Elijah Muhammad is making our people, for the first time, proud to be black, and that is most important. I just wanted to point out that whites are a race of devils. It's left up to you and me to decide if we want to integrate with this wicked race or separate to be on our own. If we separate then we have a chance for salvation.

61. Evaluate the usefulness of **Source A** as evidence of the beliefs of Malcolm X.

    6

    (You may want to comment on who wrote it, when they wrote it, why they wrote it, what they say or what has been missed out.)

MARKS

SECTION 3 — EUROPEAN AND WORLD CONTEXTS — 20 marks

Part H — Appeasement and the Road to War, 1918–1939

Answer the following questions using recalled knowledge and information from the sources where appropriate.

62. Explain the reasons why Hitler rearmed Germany after 1933.   **6**

63. To what extent was public opinion the main reason why Chamberlain followed a policy of appeasement?   **8**

    (You must use recalled knowledge to present a **balanced assessment** of the influence of different factors and come to a **reasoned conclusion**.)

Source A is from a book by a modern historian published in 1989.

> On 15th March 1939, German troops marched in to Prague and within two days Czechoslovakia ceased to exist. After destroying Czechoslovakia, Hitler turned his attention to Poland. On 29th March the British government gave Poland a guarantee to protect it against any threat to its independence. On 22nd May Hitler and Mussolini strengthened the ties between their two countries by signing an agreement which required them to help each other in time of war.

64. Evaluate the usefulness of **Source A** as evidence of the events leading to the outbreak of war in 1939.   **6**

    (You may want to comment on who wrote it, when they wrote it, why they wrote it, what they say or what has been missed out.)

SECTION 3 — EUROPEAN AND WORLD CONTEXTS — 20 marks

Part I — World War II, 1939–1945

Answer the following questions using recalled knowledge and information from the sources where appropriate.

Source A is from an interview with a sailor who was on board an evacuation ship at Dunkirk in May 1940.

> The thing that shocked me most was seeing all the soldiers coming back without their equipment. We began to think it was the end of our way of life. We didn't know how long we'd be able to hold Jerry off in England. We knew we had the Navy, and that we could fight. However we didn't know what our soldiers would be able to do if Jerry invaded, because they had nothing.

65. Evaluate the usefulness of **Source A** as evidence of what happened at Dunkirk in May 1940.

    (You may want to comment on who wrote it, when they wrote it, why they wrote it, what they say or what has been missed out.)

    6

66. Explain the reasons why the Japanese attacked the US naval base at Pearl Harbour in December 1941.

    6

67. To what extent was effective planning by the Allies the main reason for the success of the Normandy landings in June 1944?

    8

    (You must use recalled knowledge to present a **balanced assessment** of the influence of different factors and come to a **reasoned conclusion**.)

MARKS

SECTION 3 — EUROPEAN AND WORLD CONTEXTS — 20 marks

Part J — The Cold War, 1945–1989

Answer the following questions using recalled knowledge and information from the sources where appropriate.

68. To what extent was a difference in political beliefs the main reason for the development of the Cold War between 1945 and 1955?

    (You must use recalled knowledge to present a **balanced assessment** of the influence of different factors and come to a **reasoned conclusion**.)

    8

Source A is from a newspaper article written by a British journalist, published on 23 October 1956.

> Today I have seen a great event. I have watched the people of Budapest come out into the streets in rebellion against their Soviet masters. As I telephone this report I can hear the roar of crowds marching, shouting complaints against Russia. "Send the Red Army home," they roar. "We want free and secret elections." Leaflets demanding the sacking of the present Government are being thrown from trams into the crowds on the streets.

69. Evaluate the usefulness of **Source A** as evidence of the reasons for the Hungarian revolution of 1956.

    (You may want to comment on who wrote it, when they wrote it, why they wrote it, what they say or what has been missed out.)

    6

70. Explain the reasons why America was unable to defeat the Vietcong.

    6

[END OF QUESTION PAPER]

NATIONAL 5

2016

N5

National
Qualifications
2016

X737/75/11 **History**

FRIDAY, 20 MAY
1:00 PM – 2:45 PM

Total marks — 60

SECTION 1 — SCOTTISH CONTEXTS — 20 marks

Attempt ONE part.

SECTION 2 — BRITISH CONTEXTS — 20 marks

Attempt ONE part.

SECTION 3 — EUROPEAN AND WORLD CONTEXTS — 20 marks

Attempt ONE part.

Write your answers clearly in the answer booklet provided. In the answer booklet you must clearly identify the question number you are attempting.

Use **blue** or **black** ink.

Before leaving the examination room you must give your answer booklet to the Invigilator; if you do not, you may lose all the marks for this paper.

SECTION 1 — SCOTTISH CONTEXTS

PARTS

SECTION 2 — BRITISH CONTEXTS

PARTS

SECTION 3 — EUROPEAN AND WORLD CONTEXTS

PARTS

MARKS

SECTION 1 — SCOTTISH CONTEXTS — 20 marks

Part A — The Wars of Independence, 1286–1328

Answer the following questions using recalled knowledge and information from the sources where appropriate.

1. Explain the reasons why King John Balliol had problems ruling Scotland between 1292 and 1296.

6

Source A is an extract from a letter written by Wallace and Murray as Guardians of Scotland in 1297.

Source A

> From Andrew Murray and William Wallace, greetings to our beloved friends the mayors in Lubeck and in Hamburg. We ask that you announce to your merchants that they may safely trade their goods to all ports in the kingdom of Scotland, because the kingdom has been freed by war from the power of the English. In return, our merchants will bring their trade to you.

2. Evaluate the usefulness of **Source A** as evidence of Wallace's leadership.

   (You may want to comment on what type of source it is, who wrote it, when they wrote it, why they wrote it, what they say and what has been missed out.)

6

3. To what extent had Bruce dealt successfully with opposition by 1314?

   (You must use recalled knowledge to present a **balanced assessment** of the influence of different factors and come to a **reasoned conclusion**.)

8

[Now go to SECTION 2 starting on *Page eight*]

MARKS

SECTION 1 — SCOTTISH CONTEXTS — 20 marks

Part B — Mary Queen of Scots and the Scottish Reformation, 1542–1587

Answer the following questions using recalled knowledge and information from the sources where appropriate.

4. Explain the reasons why Protestantism grew in Scotland up to 1560.　　6

5. To what extent did Mary's marriage to Darnley play a part in her downfall in 1567?　　8

    (You must use recalled knowledge to present a **balanced assessment** of the influence of different factors and come to a **reasoned conclusion**.)

Source A is from a letter written in 1586 by Mary Queen of Scots to Anthony Babington.

Source A

> When everything is prepared and the forces are ready both in this country and abroad, then you must set the six gentlemen to work. Give orders that when the act is done, they get me away from here. At the same time get all your forces into battle order to protect me while we wait for help from abroad. May God grant success to our plans.

6. Evaluate the usefulness of **Source A** as evidence of why Mary Queen of Scots was executed in 1587.　　6

    (You may want to comment on what type of source it is, who wrote it, when they wrote it, why they wrote it, what they say and what has been missed out.)

[Now go to SECTION 2 starting on *Page eight*]

MARKS

SECTION 1 — SCOTTISH CONTEXTS — 20 marks

Part C — The Treaty of Union, 1689–1715

Answer the following questions using recalled knowledge and information from the sources where appropriate.

7. To what extent was anger over the Darien Scheme the most important reason in explaining worsening relations between Scotland and England by 1707?

    (You must use recalled knowledge to present a **balanced assessment** of the influence of different factors and come to a **reasoned conclusion.**)

8

Source A is from a petition by Stirling Town Council against the Union presented on 18 November 1706.

Source A

> We want a lasting friendship with England. But we judge that this Union will bring a high burden of taxation upon this land. Scotland would be under the rules of the English in the Parliament of Britain. The English may discourage our trade, if they think it will be in competition with their own. The Union will ruin our industry, our religion, laws and liberties.

8. Evaluate the usefulness of **Source A** as evidence of the arguments used by Scots against the Union.

    (You may want to comment on what type of source it is, who wrote it, when they wrote it, why they wrote it, what they say and what has been missed out.)

6

9. Explain the reasons why the Scots Parliament passed the Treaty of Union.

6

[Now go to SECTION 2 starting on *Page eight*]

MARKS

SECTION 1 — SCOTTISH CONTEXTS — 20 marks

Part D — Migration and Empire, 1830–1939

Answer the following questions using recalled knowledge and information from the sources where appropriate.

10. To what extent were the Clearances the most important factor for people leaving the Highlands?

    (You must use recalled knowledge to present a **balanced assessment** of the influence of different factors and come to a **reasoned conclusion**.)

    8

11. Explain the reasons why so many immigrants came to Scotland after 1830.

    6

Source A is from a song written by a Scottish emigrant to Canada in the 1920s.

Source A

> The winter night is long for me.
> I see only bleak empty prairie,
> There's no sound of waves breaking on the shore.
> In the evening darkness
> My spirit sinks with homesickness
> Thinking how far away
> Is everything I want to be visiting -
> The happy wee *ceilidh** house
> With the peat fire on the floor
> Where cheerful folk gathered for a gossip.
> But there's no *ceilidh** on the prairie.
> It seems like forever since I left Lewis.
>
> **ceilidh* = a friendly gathering, like a party

12. Evaluate the usefulness of **Source A** as evidence of how well Scots settled in their new countries.

    6

    (You may want to comment on what type of source it is, who wrote it, when they wrote it, why they wrote it, what they say and what has been missed out.)

[Now go to SECTION 2 starting on *Page eight*]

SECTION 1 — SCOTTISH CONTEXTS — 20 marks

Part E — The Era of the Great War, 1900—1928

Answer the following questions using recalled knowledge and information from the sources where appropriate.

13. Explain the reasons why so many Scots volunteered to fight in the Great War.   6

14. To what extent did food shortages have the biggest impact on Scottish civilians during the Great War?   8

    (You must use recalled knowledge to present a **balanced assessment** of the influence of different factors and come to a **reasoned conclusion**.)

Source A is from *"Scotland and the Impact of the Great War 1914—1928"* a book written by the historian John Kerr in 2010.

Source A

> The 1918 Representation of the People Act gave some women over 30 the vote in national elections. They had to be either householders or the wives of householders, occupiers of property with an annual rent of £5 or graduates of British universities. The electorate increased to about 21 million, of which 8·4 million were women. By the end of the 1920s women over 21 were also given the vote.

15. Evaluate the usefulness of **Source A** as evidence of the extension of the right to vote by 1918.   6

    (You may want to comment on what type of source it is, who wrote it, when they wrote it, why they wrote it, what they say and what has been missed out.)

[Now go to SECTION 2 starting on *Page eight*]

MARKS

SECTION 2 — BRITISH CONTEXTS — 20 marks

Part A — The Creation of the Medieval Kingdoms, 1066–1406

Answer the following questions using recalled knowledge and information from the sources where appropriate.

16. Explain the reasons why William, Duke of Normandy, claimed he had a right to the English throne.

5

Sources **A** and **B** are about how William I dealt with rebellion.

Source A

> When William's army reached York it brutally crushed the rebellion. Every home and farmland was burnt and all livestock destroyed. So many people were massacred that their bodies filled the streets. William made no attempt to control his anger and punished everyone whether they were innocent or guilty. Within weeks the whole of Yorkshire had become a wasteland. The few who had survived now faced starvation.

Source B

> William marched north with an army of experienced soldiers. Hundreds of people were slaughtered when William's men went from village to village to end the uprising. Crops were set on fire, herds of animals were slaughtered and supplies of food ruined. Whole families died of hunger as a result of William's harsh actions. The north never rebelled again and William was able to spend his time dealing with problems elsewhere in his kingdom.

17. Compare the views of **Sources A** and **B** about how William I dealt with rebellion. (Compare the sources overall and/or in detail.)

4

18. Describe the actions taken by Henry II to increase his power when he became king in 1154.

5

MARKS

Source C explains why the Church was important in medieval times.

Source C

> Harvest failure and disease meant life was often short and brutal for medieval people. The Church offered support and comfort during difficult times and encouraged people not to give up. Every Sunday, priests preached about the afterlife and taught people how to be good Christians. Priests also heard confessions and issued penance for those who wanted their sins forgiven. In this way the Church was able to control the way people behaved in society allowing most communities to live in peace.

19. How fully does **Source C** explain why the Church was important in medieval times? (Use the source and recall to reach a judgement.)   **6**

[Now go to SECTION 3 starting on *Page eighteen*]

SECTION 2 — BRITISH CONTEXTS — 20 marks

Part B — War of the Three Kingdoms, 1603–1651

Answer the following questions using recalled knowledge and information from the sources where appropriate.

Sources **A** and **B** are about the reign of King Charles I.

Source A

> The reign of Charles I began with an unpopular friendship with the Duke of Buckingham. He used his influence with the King to control the nobility. Buckingham was assassinated in 1628. There was ongoing tension with Parliament over money, made worse by the costs of war abroad. Religious tensions led to further resentment of Charles I as he preferred Anglican forms of worship which made Puritans suspicious.

Source B

> Charles I was a very religious man who enjoyed Anglican church services full of ritual, and this led to clashes with Puritans who preferred plain and simple services. Charles also angered many by having favourites at court, particularly the Duke of Buckingham. In 1628 Buckingham was assassinated. Charles' constant arguments with Parliament led him to rule without Parliament for eleven years. Charles also angered many with the methods he used to raise money.

20. Compare the views of **Sources A** and **B** about the reign of King Charles I. (Compare the sources overall and/or in detail.)   **4**

21. Explain the reasons why there was opposition to the methods used by Charles I to raise money.   **5**

22. Describe the reaction in Scotland to the introduction of the New Prayer Book in 1637.   **5**

MARKS

Source C is about the Battle of Edgehill in 1642.

Source C

> The King ordered his army to occupy the high ridge on Edgehill, hoping that the Parliamentarian army would be forced to attack uphill. Instead the Parliamentarian army was arranged on flat ground 2 miles away, waiting for the King to make the first move. The Parliamentary army was commanded by the Earl of Essex who had gained experience of commanding an army during the First Bishops' War. Essex's decision to wait forced the King to take action. The King moved his army down off the ridge and attacked.

23. How fully does **Source C** describe the events of the Battle of Edgehill in 1642? (Use the source and recall to reach a judgement.)

6

[Now go to SECTION 3 starting on *Page eighteen*]

MARKS

SECTION 2 — BRITISH CONTEXTS — 20 marks

Part C — The Atlantic Slave Trade, 1770—1807

Answer the following questions using recalled knowledge and information from the sources where appropriate.

Source A is about conditions on board ships during the Middle Passage.

Source A

> Slave ships left from British ports on the triangular trade. When the ships arrived in Africa, captains exchanged guns or alcohol for slaves. Slaves were often tightly packed below deck for the journey across the Atlantic Ocean. This was known as the middle passage. Conditions below deck were horrendous and slaves were denied basic sanitation. Disease was common and many died from conditions such as dysentery. Slaves were given enough food to sustain them during the voyage. However, the food was unfamiliar and many slaves simply refused to eat.

24. How fully does **Source A** describe the conditions on board ships during the Middle Passage? (Use the source and recall to reach a judgement.)   6

25. Explain the reasons why the slave trade was important to British cities.   5

MARKS

Sources **B** and **C** are about resistance on the plantations.

Source B

> Slaves hated the way they were treated. They were not paid for their work and saw no reason for working hard. They sabotaged their owners by working slowly and inefficiently. They broke tools and let animals loose. They were harshly punished for such behaviour. As well as whipping, some slaves had their ears, noses and limbs cut off. Many slaves attempted to run away. In mountainous islands like Jamaica, runaways fled to the mountains.

Source C

> The West Indian plantations relied on slaves to do the work. Although the slaves outnumbered the Whites they still felt isolated and powerless. However, they resisted their situation in many ways. The mildest forms of resistance were doing a job slowly or badly. Other slaves ran away when they saw a chance. The punishments for slaves who resisted were very harsh. Plantation records show that punishments such as hanging, mutilation or lashing were common.

26. Compare the views of **Sources B** and **C** about resistance on the plantations. (Compare the sources overall and/or in detail.)   4

27. Describe the methods used by abolitionists to try and end the slave trade.   5

[Now go to SECTION 3 starting on *Page eighteen*]

MARKS

SECTION 2 — BRITISH CONTEXTS — 20 marks

Part D — Changing Britain, 1760–1914

Answer the following questions using recalled knowledge and information from the sources where appropriate.

Sources **A** and **B** are about the Peterloo massacre in 1819.

Source A

> In 1819 a meeting was due to be addressed by Henry Hunt in Manchester. People had gathered from all over Lancashire in St Peter's Fields. The magistrates wrongly believed that people had been marching and drilling like soldiers in preparation. They ordered the army to charge the crowd. In the stampede that followed, 11 people were killed and hundreds injured. The press nicknamed the tragedy "Peterloo" in mocking memory of the Battle of Waterloo.

Source B

> I saw a large crowd that had gathered from miles around and was moving towards St Peter's Fields. I laughed at the fears of the magistrates as the so-called "marching" protest was actually a procession of men with their wives, sisters and children. After that there was just noise and confusion and I could see that many people had been hurt. I will always be haunted by the sight of those trampled bodies.

28. Compare the views of **Sources A** and **B** about the events of the Peterloo massacre in 1819. (Compare the sources overall and/or in detail.) **4**

29. Explain the reasons why working in mills was harmful to the health of textile workers. **5**

MARKS

Source C describes the benefits that railways brought to Britain.

Source C

> Railways changed the lives of nearly everyone in Britain. As early as 1852, all the present-day main lines had been laid. Even the most remote country areas were brought into contact with towns and cities. Industries benefited greatly from being able to transport their raw materials and goods quickly and cheaply. Farmers were able to sell their fresh produce over greater distances. Faster travel meant that people could live further from their jobs, so towns spread as suburbs were built.

30. How fully does **Source C** explain the benefits brought to Britain by railways? (Use the source and recall to reach a judgement.)   6

31. Describe the changes made to voting and representation by 1867.   5

[Now go to SECTION 3 starting on *Page eighteen*]

MARKS

SECTION 2 — BRITISH CONTEXTS — 20 marks

Part E — The Making of Modern Britain, 1880–1951

Answer the following questions using recalled knowledge and information from the sources where appropriate.

32. Describe the problems facing the poor by the early 1900s.   **5**

Source A is about changing attitudes to poverty.

Source A

> In 1900 the Labour Party was formed. This new party campaigned for reforms to tackle poverty. Other parties were afraid that they might lose votes to Labour if they did not show that they wanted to help the poor. Most working class men now had the vote, so it was possible that they could vote for Labour. Trade unions put pressure on the Liberals and Conservatives to do more to help the poor. Society was beginning to accept that some people became poor through no fault of their own.

33. How fully does **Source A** explain the reasons for changing attitudes to poverty by the 1900s? (Use the source and recall to reach a judgement.)   **6**

34. Explain the reasons why the reforms of the Liberal government of 1906–1914 did not fully meet the needs of the British people.   **5**

Sources **B** and **C** are about the success of the reforms of the Labour Government of 1945—1951.

Source B

> There is some disagreement amongst historians about how successful the Labour reforms actually were. However, their record of success is difficult to argue with. The National Health Service was the greatest achievement of the Labour welfare state, giving free medical and dental treatment to all. Considerable progress was made in tackling the housing shortage. Between 1948 and 1951, around 200,000 homes were built per year.

Source C

> Labour came to power in 1945. Their reputation of being the creator of the modern welfare state is not entirely deserved. Labour's record on house building was poor when compared to previous governments. Labour claimed the credit for maintaining low levels of unemployment, but this was mainly due to booming private industry and exports. By 1951, charges had to be introduced for some dental treatment, spectacles and prescriptions, meaning the NHS was not entirely free.

35. Compare the views of **Sources B** and **C** about the success of the reforms of the Labour Government of 1945—1951. (Compare the sources overall and/or in detail.)   4

[Now go to SECTION 3 starting on *Page eighteen*]

MARKS

SECTION 3 — EUROPEAN AND WORLD CONTEXTS — 20 marks

Part A — The Cross and the Crescent: the Crusades, 1071–1192

Answer the following questions using recalled knowledge and information from the sources where appropriate.

36. Describe the role of a knight in medieval times. **5**

37. Explain the reasons why the People's Crusade failed. **5**

Source A describes Muslim disunity.

Source A

> After capturing Antioch, the Crusader army had an easy march south. Local Muslim communities did not attack the Crusaders and some even gave them money to keep the peace. Unwilling to end their bitter rivalries, the Muslim leaders refused to join together and thought only of their own land. By the time the Crusaders reached Jerusalem, the Seljuk Turks had been defeated by an Egyptian force and had lost the city. The Egyptians asked for help but no Muslim armies came to their aid.

38. How fully does **Source A** describe Muslim disunity during the First Crusade? (Use the source and recall to reach a judgement.) **5**

Source B is from a chronicle written by a Crusader in 1187.

Source B

> Desperate to help the Christians in Tiberias, King Guy gathered a large Crusader army and left for the city. Whilst on their way, the Crusaders were constantly attacked by Saladin's men. Exhausted by their journey, King Guy made a terrible mistake and made camp near Hattin. Without water and supplies the Crusaders could neither carry on nor turn back. Saladin's army surrounded the Crusaders' camp and slaughtered nearly all those inside.

39. Evaluate the usefulness of **Source B** as evidence of the Battle of Hattin. **5**

   (You may want to comment on what type of source it is, who wrote it, when they wrote it, why they wrote it, what they say and what has been missed out.)

MARKS

SECTION 3 — EUROPEAN AND WORLD CONTEXTS — 20 marks

Part B — "Tea and Freedom": the American Revolution, 1774–1783

Answer the following questions using recalled knowledge and information from the sources where appropriate.

40. Explain the reasons why the colonists had become unhappy with British rule by the 1770s.   **5**

41. Describe the events at Bunker Hill in 1775.   **5**

Source A is about the events in Lexington and Concord in 1775.

Source A

> By early 1775 many in the colonies had started to prepare for war. Spies had informed the British commander in Boston about a store of gunpowder and weapons that the colonists had been collecting at Concord. British soldiers were dispatched to seize the supplies. When the British arrived at Lexington they were confronted by a group of minutemen. These were colonists who had been training and preparing for war. Shots were fired and several colonists were killed. The British then marched on to Concord where they destroyed any remaining supplies.

42. How fully does **Source A** describe the events at Lexington and Concord in 1775? (Use the source and recall to reach a judgement.)   **5**

Source B is from a diary written by an American army officer in December 1777.

Source B

> The army now continues to grow sickly from the exhaustion they have suffered in this campaign. We are sick — discontented — and out of humour. Poor food — cold weather — nasty clothes — nasty cooking — the Devil's in it! I can't endure it! Why are we sent here to starve and freeze? Despite all of this, the men still show a spirit not to be expected from such young troops.

43. Evaluate the usefulness of **Source B** as evidence of the condition of the American army during the winter of 1777.   **5**

    (You may want to comment on what type of source it is, who wrote it, when they wrote it, why they wrote it, what they say and what has been missed out.)

MARKS

SECTION 3 — EUROPEAN AND WORLD CONTEXTS — 20 marks

Part C — USA, 1850–1880

Answer the following questions using recalled knowledge and information from the sources where appropriate.

44. Describe the problems faced by the different groups who travelled west after 1850. **5**

45. Explain the reasons why the Southern States seceded from the Union in 1861. **5**

Source A is from a letter written by George Fitzhugh, a Southern lawyer, in 1857.

Source A

> The slaves of the South are the happiest and are, in many ways, the most free people in the world. The children, the aged and the sick do not work at all. They have all the comforts and necessaries of life provided for them such as food and housing. The slave women do little hard work. On average the slave men and boys do not work more than nine hours a day in good weather.

46. Evaluate the usefulness of **Source A** as evidence of slave life on plantations before 1861. **5**

   (You may want to comment on what type of source it is, who wrote it, when they wrote it, why they wrote it, what they say and what has been missed out.)

Source B is part of a speech made by Frederick Douglass, a former slave, in 1880.

Source B

> Slaves were made free in 1865. At first there were great hopes for change. But today, in most of the Southern States, the Fourteenth and Fifteenth Amendments to the Constitution are almost totally ignored. The right of citizenship granted in the Fourteenth Amendment is practically a mockery. The right to vote, provided for in the Fifteenth Amendment, is under attack. The old ruling class is victorious today and the newly freed slaves are little better off than they were before the rebellion of the Southern States against the Union.

47. How fully does **Source B** describe the impact of Reconstruction in the South after 1865? (Use the source and recall to reach a judgement.) **5**

MARKS

SECTION 3 — EUROPEAN AND WORLD CONTEXTS — 20 marks

Part D — Hitler and Nazi Germany, 1919—1939

Answer the following questions using recalled knowledge and information from the sources where appropriate.

48. Explain the reasons why the German people were opposed to the Treaty of Versailles.

5

49. Describe the treatment of the Jews in Nazi Germany.

5

Source A is from the diary of Ernst Thalmann, a Communist leader writing about his arrest in 1933 by the Gestapo.

Source A

> Every cruel method of blackmail was used against me to obtain details about my comrades. But the approach proved unsuccessful. I was then assaulted and in the process had four teeth knocked out. They tried hypnosis which was also ineffective. Finally, a Gestapo officer with a whip in his hand beat me with measured strokes. Driven wild with pain, I screamed at the top of my voice.

50. Evaluate the usefulness of **Source A** as evidence of the use of intimidation by the Nazis.

5

(You may want to comment on what type of source it is, who wrote it, when they wrote it, why they wrote it, what they say and what has been missed out.)

Source B is about the activities of the Hitler Youth.

Source B

> Boys learned military skills such as practising with weapons. To toughen them up, they were taken on cross country hikes and runs. One member of the Hitler Youth remembered that anyone who got a stitch while running was punished and humiliated as a weakling. Boys were also tested on their knowledge of Nazism and those who passed the test were given a dagger marked "Blood and Honour". Most members of the Hitler Youth joined because they thought it was fun and exciting. However they did not all enjoy the endless marching.

51. How fully does **Source B** describe the activities of the Hitler Youth? (Use the source and recall to reach a judgement.)

5

MARKS

SECTION 3 — EUROPEAN AND WORLD CONTEXTS — 20 marks

Part E — Red Flag: Lenin and the Russian Revolution, 1894—1921

Answer the following questions using recalled knowledge and information from the sources where appropriate.

Source A is about the conditions for workers and peasants in Russia before 1905.

Source A

> Tsar Nicholas II, I do not wish to die without having told you and the people of Russia what I think of your activities up to the present. Police brutality is steadily growing. The prisons are filled to overflowing with hundreds of thousands of common criminals. Many workers are now imprisoned along with political prisoners. The treatment of millions of peasants, on whom the power of Russia depends, leads to them becoming poorer every year. Famine is now normal throughout the country.

52. How fully does **Source A** describe the conditions of workers and peasants in Russia before 1905? (Use the source and recall to reach a judgement.)   **5**

53. Describe the reforms which were introduced in Russia after the 1905 Revolution.   **5**

54. Explain the reasons why the Bolsheviks were able to seize power in Petrograd in October 1917.   **5**

Source B is from the diary of Leon Trotsky written in 1921.

Source B

> We formed an army out of peasants, workers and refugees escaping from the Whites. We believed that this flabby, panicky mob could be changed into a useful force. What was needed were good commanders and a few experienced fighters. The mob would fight as long as they had boots for the barefooted, a bathhouse, food, underwear, tobacco and a dozen or so Communists ready to make any sacrifice to inspire them.

55. Evaluate the usefulness of **Source B** as evidence of the reasons for the Bolshevik victory in the Civil War.   **5**

(You may want to comment on what type of source it is, who wrote it, when they wrote it, why they wrote it, what they say and what has been missed out.)

MARKS

SECTION 3 — EUROPEAN AND WORLD CONTEXTS — 20 marks

Part F — Mussolini and Fascist Italy, 1919—1939

Answer the following questions using recalled knowledge and information from the sources where appropriate.

56. Explain the reasons why Mussolini was able to secure power in Italy by 1925.   5

57. Describe the policies introduced by Mussolini to try to control the lives of young Italians.   5

Source A is about the cult of "Il Duce".

Source A

> When the Fascists came to power in 1922, a leadership cult was established in Italy. The media played a very important role, making Mussolini the centre of every story. The cult built popular support for him and secured continuing support for his dictatorship. Benito Mussolini was shown as a man chosen by destiny to save Italy and its people from Communism and Socialism. He was the new Caesar — a man of genius, a man of action.

58. How fully does **Source A** describe the cult of "Il Duce". (Use the source and recall to reach a judgement.)   5

Source B is part of a speech made by Mussolini in 1922.

Source B

> There is much for us to do in this country. Perfect unity in Italy cannot be spoken of until Fiume and Dalmatia and other territories have come back to us, fulfilling the proud dream which we carry in our hearts. Violence may have to be used. Violence is sometimes necessary. Italy, in order to become a Mediterranean power, must have control over the Adriatic Sea.

59. Evaluate the usefulness of **Source B** as evidence of Mussolini's foreign policy.   5

   (You may want to comment on what type of source it is, who wrote it, when they wrote it, why they wrote it, what they say and what has been missed out.)

MARKS

SECTION 3 — EUROPEAN AND WORLD CONTEXTS — 20 marks

Part G — Free at Last? Civil Rights in the USA, 1918—1968

Answer the following questions using recalled knowledge and information from the sources where appropriate.

60. Describe the ways that the Jim Crow laws segregated black and white Americans. **5**

61. Explain the reasons why many Americans were against immigration by the 1920s. **5**

Source A is about the actions of the Ku Klux Klan.

Source A

> The original Ku Klux Klan was a white supremacist organisation founded in 1866. Wearing white robes and pointed hats, the Klan of the 1920s looked similar to the original. During elections, the Klan would wait outside the voting place to beat up blacks if they came near. Women considered immoral were also targeted by the Klan. A divorced woman in Texas was tarred and feathered for remarrying. A massive march in Washington DC in 1925 was a demonstration of the Klan's power.

62. How fully does **Source A** describe the actions of the Ku Klux Klan in the 1920s? (Use the source and recall to reach a judgement.) **5**

Source B is from a newspaper interview with a black American taxi driver from New York in 1961.

Source B

> I like Malcolm the best. I can believe in a leader who comes from the street, Malcolm is one of us. Malcolm isn't afraid to stand up to the FBI and the cops. Those black Muslims make more sense than the NAACP and all of the rest of them put together, you don't see Malcolm tip-toeing around the whites like he's scared of them.

63. Evaluate the usefulness of **Source B** as evidence of the reasons why Malcolm X was popular amongst many black Americans. **5**

(You may want to comment on what type of source it is, who wrote it, when they wrote it, why they wrote it, what they say and what has been missed out.)

MARKS

SECTION 3 — EUROPEAN AND WORLD CONTEXTS — 20 marks

Part H — Appeasement and the Road to War, 1918—1939

Answer the following questions using recalled knowledge and information from the sources where appropriate.

64. Describe the ways in which Hitler rearmed Germany between 1933 and 1935.

5

Source A is from an article by the historian Professor Neil Gregor in *"20th Century History Review"*, published in 2008.

Source A

> The Anschluss had a number of significant consequences and was notable for several reasons. Most obviously, it marked the beginning of Germany's territorial expansion, starting a chain of events which continued with the occupation of the Sudetenland. The lack of meaningful opposition from Britain and France underlined again for Hitler that he could do as he pleased. The persecution of Jews by the Nazis was greatly intensified following the Anschluss, especially in Austria.

65. Evaluate the usefulness of **Source A** as evidence of the consequences of the Anschluss.

5

(You may want to comment on what type of source it is, who wrote it, when they wrote it, why they wrote it, what they say and what has been missed out.)

Source B is about the British policy of appeasement in the 1930s.

Source B

> Appeasement was a policy which involved making concessions to Hitler. The main reason for such a stance was a belief that given the harsh treatment of Germany at Versailles, Hitler's demands were not unreasonable. The policy was motivated by several other factors. The British public were still haunted by memories of World War One and unwilling to back military action. Chiefs of the armed forces advised that the British military was unprepared for war. The Treasury meanwhile warned against the financial consequences of war.

66. How fully does **Source B** explain the reasons why Britain followed a policy of appeasement? (Use the source and recall to reach a judgement.)

5

67. Explain the reasons why Hitler declared war on Poland in 1939.

5

MARKS

SECTION 3 — EUROPEAN AND WORLD CONTEXTS — 20 marks

Part I — World War II, 1939—1945

Answer the following questions using recalled knowledge and information from the sources where appropriate.

68. Explain the reasons why Hitler launched an attack on Russia in June 1941.

5

69. Describe the attack on Pearl Harbour by Japanese forces in December 1941.

5

Source A is about the preparation for the Normandy Landings of June 1944.

Source A

> Operation Overlord was a complex operation. It involved the land, sea and air forces of the USA, Britain and Canada. Preparations began in 1943 under the overall command of General Eisenhower of the United States. Normandy was chosen as the site for the landings because of its open beaches that were not as well defended as those at Calais. Normandy was also chosen because it had a fairly large port, Cherbourg. It was also opposite the main ports of southern England. The intended date for the invasion was May 1944.

70. How fully does **Source A** describe the preparations for the Normandy Landings of June 1944? (Use the source and recall to reach a judgement.)

5

Source B is from a leaflet dropped by the US Government over Japan on 16 August 1945.

Source B

> TO THE JAPANESE PEOPLE: We are in possession of the most destructive explosive devised by man. We have just begun to use this weapon against your country. If you still have any doubts, ask what happened to Hiroshima when just one atomic bomb fell on that city. You should take steps now to surrender. Otherwise we shall use this bomb again to promptly and forcefully end the war. EVACUATE YOUR CITIES.

71. Evaluate the usefulness of **Source B** as evidence of the use of atomic bombs against Japan in 1945.

5

(You may want to comment on what type of source it is, who wrote it, when they wrote it, why they wrote it, what they say and what has been missed out.)

MARKS

SECTION 3 — EUROPEAN AND WORLD CONTEXTS — 20 marks

Part J — The Cold War, 1945–1989

Answer the following questions using recalled knowledge and information from the sources where appropriate.

Source A is from a leaflet published by the East German Government in 1962.

Source A

> We could no longer stand by and see so many of our doctors, engineers and skilled workers persuaded by corrupt methods to work in West Germany or West Berlin. These dirty tricks cost East Germany annual losses amounting to 3·5 thousand million marks. But we prevented something much more important with the Wall — West Berlin could have become the starting point for military conflict.

72. Evaluate the usefulness of **Source A** as evidence of why the Berlin Wall was built.

    (You may want to comment on what type of source it is, who wrote it, when they wrote it, why they wrote it, what they say and what has been missed out.)

    5

Source B is about the Cuban missile crisis.

Source B

> During the Cuban missile crisis it was said that the world held its breath. There was a crisis in Cuba because by the early 1960s the USA and the Soviet Union were bitter rivals. Many in the United States believed that the Soviet actions in Cuba provided proof of a determination to spread Communism all around the world. Cuba was very close to the American mainland and this explains why Americans were so concerned by events there. Both sides were afraid to back down in case they lost face.

73. How fully does **Source B** explain the reasons for the Cuban missile crisis? (Use the source and recall to reach a judgement.)

    5

74. Describe the differing American views on the Vietnam War.

    5

75. Explain the reasons why the USA and the Soviet Union followed a policy of détente after 1968.

    5

[END OF QUESTION PAPER]

[BLANK PAGE]

DO NOT WRITE ON THIS PAGE

NATIONAL 5
Answers

NATIONAL 5 HISTORY 2014

Section 1, Context A, The Wars of Independence, 1286-1328

1. *Candidates can be credited in a number of ways up to a maximum of 5 marks.*

Candidates must show a causal relationship between events.

Up to a **maximum of 5 marks in total**, **1 mark** should be given for each accurate, relevant reason, and a **second mark** should be given for reasons that are developed. Candidates may achieve full marks by providing five straightforward reasons, three developed reasons, or a combination of these.

Possible reasons may include:
1. Alexander III had died without a surviving male heir/ Scots had agreed the infant Margaret was his heir, Edward approached for help
2. Edward had been Alexander's brother-in-law and a friend
3. Edward was a strong king who could use his authority to subdue Scottish troublemakers/there was a threat of civil war
4. Edward was Margaret's great uncle so could claim an interest as a relative
5. The Scots agreed to the Treaty of Birgham and the marriage of Margaret to Edward's infant son
6. Margaret died before she reached Scotland so there was now no direct heir – a further opportunity for Edward's involvement
7. Bishop Fraser invited Edward to help choose from the claimants to the throne
8. Edward insisted the claimants/competitors accepted him as their overlord before he would begin to judge the claims
9. Edward insisted the Scottish castles be handed over to him, to hold for the eventual king
10. All the competitors accepted that Edward was overlord
11. Edward judged that John Balliol had the best claim
12. Balliol paid homage to Edward for Scotland after his coronation, making Edward's superiority clear

2. *Candidates can be credited in a number of ways up to a maximum of 5 marks.*

They may take different perspectives on the events and may describe a variety of different aspects of the events.

1 mark should be given for each accurate relevant key point of knowledge. **A second mark** should be given for each point that is developed, up to a maximum of **5 marks**. Candidates may achieve full marks by providing five straightforward points, by making three developed points, or a combination of these.

Possible points of knowledge may include:
1. Wallace and Murray joined forces on the north side of the River Forth
2. The Scots were on the high ground of Abbey Craig/the English assembled on the south side of the river
3. The English delayed the start of the battle/Surrey slept in
4. The English could not decide whether to use the narrow bridge or travel further upstream and cross at the broader ford
5. Cressingham did not want any further expenses and wanted to get the battle over as quickly as possible in case the Scots escaped so opted for the bridge
6. The English partly crossed, turned back and then began again, making their plans clear to the Scots
7. The English crossed the bridge slowly/only three abreast
8. The Scots attacked before all the English were over
9. The Scots attacked the end of the bridge trapping the English who had crossed and preventing the rest from crossing to help them
10. English soldiers who attempted to escape across the river were drowned/weighed down by waterlogged tunics
11. Bridge collapsed and English fled
12. The English were defeated/Cressingham was killed

3. *Candidates can be credited in a number of ways up to a maximum of 5 marks.*

Candidates must make a judgement about the usefulness of the source and support this by making evaluative comments on identified aspects of the source.

1 mark should be given for each relevant comment made, up to a **maximum of 5 marks in total**.

- A maximum of **4 marks** can be given for evaluative comments relating to the author, type of source, purpose and timing.
- A maximum of **2 marks** may be given for comments relating to the content of the source.
- A maximum of **2 marks** may be given for comments relating to points of significant omission.

Examples of aspects of the source and relevant comments:

Aspect of the source	Possible comment
Author: Walter of Guisborough	Churchman in Guisborough Priory in Yorkshire, so not an eyewitness, so perhaps less useful
Type of Source: Chronicle	Contains details of events, generally thought to be reliable so more useful
Purpose: To record	Keep a record of events as a history, so may be more useful, but an English version so may be biased against Bruce
Timing: Early 14th century	Written during the Wars of Independence at the time of Bruce taking the throne, so more useful.

Content	Possible comment
He lured him to a meeting in Greyfriars Church	Suggests Bruce planned a deception so shows bias so less useful
Bruce accused Comyn of telling lies about him	May not be accurate so less useful
He struck him with his sword	Puts blame on Bruce so may be biased and less useful

Possible points of significant omission may include:
1. Comyn was his main rival so more useful
2. Comyn was killed by Bruce/Bruce's men
3. Comyn's body was left at the altar
4. Bruce was excommunicated for sacrilege
5. Bruce had himself crowned king

4. *Candidates can be credited in a number of ways up to a maximum of 5 marks.*

Candidates must make an overall judgement about how fully the source explains the events. **1 mark** may be given for each valid point interpreted from the source or each valid point of significant omission provided. The candidate can achieve **up to 3 marks** for their interpretation of the parts of the source they consider are relevant in terms of the proposed question where there is also at least one point of significant omission identified to imply a judgement has been made about the limitations of the source. For full marks to be given each point needs to be discretely mentioned in terms of the question.

A maximum of 2 marks may be given for answers which refer only to the source or in which no judgement has been made.

Possible points which may be identified in the source include:
1. Bruce's parliament agreed that Scots nobles who had not made peace with him would lose their lands in Scotland
2. Bruce gave this forfeited land to his own supporters
3. Scots nobles would no longer be allowed to have English estates so their loyalties would not be divided
4. Continued to raid the north of England to put pressure on Edward

Possible points of significant omission may include:
1. Defeated English army at Bannockburn
2. Secured release of his wife and daughter/Wishart, in exchange for ransomed English prisoners
3. Recaptured Berwick from English occupation
4. Added to Scottish exchequer by accepting protection money from northern English towns
5. Encouraged production of Declaration of Arbroath
6. Renewed Alliance with France
7. Agreed Treaty of Edinburgh with England in 1328
8. Made a marriage treaty for his son/heir

Section 1, Context B, Mary Queen of Scots and the Scottish Reformation, 1542-1587

1. *Candidates can be credited in a number of ways up to a maximum of 5 marks.*

They may take different perspectives on the events and may describe a variety of different aspects of the events.

1 mark should be given for each accurate relevant key point of knowledge. **A second mark** should be given for each point that is developed, up to a maximum of **5 marks**. Candidates may achieve full marks by providing five straightforward points, by making three developed points, or a combination of these.

Possible points of knowledge may include:
1. English wanted Mary to marry Edward, son of Henry VIII, Treaty of Greenwich
2. Scots cancelled their agreement for Mary to marry Edward, this angered Henry
3. Henry VIII sent armies to destroy Scottish cities/punish the Scots – known as the 'Rough Wooing'

4. English armies tried to capture Mary
5. English armies burned Edinburgh/Borders Abbeys, St Andrews etc
6. English defeated the Scots at the Battle of Pinkie, 1547
7. Scots needed French help/French agreed if Mary married the French Dauphin (Treaty of Haddington)
8. Mary left for France from Dumbarton in August 1548

2. *Candidates can be credited in a number of ways up to a maximum of 5 marks.*

Candidates must make an overall judgement about how fully the source explains the events. **1 mark** may be given for each valid point interpreted from the source or each valid point of significant omission provided. The candidate can achieve **up to 3 marks** for their interpretation of the parts of the source they consider are relevant in terms of the proposed question where there is also at least one point of significant omission identified to imply a judgement has been made about the limitations of the source. For full marks to be given each point needs to be discretely mentioned in terms of the question.

A maximum of 2 marks may be given for answers which refer only to the source or in which no judgement has been made.

Possible points which may be identified in the source include:
1. The Protestant form of worship meant that people could participate much more in services.
2. The Bible was available in English, not Latin; therefore people who could not read Latin could still understand it
3. Some people began to criticise the Catholic Church because of its great wealth
4. Local priests were resented for charging people for christening their children.

Possible points of significant omission may include:
1. Some Scots began to resent the wealth of the Catholic Church eg excessive spending on decoration
2. Some priests & nuns attacked for setting bad example eg spent wealth on themselves not the poor/broke vow of chastity
3. Resentment at the way Protestant preachers had been treated led to more sympathy for Protestants eg Wishart burned as a heretic
4. Resentment at Catholic foreign influence at court (French)
5. Creation of the Lords of the Congregation/many favoured Protestantism
6. Scottish Parliament that met in 1560 was controlled by men who had sympathised with the Reformation
7. Scottish Parliament banned the celebration of mass in 1560/agreed to end the power of the Pope over the Church in Scotland
8. Lack of priests or poor quality of priests caused resentment

3. *Candidates can be credited in a number of ways up to a maximum of 5 marks.*

Candidates must make a judgement about the usefulness of the source and support this by making evaluative comments on identified aspects of the source.

1 mark should be given for each relevant comment made, up to a **maximum of 5 marks in total**.
- A maximum of 4 marks can be given for evaluative comments relating to the author, type of source, purpose and timing.

- A maximum of 2 marks may be given for comments relating to the content of the source.
- A maximum of 2 marks may be given for comments relating to points of significant omission.

Examples of aspects of the source and relevant comments:

Aspect of the source	Possible comment
Author: John Knox	Useful as he was an influential Protestant reformer/hated Mary as a Catholic ruler
Type of Source: Sermon	Useful as heard by Protestant followers/ public expression of Knox's views
Purpose: To persuade	Less useful as it is biased/ enthusiastically condemns Mary and her Catholic religion/to persuade people to turn against Mary
Timing: 1560s	Useful as it was delivered when the Protestant faith was growing in Scotland

Content	Possible comment
In the north of the country, where Mary had travelled before harvest time, the famine was hardest with great suffering. Many people died	Less useful as Knox blames Mary for causing famine – extreme and much exaggerated view/but perhaps useful as many Protestants also held these views
Thus did God punish the many sins of our wicked Queen and her followers	Less useful as he claims God is punishing Scotland for having a Catholic Queen – extreme and much exaggerated view/but perhaps useful as many Protestants also held these views
The excessive celebrations and huge feasts in the palace and in the country provoked God into this action	Less useful as he claims God punished Scotland because of Mary's behaviour – extreme and much exaggerated view/but perhaps useful as many Protestants also held these views

Possible points of significant omission may include:
1. John Knox denounced Mary for her whole way of life, she was an 'ungodly ruler', eg dancing criticised
2. Knox would often lecture Mary on religion, condemning Catholicism (Mary reduced to tears by him on one occasion)
3. Some Protestants were happy with Mary eg she tolerated their religion/ ensured the Protestant Church had an income

4. *Candidates can be credited in a number of ways up to a maximum of 5 marks.*

Candidates must show a causal relationship between events.

Up to a **maximum of 5 marks in total**, **1 mark** should be given for each accurate, relevant reason, and a **second mark** should be given for reasons that are developed. Candidates may achieve full marks by providing five straightforward reasons, three developed reasons, or a combination of these.

Possible reasons may include:
1. Nobles persuaded Darnley that Riccio was too friendly with Mary/implied they were having an affair
2. Riccio was humiliating the Scottish nobles by making them ask him to see Mary

3. Riccio was boasting about his influence over Mary
4. Riccio was dressing and behaving like a nobleman which angered the nobles as he was below them in status
5. Darnley thought Riccio had persuaded Mary not to give him the crown matrimonial, which angered Darnley
6. Some nobles thought Riccio was a spy sent by the Pope so were suspicious of Riccio

Section 1, Context C, The Treaty of Union, 1689-1715

1. *Candidates can be credited in a number of ways up to a maximum of 5 marks.*

They may take different perspectives on the events and may describe a variety of different aspects of the events.

1 mark should be given for each accurate relevant key point of knowledge. **A second mark** should be given for each point that is developed, up to a maximum of **5 marks**. Candidates may achieve full marks by providing five straightforward points, by making three developed points, or a combination of these.

Possible points of knowledge may include:
1. King William wanted to remain on good terms with the Spanish and so deliberately sabotaged the Darien colony
2. English officials prevented investment in the Darien scheme
3. There was a feeling that the English had not done enough to help Scotland during the Ill Years of the 1690s
4. William took little positive interest in Scotland eg Glencoe massacre
5. Anne had declared herself to be "entirely English"
6. The strength of Jacobitism in Scotland caused tension
7. Scots loyalties were suspect after the rebellion of 1689
8. The Scots were angry that the English Parliament passed the succession to Sophia of Hanover without consulting them
9. The English were angry when the Scots Parliament passed the Act of Security
10. Scottish trade badly affected by England's French wars (no Scottish gains in the peace treaties)
11. Worcester incident

2. *Candidates can be credited in a number of ways up to a maximum of 5 marks.*

Candidates must make a judgement about the usefulness of the source and support this by making evaluative comments on identified aspects of the source.

1 mark should be given for each relevant comment made, up to a **maximum of 5 marks in total**.
- A maximum of **4 marks** can be given for evaluative comments relating to the author, type of source, purpose and timing.
- A maximum of **2 marks** may be given for comments relating to the content of the source.
- A maximum of **2 marks** may be given for comments relating to points of significant omission.

Examples of aspects of the source and relevant comments:

Aspect of the source	Possible comment
Author: Andrew Fletcher	Useful as he was one of the leading opponents of the Union.
Type of Source: Leaflet	Useful as this was a common method of trying to communicate political ideas at this time.

Purpose: To persuade	Less useful as the writer is biased against the Union/designed to persuade the reader that the Union will be bad for Scotland
Timing: One year before Union was agreed	Useful as it is written when the Union was being debated in Scotland.

Content	Possible comment
Scotland needs to keep its own separate law and church	Useful as it was a commonly held view at the time.
If the Scots agree to these interests being controlled by a single Parliament they will surrender control to the English	Useful as it reflects the fears of many Scots.
The English will have a vast majority.	Useful as it is an accurate statement about the parliamentary arithmetic after Union.

Possible points of significant omission may include:

1. Scotland had always been an independent nation and its identity would be subsumed if there was a new united Parliament.
2. Public opinion in Scotland was against a union.
3. Some Scots would have preferred a Federal Union eg Andrew Fletcher.
4. Episcopalians in Scotland opposed union as it would secure the Hanoverian succession and only a return to the Stuart dynasty could restore episcopacy to the Scottish church.
5. Some Presbyterians feared over the position of the Church of Scotland. The English Parliament was dominated by the Episcopalian church with Bishops' seats in the House of Lords.

3. *Candidates can be credited in a number of ways up to a maximum of 5 marks.*

Candidates must make an overall judgement about how fully the source explains the events. **1 mark** may be given for each valid point interpreted from the source or each valid point of significant omission provided. The candidate can achieve **up to 3 marks** for their interpretation of the parts of the source they consider are relevant in terms of the proposed question where there is also at least one point of significant omission identified to imply a judgement has been made about the limitations of the source. For full marks to be given each point needs to be discretely mentioned in terms of the question.

A maximum of 2 marks may be given for answers which refer only to the source or in which no judgement has been made.

Possible points which may be identified in the source include:

1. By this union we will all have access to all the advantages of trade that the English enjoy at the moment
2. We will be able to improve our wealth
3. We will have our liberty, our property and our religion secured
4. Scotland will be under the protection of one sovereign and one Parliament of Great Britain.

Possible points of significant omission may include:

- If Scotland failed to accept Union voluntarily they might be forced to accept it on unfavourable terms after an English invasion.
- The Scots knew that Ireland had been conquered by England and wanted to avoid this fate.
- Presbyterians wanted to solve the problem of the succession and ensure that the exiled Stuarts did not return
- The Union guaranteed the position of the Presbyterian Church
- Fear of the reintroduction of the Alien Act if Union was not approved by the Scots
- Many Scots believed the Scottish economy would benefit from Union
- Scots attracted by guarantee of free trade with the UK and the colonies
- Some felt that failure of Darien proved that Scotland could no longer go it alone/some influential Scots saw it as only way to recover from the financial disaster of the Darian Scheme
- The position of Scots Law had been guaranteed

4. *Candidates can be credited in a number of ways up to a maximum of 5 marks.*

Candidates must show a causal relationship between events.

Up to a **maximum of 5 marks in total**, **1 mark** should be given for each accurate, relevant reason, and a **second mark** should be given for reasons that are developed. Candidates may achieve full marks by providing five straightforward reasons, three developed reasons, or a combination of these.

Possible reasons may include:

1. The 1707 Union was deeply unpopular. It had failed to bring economic prosperity to Scotland
2. Many participated as they were anti-Union. James VIII promised to end the Union
3. Dislike of the Campbells (especially in the Highlands)
4. Episcopalians offered support as the return of James seemed to provide the best prospect of an Episcopalian church settlement
5. Loyalty to the House of Stuart. Jacobites did not accept William, Anne or George. They believed James was the rightful King
6. Highland clansmen felt loyalty to the exiled King
7. Some participants were "forced out"
8. The Earl of Mar fought for selfish political reasons as he had lost his government position under George I
9. Dislike of new currency, weights etc
10. Disappointment at failure of payment of the Equivalent motivated some to participate

Section 1, Context D, Migration and Empire, 1830-1939

1. *Candidates can be credited in a number of ways up to a maximum of 5 marks.*

Candidates must show a causal relationship between events.

Up to a **maximum of 5 marks in total**, **1 mark** should be given for each accurate, relevant reason, and a **second mark** should be given for reasons that are developed. Candidates may achieve full marks by providing five straightforward reasons, three developed reasons, or a combination of these.

Possible reasons may include:

1. Scots accused them of taking Scots' jobs, so resented immigrants
2. Scots accused them of working for less money/lowering wages, so suspicious of immigrants
3. Immigrants were exploited as strike breakers/did not join in with strikes so were unpopular
4. Some had a reputation for drunkenness, so many Scots were wary of immigrants
5. Some had a reputation for violence/fighting, so some Scots were afraid of immigrants
6. Accused them of causing overcrowding/pressure on limited housing stock/ putting up rents, which caused resentment
7. Immigrants were said to spread disease/unhygienic way of life/'brought down' the Scots, so viewed with suspicion
8. Accused some of claiming poor relief intended for Scots, so were resented
9. Some immigrants practised a different religion, which made Scots suspicious of them
10. Some immigrants failed to fit in/kept to themselves/ kept their own customs, so were viewed with suspicion

2. *Candidates can be credited in a number of ways up to a maximum of 5 marks.*

They may take different perspectives on the events and may describe a variety of different aspects of the events.

1 mark should be given for each accurate relevant key point of knowledge. **A second mark** should be given for each point that is developed, up to a maximum of **5 marks**. Candidates may achieve full marks by providing five straightforward points, by making three developed points, or a combination of these.

Possible points of knowledge may include:

1. Fares were paid by landlords in the Highlands
2. HIES – sent poor crofter families to Australia
3. Glasgow Emigration Society – gave assistance to settle in Canada
4. British Government/Colonial Land and Emigration Commissioners – 'Bounty' settlers to Australia
5. Emigrants' Information Office – gave advice and assistance on aspects of emigration
6. Empire Settlement Act 1922 – gave loans and grants to help with passages and training
7. Barnardos/Quarriers – sent orphan boys and girls to Australia and Canada
8. YMCA – helped young men to emigrate as farm workers/Big Brother scheme supported boys who emigrated/'Dreadnought' boys supported as farm workers
9. Personal loans from family paid for fares etc
10. Cheap rail/steamer fares offered by transport companies eg Anchor-Donaldson Line
11. Subsidised passages paid for by Australian and Canadian governments
12. Free passage for domestic servants to New Zealand, Lewis girls as servants to Canada etc

3. *Candidates can be credited in a number of ways up to a maximum of 5 marks.*

Candidates must make an overall judgement about how fully the source explains the events. **1 mark** may be given for each valid point interpreted from the source or each valid point of significant omission provided. The candidate can achieve **up to 3 marks** for their interpretation of the parts of the source they consider are relevant in terms of

the proposed question where there is also at least one point of significant omission identified to imply a judgement has been made about the limitations of the source. For full marks to be given each point needs to be discretely mentioned in terms of the question.

A maximum of 2 marks may be given for answers which refer only to the source or in which no judgement has been made.

Possible points which may be identified in the source include:

1. Alexander Spark was a leading member of the business community/ prominent in banking
2. By 1840 owned £40,000 of land
3. Became the local agent for a variety of companies
4. Scottish Agents in Australia handled the interests of many Scots who invested money in Australian businesses without ever leaving Scotland.

Possible points of significant omission may include:

1. Scots introduced merino sheep to Australia/developed sheep farming in New Zealand
2. Scots developed shipping companies/developed refrigerated sea transport for meat
3. Scots pioneered the sugar industry in Australia/ introduced sugar mills/ refineries
4. Scots were involved in developing the wine industry/ brewing in Australia
5. Scots set up universities in Canada/New Zealand/ education systems variously
6. Scots developed engineering companies in Canada, Australia/developed shipbuilding in New Zealand
7. Scots developed Canadian Pacific railroad as engineers and financiers
8. Scots cleared and developed virgin land in Canada, Australia, New Zealand
9. Scots masons built prestigious public buildings in new cities
10. Scots developed the jute industry in India
11. Scots' were active in politics/reached high positions eg JA MacDonald, Prime Minister of Canada

4. *Candidates can be credited in a number of ways up to a maximum of 5 marks.*

Candidates must make a judgement about the usefulness of the source and support this by making evaluative comments on identified aspects of the source.

1 mark should be given for each relevant comment made, up to a **maximum of 5 marks in total**.

- A maximum of **4 marks** can be given for evaluative comments relating to the author, type of source, purpose and timing.
- A maximum of **2 marks** may be given for comments relating to the content of the source.
- A maximum of **2 marks** may be given for comments relating to points of significant omission.

Examples of aspects of the source and relevant comments:

Aspect of the source	Possible comment
Author: Mary Contini	Personal recollection of her own family history so useful
Type of Source: Memoirs about her grandparents' experience	Not describing a first-hand experience so may be less accurate, so less useful

Purpose: Informs why they worked hard	Simple explanation, not exaggerated, so useful
Timing: Reflection on early 20th century	Grandparents arrived around time of peak Italian immigration to Scotland so fairly typical and more useful/looking back with the benefit of hindsight

Content	Possible comment
Many of them made their living selling fish and chips	Useful as true of many Italian immigrants
Debt worried them and made them work even harder	Useful as explains concerns of immigrants to succeed
Shops were open long hours/the whole family helped serve customers/shops became the focus of social life	Useful as explains why families had so much contact with new communities/useful as accurate

Possible points of significant omission may include:

1. Italian cafes became very stylish and fashionable eg Nardini's in Largs
2. Names changed to Scottish versions/nicknames were used to seem less foreign
3. Second generation immigrants spoke Scots English
4. Some intermarriage, especially Scots and Irish
5. Worked with Scots in Trade Union movement/ Temperance movement
6. Worked with Scots in politics/Women's suffrage movement
7. Scots and immigrants served together in the Great War

Section 1, Context E, The Era of the Great War, 1910-1928

1. *Candidates can be credited in a number of ways up to a maximum of 5 marks.*

They may take different perspectives on the events and may describe a variety of different aspects of the events.

1 mark should be given for each accurate relevant key point of knowledge. **A second mark** should be given for each point that is developed, up to a maximum of **5 marks**. Candidates may achieve full marks by providing five straightforward points, by making three developed points, or a combination of these.

Possible points of knowledge may include:
1. **Use of Tanks:**
   - Able to cross trenches/crush barbed wire
   - Use fascines to cross trenches
   - Scattered German infantry
   - Achieved some success/at Cambrai
   - Protected the infantry going forward
   - Were armoured/bullet proof/equipped with machine guns/six pound guns
   - However were easily bogged down/inefficient/ unreliable/dangerous or uncomfortable for the crew
2. **Use of Machine guns:**
   - Vickers was highly efficient/successful/accurate weapon
   - Could fire up to 600 bullets a minute
   - Killed thousands of men
   - Development of portable machine guns

3. **Use of Aircraft**
   - Used for reconnaissance, ascertain enemy actions
   - Used to photograph enemy lines
   - Used to protect troops in the trenches
   - Fighter planes built to shoot down enemy planes
   - Used to bomb enemy trenches
   - Used to strafe enemy trenches
4. **Use of Gas**
   - Germans were first to use gas at Ypres in 1915 British use of gas eg ...
   - operation of gas canisters/shells; delivery; unreliability
   - different types of gas used (chlorine, mustard, phosgene, tear)
   - surprise/fear/panic factor of gas
   - importance of weather/wind direction
   - effects of gas (suffocating/choking, blinding, blisters/ burns)
   - use of gas masks; soldiers urinated on hankies
   - gas rarely used after 1917 as the Germans ran out of chemicals
   - (initially) killed thousands
   - (overall) more injuries than deaths
5. Development of range finding techniques for heavy artillery
6. Flamethrowers used to clear out enemy trenches

2. *Candidates can be credited in a number of ways up to a maximum of 5 marks.*

Candidates must make a judgement about the usefulness of the source and support this by making evaluative comments on identified aspects of the source.

1 mark should be given for each relevant comment made, up to a **maximum of 5 marks in total**.
- A maximum of 4 marks can be given for evaluative comments relating to the author, type of source, purpose and timing.
- A maximum of 2 marks may be given for comments relating to the content of the source.
- A maximum of 2 marks may be given for comments relating to points of significant omission.

Examples of aspects of the source and relevant comments:

Aspect of the source	Possible comment
Author: David Lloyd George	Useful as he is an eyewitness/a government minister soon to be Prime Minister so an expert on women's war effort
Type of Source: Memoir extract	Useful as based on Lloyd George's feelings/as a memoir could be less useful as could be coloured by subsequent events
Purpose: To record	Useful as it is an accurate account of the dangers faced by the women/ to record DLG's admiration of the women who worked in the munitions factories
Timing: Memoir from his time as Minister of Munitions (from 1915)	Useful as it is an account of his wartime experiences

Content	Possible comment
They had to work under conditions of real danger to life	Useful as it tells of the dangers of explosions which were common

One of the risks of shell filling factories was toxic jaundice resulting from the TNT poisoning/ The poor girls were nicknamed 'canaries'	Useful as it explains the dangers of the TNT poisoning
They were quite proud of this/They had earned it in the path of duty	Useful as it shows the women were proud of the jobs they were doing, despite the danger

Possible points of significant omission may include:
1. Details of other jobs done by women eg the Land Army, Nursing etc
2. Mourning for lost loved ones
3. Women became head of the family/struggled to juggle children, jobs, bills etc
4. Women got the vote as a result of contribution

3. *Candidates can be credited in a number of ways **up to a maximum of 5 marks**.*

Candidates must make an overall judgement about how fully the source explains the events. **1 mark** may be given for each valid point interpreted from the source or each valid point of significant omission provided. The candidate can achieve **up to 3 marks** for their interpretation of the parts of the source they consider are relevant in terms of the proposed question where there is also at least one point of significant omission identified to imply a judgement has been made about the limitations of the source. For full marks to be given each point needs to be discretely mentioned in terms of the question.

A maximum of 2 marks may be given for answers which refer only to the source or in which no judgement has been made.

Possible points which may be identified in the source include:
1. Men who refused to enlist in the army had to face military discipline
2. Some were sentenced to death for refusing orders although the sentence was always reduced if the 'conchie' still refused to give in
3. Special prisons and work camps were opened up in addition to the ordinary prisons to which many objectors were sent
4. Twenty four objectors died while detained at work camps

Possible points of significant omission may include:
1. In their communities conscientious objectors were often subject to a torrent of verbal and sometimes physical abuse
2. They were often ignored or refused service in shops
3. Women would give these men white feathers to signify cowardice

4. *Candidates can be credited in a number of ways up to a maximum of 5 marks.*

Candidates must show a causal relationship between events.

Up to a **maximum of 5 marks in total**, **1 mark** should be given for each accurate, relevant reason, and a **second mark** should be given for reasons that are developed. Candidates may achieve full marks by providing five straightforward reasons, three developed reasons, or a combination of these.

Possible reasons may include:
1. Post-war lack of demand/orders for shipbuilding eg 1921–23 tonnage of ships built on the Clyde declined/ from 510,000 to 170,000
2. Poor industrial relations (eg demarcation disputes) created difficulties
3. Failure to invest in new technology/lack of investment
4. Lack of demand led to iron and steel production declining/plants closing
5. Lack of orders led to decline in railway production eg by two-thirds at the North British Locomotive company
6. New fuels, so coal production also declined/pits closed
7. Foreign competition challenged Scottish industry
8. International markets lost during the war were not recovered
9. The jute factories in Dundee were in need of fresh investment and repair/lack of demand for sandbags reduced demand for jute
10. At the same time jute prices fell around the world
11. The management of Scottish industry suffered from disproportionate effect of losses of middle-class officers

Section 2, Context A, The Creation of the Medieval Kingdoms, 1066-1406

1. *Candidates can be credited in a number of ways **up to a maximum of 8 marks**.*

Candidates must use knowledge to present a balanced assessment of the influence of different possible factors and come to a reasoned conclusion.

Up to 5 marks are allocated for relevant points of knowledge used to address the question. **1 mark** should be given for each relevant, factual key point of knowledge used to support a factor. **If only one factor is presented, a maximum of 3 marks should be given for relevant points of knowledge.**

Possible factors may include:	Relevant, factual, key points of knowledge to support this factor may include:
William's leadership skills	1. William was experienced in battle and had previously defeated the French king 2. William feigned retreat during the battle tricking the Anglo-Saxons
William's superior army	3. William's army was well trained and wore chain mail armour 4. William's cavalry rode specially bred horses. The horses also had a saddle on them keeping the knights in position and allowing them to fight 5. William had brought supplies with him from Normandy and so his army was well fed and rested
Harold's inferior army	6. Harold's army was a mixture of professional soldiers/bodyguards and ordinary men 7. The army was not as well trained as the Normans 8. Death of Harold and his brothers meant there was no clear leadership during the battle

Harold's army were tired	9. Harold's army had only just fought the Battle of Stamford Bridge
	10. Harold's army had been forced to march quickly to the south to meet the Normans
Any other valid factor	

Up to 3 marks should be given for presenting the answer in a structured way, leading to a conclusion which addresses the question, as follows:

1 mark for the answer being presented in a structured way, with knowledge being organised in support of different factors.
1 mark given for a valid judgement or overall conclusion.
1 mark given for a reason being provided in support of the conclusion.

2. *Candidates can be credited in a number of ways up to a maximum of 6 marks.*

Candidates must make a judgement about the usefulness of the source and support this by making evaluative comments on identified aspects of the source.

1 mark should be given for each relevant comment made, up to a **maximum of 6 marks in total.**
• A maximum of 4 marks can be given for evaluative comments relating to the author, type of source, purpose and timing.
• A maximum of 2 marks may be given for comments relating to the content of the source.
• A maximum of 2 marks may be given for comments relating to points of significant omission.

Examples of aspects of the source and relevant comments:

Aspect of the source	Possible comment
Author: Royal clerk	Useful because he was well placed to gather information
Type of Source: Chronicle	Useful because it was an official record of events
Purpose: To describe	Less useful as clearly biased description of rebellions/author may have exaggerated when describing the actions of the Scots
Timing: 1174	At the time that Henry II was facing rebellion

Content	Possible comment
William rebelled and attacked Northumberland	Useful because it gives details of William's rebellion
Women and children were slaughtered/ priests murdered inside their own churches	Less useful because it could be exaggerating what happened.
His army besieged the castle/by cutting off their supplies/forced the English to make a treaty with the Scots.	Useful because it provides details on what William did next.

Possible points of significant omission may include:
1. Henry II's sons rebelled against him/the Great Rebellion 1173
2. Further rebellions by Henry's sons in 1183 and 1187

3. *Candidates can be credited in a number of ways up to a maximum of 6 marks.*

Candidates must show a causal relationship between events.

Up to a **maximum of 6 marks in total**, **1 mark** should be given for each accurate, relevant reason, and a **second mark** should be given for reasons that are developed. Candidates may achieve full marks by providing five straightforward reasons, three developed reasons, or a combination of these.

Possible reasons may include:
1. Effects of the Black Death eg some peasants were free some were not
2. Peasants prevented from earning higher wages than they had before the Black Death eg 1351 Statute of Labour (ie wages were cut), so unhappy
3. Peasants' discontent with war with France
4. Peasants had been taxed in 1377, 1379 and 1381, so unhappy
5. 1381 tax targeted new groups eg over 15s/craftsmen/ women taxed whether they worked or not, which was resented
6. Peasants unhappy as wanted an end to forced labour/ greater access to forests
7. Lack of faith in King Richard II who was a boy
8. Hatred of the King's advisor/allegations of corruption
9. Inspired by speakers who criticised the Church and monarchy eg John Ball/ Waldergrave

Section 2, Context B, War of the Three Kingdoms, 1603-1651

1. *Candidates can be credited in a number of ways up to a maximum of 8 marks.*

Candidates must use knowledge to present a balanced assessment of the influence of different possible factors and come to a reasoned conclusion.

Up to 5 marks are allocated for relevant points of knowledge used to address the question. **1 mark** should be given for each relevant, factual key point of knowledge used to support a factor. **If only one factor is presented, a maximum of 3 marks should be given for relevant points of knowledge.**

Possible factors may include:	Relevant, factual, key points of knowledge to support this factor may include:
Religious differences	1. Some in Parliament were offended by James' belief in the Divine Right of Kings 2. Millenary Petition 1603 demanded changes to church practices – rejected by James VI and I
Religious differences (continued)	3. Archbishops Canons – clergy had to subscribe to 39 articles and Prayer Book, James licensed the Canons, which provoked the clergy 4. 1622 – Direction of Preachers issued, gave Bishops more control, which worried Puritans 5. Demands of Presbyterians for the removal of Bishops 6. Demands from Catholics for more lenient treatment 7. Gunpowder plot

Financial grievances	8. Extravagant spending and debts built up by James eg clothing banquets 9. Gave money and power to his favourites at court 10. Bates Case 1606 – judges agreed that impositions (new source of revenue of additional tax on imports and exports) were legal 11. Failure of Great Contract 1610 – reciprocal distrust 12. Monopolies caused anger and resentment
Political factors	13. James dismissed Parliament in 1610 14. Failure of 'Addled Parliament' in 1614 15. James' insistence on creating a legal and administrative Union with Scotland caused suspicions in England
Any other relevant factor	

Up to 3 marks should be given for presenting the answer in a structured way, leading to a conclusion which addresses the question, as follows:
1 mark for the answer being presented in a structured way, with knowledge being organised in support of different factors.
1 mark given for a valid judgement or overall conclusion.
1 mark given for a reason being provided in support of the conclusion.

2. *Candidates can be credited in a number of ways up to a maximum of 6 marks.*

Candidates must show a causal relationship between events.

Up to a **maximum of 6 marks in total**, **1 mark** should be given for each accurate, relevant reason, and a **second mark** should be given for reasons that are developed. Candidates may achieve full marks by providing six straightforward reasons, three developed reasons, or a combination of these.

Possible reasons may include:
1. Believed in the Divine Right of Kings, which was resented
2. Married to Henrietta Maria – a Catholic, unpopular with Protestants
3. Spending habits eg paintings and expensive clothes were resented
4. 1629-1640 – ruled without Parliament (Personal Rule), so was unpopular
5. Forced Ship Money, those who refused went to prison, created resentment
6. Appointed Laud as Archbishop of Canterbury, who was unpopular
7. Laud changed Church of England services (statues, music and candles introduced) – offended some Protestants
8. Introduced New Prayer Book – in Scotland this caused riots
9. Scots attacked English because of religious changes (Bishops' Wars)

10. Charles called Parliament to get money to fight the Scots, which was resented
11. Earl of Strafford ruled Ireland for Charles – Strafford unpopular with the Irish and the Long Parliament

3. *Candidates can be credited in a number of ways up to a maximum of 6 marks.*

Candidates must make a judgement about the usefulness of the source and support this by making evaluative comments on identified aspects of the source.

1 mark should be given for each relevant comment made, up to a **maximum of 6 marks in total**.
- A maximum of 4 marks can be given for evaluative comments relating to the author, type of source, purpose and timing.
- A maximum of 2 marks may be given for comments relating to the content of the source.
- A maximum of 2 marks may be given for comments relating to points of significant omission.

Examples of aspects of the source and relevant comments:

Aspect of the source	Possible comment
Author: Oliver Cromwell	Useful as he was the leader of the Parliamentary forces (who was an extreme Puritan and who hated the Irish Catholics)
Type of Source: Letter (to the House of Commons)	Useful as an official account of the events of the battle, so should be accurate/less useful as may be biased based on Cromwell's actions
Purpose: To inform	Useful as provides reasons for victory at Drogheda/ Cromwell justifying his actions
Timing: September 1649	Useful as written soon after the battle took place

Content	Possible comment
On Monday 9th the battering guns began/Our guns then beat down the corner tower, and made gaps in the east and south walls	Useful as it provides accurate details of when the battle began/weapons used
I sent Sir Arthur Aston a request to surrender the town but received no satisfactory answer	Useful as Sir Arthur Aston ignored Cromwell's order to surrender
On the following day, after some fierce fighting, we entered the town/several of the enemy, including Sir Arthur Aston, retreated into Mill Mount	Useful as it describes the successful storming of the city by Cromwell's forces

Possible points of significant omission may include:
1. Cromwell ordered his men to kill everyone remaining in the town who had weapons
2. Cromwell's men killed approximately 2000 men after the surrender
3. The Church of St. Peters was set on fire, burning alive a group of defenders who had barricaded themselves in
4. Parliamentarian losses are regarded to be around 150
5. Sir Arthur Aston reported to have been beaten to death with his own wooden leg

Section 2, Context C, The Atlantic Slave Trade, 1770-1807

1. *Candidates can be credited in a number of ways up to a maximum of 8 marks.*

Candidates must use knowledge to present a balanced assessment of the influence of different possible factors and come to a reasoned conclusion.

Up to 5 marks are allocated for relevant points of knowledge used to address the question. **1 mark** should be given for each relevant, factual key point of knowledge used to support a factor. **If only one factor is presented, a maximum of 3 marks should be given for relevant points of knowledge.**

Possible factors may include:	Relevant, factual, key points of knowledge to support this factor may include:
Role of Thomas Clarkson	1. Visited ports such as Liverpool to collect evidence about the cruelties of the slave trade 2. Interviewed sailors who were involved in the slave trade 3. Risked his life to campaign for the abolition of slavery 4. Clarkson published his evidence about the slave trade 5. Clarkson's influence on Wilberforce and others
Role of other campaigners	6. William Wilberforce led the campaign against the slave trade in parliament. 7. Wilberforce presented bills to abolish the slave trade 8. Wilberforce used his friendship with the prime minister and the monarchy to win support for abolition 9. Wilberforce became leader of the Society for the Abolition of the Slave Trade 10. Former slave ship captain, John Newton, preached against the evils of the trade/wrote the hymn, Amazing Grace 11. Freed slaves such as Olaudah Equiano published personal accounts about the terrible nature of the slave trade 12. Granville Sharp campaigned against slavery in British courts 13. Many people across Britain signed petitions against the slave trade.
Role of other campaigners *(continued)*	14. Pamphlets, posters, newspaper adverts were used to campaign against the slave trade 15. Slogans such as 'Am I not a man and a brother' were used/appeared on Wedgwood crockery 16. Boycotts of slave produced goods such as sugar
Changing attitudes	17. Christian teaching led people to change their attitudes to the slave trade 18. People began to think of Africans as fellow human beings 19. Plantation agriculture became less important to the British economy 20. People began to regard slave labour as an inefficient way to produce goods
Any other relevant factor	

Up to 3 marks should be given for presenting the answer in a structured way, leading to a conclusion which addresses the question, as follows:

1 mark for the answer being presented in a structured way, with knowledge being organised in support of different factors.
1 mark given for a valid judgement or overall conclusion.
1 mark given for a reason being provided in support of the conclusion.

2. *Candidates can be credited in a number of ways up to a maximum of 6 marks.*

Candidates must show a causal relationship between events.

Up to a **maximum of 6 marks in total**, **1 mark** should be given for each accurate, relevant reason, and a **second mark** should be given for reasons that are developed. Candidates may achieve full marks by providing six straightforward reasons, three developed reasons, or a combination of these.

Possible reasons may include:
1. The slave trade brought wealth to Britain, so was popular with those who became wealthy
2. The slave trade brought employment to Britain in areas such as shipyards, ports, mills, manufacturing, so was supported by many involved in these industries
3. Cities profited from the slave trade (eg Bristol, Liverpool and Glasgow), so many in these cities wished to see slavery continue
4. The products of the slave trade were in great demand (eg cotton, tobacco and sugar) and many believed that slavery was needed in order to meet demand for these products
5. Involvement in the slave trade helped Britain to remain a world power, so many continued to support slavery
6. The slave trade was seen as a valuable training ground for the Royal Navy, so it was supported
7. Many MPs had financial interests in the slave trade, so wished to see it continue
8. Many MPs were being bribed to ensure that they continued to give their support for the continuation of the trade
9. The slave trade still enjoyed the support of the King
10. Profits from the trade were essential to fund the war with France

3. *Candidates can be credited in a number of ways up to a maximum of 6 marks.*

Candidates must make a judgement about the usefulness of the source and support this by making evaluative comments on identified aspects of the source.

1 mark should be given for each relevant comment made, up to a **maximum of 6 marks in total**.
- A maximum of **4 marks** can be given for evaluative comments relating to the author, type of source, purpose and timing.
- A maximum of **2 marks** may be given for comments relating to the content of the source.
- A maximum of **2 marks** may be given for comments relating to points of significant omission.

Examples of aspects of the source and relevant comments:

Aspect of the source	Possible comment
Author: Historian	Useful as modern historians are likely to be experts on the issue and have carried out research
Type of Source: Textbook	Factual account of the treatment of slaves on the plantations
Purpose: To inform	Useful as evidence of harsh treatment of slaves on the plantations
Timing: 1995	A secondary source written with the benefit of hindsight

Content	Possible comment
They followed a policy of control through fear	Useful as this shows how harsh the treatment of slaves was
Slaves had no rights. They were seen as possessions rather than human beings	Useful as this shows slaves were not treated equally
There was no punishment for owners who worked their slaves to death/ no one questioned owners burning or torturing their slaves	Useful as this shows how cruel plantation owners were/not answerable for their actions towards their slaves

Possible points of significant omission may include:
1. Slaves were forced to work long hours
2. Slaves were often whipped for not working hard enough
3. Slave families were often broken up when slaves were bought and sold from plantations

Section 2, Context D, Changing Britain, 1760–1900

1. *Candidates can be credited in a number of ways up to a maximum of 6 marks.*

Candidates must make a judgement about the usefulness of the source and support this by making evaluative comments on identified aspects of the source.

1 mark should be given for each relevant comment made, up to a **maximum of 6 marks** in total.
- A maximum of **4 marks** can be given for evaluative comments relating to the author, type of source, purpose and timing.
- A maximum of **2 marks** may be given for comments relating to the content of the source.
- A maximum of **2 marks** may be given for comments relating to points of significant omission.

Examples of aspects of the source and relevant comments:

Aspect of the source	Possible comment
Author: Doctor	Useful as it was written by an eyewitness to poor housing conditions in Manchester
Type of Source: Report	Useful as it was part of an official document by someone with medical expertise/reports tend to be factual
Purpose: To record	May be less useful, as report only focuses on one area of Manchester/ but useful because factual record of poor housing conditions in Manchester
Timing: 1832	Useful as it was written at the time of urbanisation/growth of cities/ industrial revolution/time when there was a lot of poor housing in British cities

Content	Possible comment
The houses that the mill workers live in are poorly ventilated and do not have toilets	Useful as fairly typical of urban housing in poorer areas at this time
The streets are narrow, unpaved and worn into deep ruts, which become the resting place of mud, refuse and rubbish	Useful as typical of cities at this time with poor sanitation
In Parliament Street there is only one toilet for 380 inhabitants. The flow of muck from this toilet infests close-by houses and must be a source of disease	May be less useful as may have been exaggerated for effect but could also say useful as fairly typical of concerns about dirt and disease at this time

Possible points of significant omission may include:
1. Lack of clean water
2. Overcrowding
3. Poorly constructed homes
4. Impact of these living conditions on health – eg rickets/ cholera/TB, vermin spread other diseases

2. *Candidates can be credited in a number of ways **up to a maximum of 8 marks.***

Candidates must use knowledge to present a balanced assessment of the influence of different possible factors and come to a reasoned conclusion.

Up to 5 marks are allocated for relevant points of knowledge used to address the question. **1 mark** should be given for each relevant, factual key point of knowledge used to support a factor. **If only one factor is presented, a maximum of 3 marks should be given for relevant points of knowledge.**

Possible factors may include:	Relevant, factual, key points of knowledge to support this factor may include:
Technology	1. Iron rails underground made it easier to transport coal 2. Steam power to raise cages 3. Wire rope to raise cages 4. Steam-powered drainage pumps 5. Davy safety lamp 6. Metal pit props 7. Gunpowder used to loosen rock 8. Technology enabled deeper shafts to be dug, reaching into seams of coal below water-bearing ground 9. Chain coal-cutting machines from the 1880s 10. Better ventilation systems 11. Electric lighting from the 1890s 12. Electric hauling from the 1890s
Legislation	13. 1842 – banned women and children under 10 from working underground/fatalities reduced as fewer children employed 14. 1850 – Mine Inspectors appointed, which improved safety 15. 1860 – boys under 12 forbidden to go underground 16. 1862 – mines must have at least two exits 17. 1872 – mine managers required a certificate, which improved safety 18. from 1894 – minimum wage for miners
Animals	19. Canaries used to detect pockets of suffocating gas (Choke Damp) 20. Ponies used (instead of putters) to move wagons of coal
Pressure groups	21. Trade unions campaigned for shorter working hours/better conditions
Any other valid factor	

Up to 3 marks should be given for presenting the answer in a structured way, leading to a conclusion which addresses the question, as follows:

1 mark for the answer being presented in a structured way, with knowledge being organised in support of different factors.
1 mark given for a valid judgement or overall conclusion.
1 mark given for a reason being provided in support of the conclusion.

3. *Candidates can be credited in a number of ways up to a maximum of 6 marks.*

Candidates must show a causal relationship between events.

Up to a **maximum of 6 marks in total**, **1 mark** should be given for each accurate, relevant reason, and a **second mark** should be given for reasons that are developed. Candidates

may achieve full marks by providing six straightforward reasons, three developed reasons, or a combination of these.

Possible reasons may include:
1. Canals very slow means of transport – railways much faster
2. Canals could not go everywhere, especially in hilly country
3. A more extensive network of railways developed
4. Canals often different widths and depths, so goods had to be transferred from one size of boat to another
5. Even short journeys involved several canal companies/inconvenient paperwork/expensive
6. Locks slowed up movement considerably
7. Canal transport more expensive than railways/railways carried more goods so more cost effective
8. Factories could have their own railway sidings – more convenient than canals
9. Canal companies failed to invest their profits back into widening and deepening canals/Investment needed to widen canals was diverted to railways

Section 2, Context E, The Making of Modern Britain, 1880-1951

1. *Candidates can be credited in a number of ways up to a maximum of 8 marks.*

Candidates must use knowledge to present a balanced assessment of the influence of different possible factors and come to a reasoned conclusion.

Up to 5 marks are allocated for relevant points of knowledge used to address the question. **1 mark** should be given for each relevant, factual key point of knowledge used to support a factor. If only one factor is presented, a maximum of **3 marks** should be given for relevant points of knowledge.

Possible factors may include:	Relevant, factual, key points of knowledge to support this factor may include:
Poor health	1. Absence from work due to sickness could lead to loss of job/earnings 2. Poor could not afford doctors/medicine 3. Many occupations dangerous/few safety precautions eg miners/shipyards so greater chance of accidents/injury
Old age	4. Those on low wages unable to save, so when too old to work, fell into poverty 5. Limited poor relief 6. Caring for elderly relatives was an added burden on poor households
Death of wage-earner	7. Death of the main wage-earner would cause families to fall into poverty 8. Only limited compensation available for illness or accidents caused through work

Family size	9. Large families often lived below poverty-line, especially when children were very young 10. No easily available child-care, so mother often prevented from working
Irregular/ low earnings/ unemployment	11. Work was often cyclical/ irregular or seasonal – causing temporary poverty 12. Wages were often below subsistence-level 13. Considerable time often had to be spent looking for work/ queuing outside factory gates 14. Women were particularly low paid half or even less of male wages 15. Unemployment meant a lack of income
Other causes	16. Secondary poverty caused when earnings spent/wasted on other things - eg drinking or gambling 17. High rents used up a lot of family income 18. Discrimination could add to unemployment eg Irish in Scotland

Up to 3 marks should be given for presenting the answer in a structured way, leading to a conclusion which addresses the question, as follows:

1 mark for the answer being presented in a structured way, with knowledge being organised in support of different factors.
1 mark given for a valid judgement or overall conclusion.
1 mark given for a reason being provided in support of the conclusion.

2. *Candidates can be credited in a number of ways up to a maximum of 6 marks.*

Candidates must make a judgement about the usefulness of the source and support this by making evaluative comments on identified aspects of the source.

1 mark should be given for each relevant comment made, up to a **maximum of 6 marks in total**.
- A maximum of **4 marks** can be given for evaluative comments relating to the author, type of source, purpose and timing.
- A maximum of **2 marks** may be given for comments relating to the content of the source.
- A maximum of **2 marks** may be given for comments relating to points of significant omission.

Examples of aspects of the source and relevant comments:

Aspect of the source	Possible comment
Author: Historians	Useful because they would have researched the subject thoroughly
Type of Source: Modern history book	Useful as published sources tend to be factual
Purpose: To inform	Useful as will be a balanced/ comprehensive account of reasons for Liberals passing reforms to help the young
Timing: Published in 2002	Useful as written with the benefit of hindsight

Content	Possible comment
The Boer War and the condition of many recruits led politicians to act	Useful as the Boer War did raise concern about the fitness of recruits/national stock/efficiency
The children would be the soldiers of the future	Useful as this was a typical/ important concern at the time of international tensions
Healthy children would grow up to be healthy soldiers and workers and the British Empire would be stronger as a result	Useful as there was great concern about Britain's status in the world

Possible points of significant omission may include:
1. Rowntree's report in particular revealed that families with young children often fell below the poverty line.
2. Children regarded as 'deserving' poor.
3. Report of the 1904 Inter-departmental Committee on Physical Deterioration recommended reforms to improve the health of children/ free school meals and medical inspections.
4. School leaving age 13/desire to improve access to free secondary education for some.
5. High levels of juvenile crime/often caused by poverty.
6. Desire to alter justice system which treated juvenile criminals in the same way as adult criminals.
7. Work of Margaret McMillan in pushing for school meals and medical inspections.

3. *Candidates can be credited in a number of ways up to a maximum of 6 marks.*

Candidates must show a causal relationship between events.

Up to a maximum of **6 marks in total**, **1 mark** should be given for each accurate, relevant reason, and a **second mark** should be given for reasons that are developed. Candidates may achieve full marks by providing six straightforward reasons, three developed reasons, or a combination of these.

Possible reasons may include:
1. Sense of determination/will to 'build a better Britain' after the war.
2. Evacuation highlighted the poor health/physical condition of children and the problem of poverty, so opened eyes/changed attitudes
3. Rich and poor subject to bombing/created need for reform
4. Rationing ensured a fair supply of food for all – rich and poor alike, levelled classes/created expectation of further government intervention
5. Social classes mixed more than ever before during the war – raised awareness of social problems and need for welfare reform
6. Government had been forced to intervene more during the war – eg Ministry of Food, rationing, and free health care for war-wounded/War forced government to change laissez-faire attitudes
7. Greater acceptance of government control during wartime was accepted to tackle post-war problems
8. War highlighted social problems that only the state could tackle - eg poverty, housing, people accepted this

9. Beveridge Report of 1942 highlighted social problems/ Beveridge Report popular and created an expectation of government action

Section 3, Context A, The Cross and the Crescent; the Crusades, 1071-1192

1. *Candidates can be credited in a number of ways **up to a maximum of 5 marks**.*
They may take different perspectives on the events and may describe a variety of different aspects of the events.

1 mark should be given for each accurate relevant key point of knowledge.

A second mark should be given for each point that is developed, up to a maximum of **5 marks**. Candidates may achieve full marks by providing five straightforward points, by making three developed points, or a combination of these.

Possible points of knowledge may include:
1. Castles used as a home
2. Castles used for protection/defence against an enemy eg control of river crossings
3. Castles were used as barracks for knights
4. Castles were a symbol of power/wealth
5. Castles were administrative centres
6. Castles were used to hold courts
7. Castles were used to store food
8. Castles held feasts

2. *Candidates can be credited in a number of ways **up to a maximum of 5 marks**.*

Candidates must show a causal relationship between events.

Up to a **maximum of 5 marks in total**, **1 mark** should be given for each accurate, relevant reason, and a **second mark** should be given for reasons that are developed. Candidates may achieve full marks by providing five straightforward reasons, three developed reasons, or a combination of these.

Possible reasons may include:
1. Inspired by the Pope's speech/preachers such as Peter the Hermit
2. To recapture Jerusalem/free eastern Christians from Muslim rule
3. Religious motives/desire to fulfil Christian duty to God eg Raymond of Toulouse
4. To have sins forgiven/to be able to enter heaven in the afterlife
5. To gain land eg younger sons or those disinherited eg Bohemond of Taranto/Baldwin of Boulogne
6. Peer pressure/to represent a family eg Hugh of Vermandois/Stephen of Blois
7. Military skills/to fight in battle with the Church's blessing eg Tancred wanted to escape the limitations of the Peace of God movement
8. Social mobility eg peasants wanted better life/"land of milk and honey"

3. *Candidates can be credited in a number of ways **up to a maximum of 6 marks**.*

Candidates must make an overall judgement about how fully the source explains the events. **1 mark** may be given for each valid point interpreted from the source or each valid point of significant omission provided. The candidate can achieve **up to 3 marks** for their interpretation of the parts of the source they consider are relevant in terms of the proposed question where there is also at least one point

of significant omission identified to imply a judgement has been made about the limitations of the source. For full marks to be given each point needs to be discretely mentioned in terms of the question.

A maximum of 2 marks may be given for answers which refer only to the source or in which no judgement has been made.

Possible points which may be identified in the source include:
1. Alexius feared they would attack his city/made them camp outside the city and only allowed them to enter in small groups
2. Offered treasure and supplies to Crusaders who agreed to fight for him
3. Any Crusader who refused was attacked and forced to surrender
4. Alexius did not trust the Crusaders/made plans to remove them from Constantinople

Possible points of significant omission may include:
1. Crusaders blamed Alexius for the failure of the People's Crusade
2. Made Crusaders take an oath of loyalty/made Crusaders take an oath they would capture land for him
3. Provided the Crusaders with a guide/troops/supplies
4. Provided the Crusaders with boats to blockade Nicaea
5. Negotiated with the Muslims inside Nicaea/took the city behind the Crusaders' back
6. Baldwin broke his oath and captured Edessa
7. Alexius did not arrive at Antioch to help the Crusaders
8. Bohemond broke his oath and claimed Antioch

4. *Candidates can be credited in a number of ways **up to a maximum of 4 marks**.*

Candidates must make direct comparisons of the two sources, either overall or in detail. A simple comparison will indicate what points of detail or overall viewpoint they agree or disagree about and should be given **1 mark**.

A developed comparison of the points of detail or overall viewpoint should be given **2 marks**. Candidates may achieve full marks by making four simple comparisons, two developed comparisons or by a combination of these.

Possible points of comparison may include:

Overall: The sources agree about the character of Richard I	
Source B	Source C
Vowed to fulfil his Christian duty	Promised he would keep his oath to God
Excellent military commander who used clever tactics to win key battles	Used his experience and leadership to force the city to surrender
Always fought alongside his men, courageously attacking the enemy	Richard showed great bravery by defending his men and killing the enemy

Section 3, Context B, "Tea and Freedom,": the American Revolution, 1774-1783

1. *Candidates can be credited in a number of ways **up to a maximum of 6 marks**.*

Candidates must make an overall judgement about how fully the source explains the events. **1 mark** may be given for each valid point interpreted from the source or each valid point of significant omission provided. The candidate can achieve **up to 3 marks** for their interpretation of the parts of the source they consider are relevant in terms of the proposed question where there is also at least one point of significant omission identified to imply a judgement has been made about the limitations of the source. For full marks to be given each point needs to be discretely mentioned in terms of the question.

A maximum of 2 marks may be given for answers which refer only to the source or in which no judgement has been made.

Possible points which may be identified in the source include:
1. The decision to increase taxes was very unpopular
2. The decision to maintain a standing army alarmed colonists
3. The Stamp Act provoked a furious reaction
4. Colonists organised a boycott of British goods

Possible points of significant omission may include:
1. Colonists felt that actions of the British government were damaging trade
2. The colonists were unhappy that the British were stopping them from moving West
3. There was anger among the colonists about the Quartering Act which allowed British soldiers to invade private property
4. There was anger among the colonists about a lack of representation in the British parliament
5. Events such as the Boston Massacre increased tension

2. *Candidates can be credited in a number of ways **up to a maximum of 5 marks.***

They may take different perspectives on the events and may describe a variety of different aspects of the events.

1 mark should be given for each accurate relevant key point of knowledge. **A second mark** should be given for each point that is developed, up to a maximum of **5 marks**. Candidates may achieve full marks by providing five straightforward points, by making three developed points, or a combination of these.

Possible points of knowledge may include:
1. Colonists were angered by the passing of the Tea Act in 1773 which allowed the East India Company to undercut colonial merchants and smugglers
2. Bostonians disguised themselves as Mohawk Indians and boarded the three tea ships
3. Tea was emptied into the water of Boston harbour
4. Some of the tea was stolen
5. King George III and Parliament were outraged when they heard of these events
6. Lord North rejected the offer of compensation from some of the colonial merchants
7. Led to the passing of the 'Intolerable Acts' eg Massachusetts Act/ Administration of Justice Act/ Quartering Act/Quebec Act
8. Port of Boston closed

3. *Candidates can be credited in a number of ways **up to a maximum of 5 marks.***

Candidates must show a causal relationship between events.

Up to a **maximum of 5 marks in total, 1 mark** should be given for each accurate, relevant reason, and a **second mark** should be given for reasons that are developed. Candidates may achieve full marks by providing five straightforward reasons, three developed reasons, or a combination of these.

Possible reasons may include:
1. The British forces were poorly led so poorer tactics/ communication
2. There were tactical errors by Britain eg at Yorktown, so battles were lost
3. British army had to rely on mercenary forces, so less loyalty
4. British soldiers were not properly trained, so less effective
5. Colonial army was effectively led by George Washington, strong leader
6. British generals underestimated the bravery of the Americans
7. Rebel tactics also made life very difficult/rebels often used guerrilla tactics against British which were successful
8. Colonists had greater forces/able to call on minutemen when required, so more effective
9. Fighting a war so far from home made it difficult to supply British forces
10. Attacks by French and Spanish weakened/distracted British forces
11. Assistance from French and Spanish navies gave colonists control of the seas

4. *Candidates can be credited in a number of ways **up to a maximum of 4 marks.***

Candidates must make direct comparisons of the two sources, either overall or in detail. A simple comparison will indicate what points of detail or overall viewpoint they agree or disagree about and should be given **1 mark**.

A developed comparison of the points of detail or overall viewpoint should be given **2 marks**. Candidates may achieve full marks by making four simple comparisons, two developed comparisons or by a combination of these.

Possible points of comparison may include:

Overall: The sources agree that there were a number of reasons for the British defeat at Saratoga	
Source B	**Source C**
Progress was then slowed by mountains and dense forest	Progress was slowed by the difficult terrain
Burgoyne had no reinforcements	Burgoyne's army was left on its own
Army was trapped against the Hudson River	British found themselves trapped at the little community of Saratoga

Section 3, Context C, USA 1850–1880

1. *Candidates can be credited in a number of ways **up to a maximum of 5 marks.***

They may take different perspectives on the events and may describe a variety of different aspects of the events.

1 mark should be given for each accurate relevant key point of knowledge.

A second mark should be given for each point that is developed, up to a maximum of **5 marks**. Candidates may achieve full marks by providing five straightforward points, by making three developed points, or a combination of these.

Possible points of knowledge may include:
1. Many subject to strict rules and regulations/had no freedom

2. Slaves could be bought and sold/seen as property
3. Worked long hours at hard work with only short breaks
4. Subject to harsh/inhuman discipline eg whipping common
5. Runaway slaves were beaten/maimed: use of dogs to hunt runaways
6. Slaves needed permission to get married
7. Slave marriages had no legal status
8. Slave owners often named slave children
9. Slave families often broken up/separated
10. Slaves unable to visit family/relatives on other plantations
11. Female slaves sometimes sexually abused by owners/overseers
12. Children born to a slave, fathered by white owner, were still slaves
13. Pregnant slaves were expected to work until the child was born.

2. *Candidates can be credited in a number of ways **up to a maximum of 5 marks**.*

Candidates must show a causal relationship between events.

Up to a **maximum of 5 marks in total**, **1 mark** should be given for each accurate, relevant reason, and a **second mark** should be given for reasons that are developed. Candidates may achieve full marks by providing five straightforward reasons, three developed reasons, or a combination of these.

Possible reasons may include:
1. Kansas – Nebrasaka Act allowed States to decide if slave state or free state, which caused tension.
2. Violence in Kansas (Bleeding Kansas) had led to a number of deaths, which increased tension
3. Dred Scott Case caused unhappiness among abolitionists and Northern States
4. Attack on Harpers Ferry by John Brown heightened tension
5. Growth of Republican Party which favoured Northern Interests upset South
6. Election of Lincoln upset South
7. South felt North was infringing on states' rights, caused resentment
8. Growth of militant abolitionism in North increased tension
9. Southern planters resented Northern trade tariffs which affected their trade
10. Expansion of Northern cities and immigration worried the South

3. *Candidates can be credited in a number of ways **up to a maximum of 6 marks**.*

Candidates must make an overall judgement about how fully the source explains the events. **1 mark** may be given for each valid point interpreted from the source or each valid point of significant omission provided. The candidate can achieve **up to 3 marks** for their interpretation of the parts of the source they consider are relevant in terms of the proposed question where there is also at least one point of significant omission identified to imply a judgement has been made about the limitations of the source. For full marks to be given each point needs to be discretely mentioned in terms of the question.

A maximum of 2 marks may be given for answers which refer only to the source or in which no judgement has been made.

Possible points which may be identified in the source include:
1. Attracted by the promise of a better life
2. Attracted by the warmer weather in California
3. Went west because they thought the land would be more fertile
4. Ranch owners realised that the plains could be used to feed their huge herds of cattle

Possible points of significant omission may include:
1. Gold in California attracted many. Later gold discoveries in Black Hills also attracted prospectors
2. Cheap land available in the west for farmers
3. Belief in Manifest Destiny eg many Americans saw it as a duty to spread their way of life
4. Mormons wished to find new lands to settle away from other people
5. Railways encouraged many settlers west
6. Government Acts offered land to settlers
7. The Homestead Act of 1862/Timber and Culture Act of 1875 each offered cheap/free land to settlers
8. Railroad companies sold land cheaply to settlers
9. Freed slaves headed west after 1865 to escape persecution
10. Shopkeepers and hotel owners travelled west to exploit the demand of the settlers
11. Overcrowding of cities in East
12. Sense of adventure

4. *Candidates can be credited in a number of ways **up to a maximum of 4 marks**.*

Candidates must make direct comparisons of the two sources, either overall or in detail. A simple comparison will indicate what points of detail or overall viewpoint they agree or disagree about and should be given **1 mark**.

A developed comparison of the points of detail or overall viewpoint should be given **2 marks**. Candidates may achieve full marks by making four simple comparisons, two developed comparisons or by a combination of these.

Possible points of comparison may include:

Overall: The sources disagree about the events which took place during the Sand Creek massacre of 1864.	
Source B	**Source C**
In the village there were 500 people	In the Cheyenne camp there were about 1200 people
Two-thirds of whom were women and children.	700 were warriors
Counted from 60 to 70 dead bodies, a large majority of whom were women and children.	I estimate there were 500 or 600 people killed/I saw only one woman who had been killed and I saw no dead children

Section 3, Context D, Hitler and Nazi Germany, 1919-1939

1. *Candidates can be credited in a number of ways **up to a maximum of 5 marks**.*

They may take different perspectives on the events and may describe a variety of different aspects of the events.
1 mark should be given for each accurate relevant key point of knowledge.

A second mark should be given for each point that is developed, up to a maximum of **5 marks**. Candidates may achieve full marks by providing five straightforward points, by making three developed points, or a combination of these.

Possible points of knowledge may include:

1. All men and women over 20 had the vote/over 35 in Presidential elections
2. All Germans were equal before the law
3. People had the right to vote by secret ballot
4. Everyone had the right of freedom of speech/to express opinions freely and openly
5. Freedom of association/people had the right to hold peaceful meetings
6. Freedom of press
7. Everyone had the right of freedom of religion
8. Letters and correspondence could not be opened and read
9. No one could be arrested without good reason/unless they broke the law
10. People had the right to join trade unions and societies
11. No one could be imprisoned without trial
12. Rights of privacy/people had the right of privacy in their own homes
13. People had the right to form political parties.

2. *Candidates can be credited in a number of ways **up to a maximum of 4 marks.***

Candidates must make direct comparisons of the two sources, either overall or in detail. A simple comparison will indicate what points of detail or overall viewpoint they agree or disagree about and should be given **1 mark**.

A developed comparison of the points of detail or overall viewpoint should be given **2 marks**. Candidates may achieve full marks by making four simple comparisons, two developed comparisons or by a combination of these.

Possible points of comparison may include:

Overall: The sources agree that hyperinflation caused people difficulties	
Source B	Source C
Workers were paid twice a day/ rushed to shops before prices went up	Some workers were paid twice a day/could spend their wages instantly.
Millions of people faced starvation due to hyperinflation	They faced homelessness and starvation.
Pensioners who were living on fixed incomes found that prices rose much faster than their earnings	Pensioners lived on fixed incomes and received the same amount each week; these incomes were now worth nothing

3. *Candidates can be credited in a number of ways **up to a maximum of 5 marks.***

Candidates must show a causal relationship between events.

Up to a **maximum of 5 marks in total**, **1 mark** should be given for each accurate, relevant reason, and a **second mark** should be given for reasons that are developed. Candidates may achieve full marks by providing five straightforward reasons, three developed reasons, or a combination of these.

Possible reasons may include:

1. Hitler appeared to offer Germany strong leadership, which was appealing

2. Offered solutions to Germany's economic problems, so popular
3. Promised to provide jobs for the unemployed , which was popular
4. Promised to overthrow the Treaty of Versailles, which was welcomed
5. Nazi rallies, eg Nuremberg, impressed people
6. Hitler was a superb speaker
7. Effective use of propaganda to get over his message
8. Hitler had a clear, simple message which appealed to many people
9. Promised support for the farmers, shopkeepers, etc, which was popular
10. Businessmen were attracted by Hitler's promise to destroy trade unions
11. Young people were attracted to the Hitler Youth
12. Promised to restore Germany as a world power, which was welcomed
13. Germany's best defence against Communism/support from middle classes
14. Discipline/uniforms of the SA impressed people
15. Widespread support from nationalists for his racial theories/anti-Semitism
16. Tired of the chaos of the Weimar Government and wanted a change/belief that democracy weak

4. *Candidates can be credited in a number of ways **up to a maximum of 6 marks.***

Candidates must make an overall judgement about how fully the source explains the events. **1 mark** may be given for each valid point interpreted from the source or each valid point of significant omission provided. The candidate can achieve **up to 3 marks** for their interpretation of the parts of the source they consider are relevant in terms of the proposed question where there is also at least one point of significant omission identified to imply a judgement has been made about the limitations of the source. For full marks to be given each point needs to be discretely mentioned in terms of the question.

A maximum of 2 marks may be given for answers which refer only to the source or in which no judgement has been made.

Possible points which may be identified in the source include:

1. The KDF (Strength through Joy Organisation) controlled most forms of entertainment
2. Each year around seven million people took part in KDF sports matches
3. Mass outings to the theatre and the opera were arranged
4. Workers were also provided with affordable holidays including cruises and walking or skiing holidays

Possible points of significant omission may include:

1. Other Strength through Joy programmes such as:
   Evening classes for adults
   The Peoples Car (Volkswagen) hire purchase scheme which turned out to be a swindle
2. Nuremberg Laws
3. Hitler Youth later made compulsory
4. Role of Gestapo
5. Propaganda (examples of)
6. Censorship of newspapers/films/books/films
7. Books considered unacceptable were burned
8. Complaining about the Nazis against the law
9. Penalty for anti-Hitler jokes was death
10. National Labour Service
11. Compulsory Military Service

Section 3, Context E, Red Flag: Lenin and the Russian Revolution, 1894–1921

1. *Candidates can be credited in a number of ways **up to a maximum of 5 marks**.*

They may take different perspectives on the events and may describe a variety of different aspects of the events.

1 mark should be given for each accurate relevant key point of knowledge.

A second mark should be given for each point that is developed, up to a maximum of **5 marks**. Candidates may achieve full marks by providing five straightforward points, by making three developed points, or a combination of these.

Possible points of knowledge may include:
1. The Pillars of Autocracy controlled the Russian people
2. The Civil Service controlled everyday life eg censorship of newspapers
3. Use of secret police the Okhrana to spy on opponents
4. Support from church who taught peasants that Tsar should be obeyed
5. Use of army/Cossacks to crush uprisings or opponents
6. Use of exile to get rid of opponents

2. *Candidates can be credited in a number of ways **up to a maximum of 5 marks**.*

Candidates must show a causal relationship between events.

Up to a **maximum of 5 marks in total**, **1 mark** should be given for each accurate, relevant reason, and a **second mark** should be given for reasons that are developed. Candidates may achieve full marks by providing five straightforward reasons, three developed reasons, or a combination of these.

Possible reasons may include:
1. Peasants unhappy due to redemption payments and high taxes (bad harvests made situation worse)
2. Peasant 'land hunger' caused discontent
3. Workers unhappy with poor wages and working conditions
4. Violent strikes due to long hours and low wages (government reaction made situation worse eg by arresting leaders)
5. Radical politics among university students caused further discontent
6. Defeat in the Russo – Japanese War led to unrest
7. Policy of Russification caused discontent amongst nationalities eg Poles
8. Some sections of military become discontented – Potemkin Mutiny.
9. Events of Bloody Sunday in January 1905 led to discontent and strikes
10. Set up of St Petersburg & Moscow Soviets
11. October Manifesto split middle classes from workers and socialists

3. *Candidates can be credited in a number of ways **up to a maximum of 6 marks**.*

Candidates must make an overall judgement about how fully the source explains the events. **1 mark** may be given for each valid point interpreted from the source or each valid point of significant omission provided. The candidate can achieve **up to 3 marks** for their interpretation of the parts of the source they consider are relevant in terms of the proposed question where there is also at least one point of significant omission identified to imply a judgement

has been made about the limitations of the source. For full marks to be given each point needs to be discretely mentioned in terms of the question.

A maximum of 2 marks may be given for answers which refer only to the source or in which no judgement has been made.

Possible points which may be identified in the source include:
1. First World War was to have a terrible impact on Russia
2. Heart-breaking losses were suffered by the Tsars armies
3. Thousands of wounded soldiers were left lying untreated on the ground for days
4. Not even quarter enough bandages

Possible points of significant omission may include:
1. Military defeat at Tannenburg and Masurian lakes
2. Collapse of the economy
3. Inflation affected prices
4. Population suffered shortages of food and fuel
5. Tsar took control of the armies and was then blamed for defeats
6. Tsarina took charge and was unpopular as she was German-born/thought to be under the influence of Rasputin
7. Political instability – regular changes to both Prime Ministers and Ministers/ministerial 'leapfrog'
8. Allegations of government corruption eg Rasputin weakened Tsar's authority
9. Conscripting millions of peasants led to shortage of grain
10. Inability of the government to organise procurement/ movement of supplies to civilians or war production for the military

4. *Candidates can be credited in a number of ways **up to a maximum of 4 marks**.*

Candidates must make direct comparisons of the two sources, either overall or in detail. A simple comparison will indicate what points of detail or overall viewpoint they agree or disagree about and should be given **1 mark**.

A developed comparison of the points of detail or overall viewpoint should be given **2 marks**. Candidates may achieve full marks by making four simple comparisons, two developed comparisons or by a combination of these.

Possible points of comparison may include:

Overall: The sources agree the situation was serious with shortages and unrest	
Source B	**Source C**
Disturbances...are becoming more serious	The situation was already very serious
Shortages of bread	They wanted bread but... many had been unable to get any
Workers are without jobs	Several thousand workmen unemployed

Section 3, Context F, Mussolini and Fascist Italy, 1919–1939

1. *Candidates can be credited in a number of ways **up to a maximum of 5 marks**.*

They may take different perspectives on the events and may describe a variety of different aspects of the events.

1 mark should be given for each accurate relevant key point of knowledge.

A **second mark** should be given for each point that is developed, up to a maximum of **5 marks**. Candidates may achieve full marks by providing five straightforward points, by making three developed points, or a combination of these.

Possible points of knowledge may include:

1. Mussolini aimed to make Italy a great power/wanted control of Mediterranean
2. Mussolini wanted to expand Italy's colonial empire in Africa/increase Italian influence in the Balkans
3. In 1924 Mussolini took control of the Yugoslavian port of Fiume
4. Wished to appear as a statesman in early years eg Locarno 1925
5. Mussolini supported King Zog in Albania (by signing a Treaty of Friendship in 1926 Mussolini made Albania into an Italian satellite state)
6. Mussolini funded Croat nationalists in order to create trouble for Yugoslavia
7. Mussolini settled the border dispute with Britain over Libya and Egypt
8. Mussolini aided Dolfuss in order to provide a bulwark against Nazi aggression
9. In 1935 concluded Stresa Front with France and Britain (wished to be recognised as a great power)
10. Launched attack on Ethiopia
11. Intervened in Spanish Civil War
12. Agreed Anti-Comintern Pact with Japan and Germany in 1937
13. Posed as mediator at Munich Conference Sept 1938
14. Invaded Albania in 1939
15. Pact of Steel with Germany concluded May 1939

2. *Candidates can be credited in a number of ways* **up to a maximum of 5 marks.**

Candidates must show a causal relationship between events.

Up to a **maximum of 5 marks in total**, **1 mark** should be given for each accurate, relevant reason, and a **second mark** should be given for reasons that are developed. Candidates may achieve full marks by providing five straightforward reasons, three developed reasons, or a combination of these.

Possible reasons may include:

1. Many were unhappy when trade unions were outlawed
2. Revaluation of the lira in 1927 led to decline in exports, causing discontent
3. Increase in unemployment 1926-28. By 1933 unemployment had reached 2 million, causing unpopularity
4. High tariffs restricted imports, so people unhappy
5. Real wages fell, so people unhappy
6. Sick pay and paid holidays were not introduced until 1938, so people were unhappy
7. The failure to make Italy self-sufficient – embarrassment/unpopularity
8. As part of the Battle For Grain land in central and southern regions was turned over to wheat production despite being unsuitable (traditional agricultural exports declined), unpopular in these areas
9. Increasing government control of industry was resented

3. *Candidates can be credited in a number of ways* **up to a maximum of 6 marks.**

Candidates must make an overall judgement about how fully the source explains the events. **1 mark** may be given for each valid point interpreted from the source or each valid point of significant omission provided. The candidate can achieve **up to 3 marks** for their interpretation of the parts of the source

they consider are relevant in terms of the proposed question where there is also at least one point of significant omission identified to imply a judgement has been made about the limitations of the source. For full marks to be given each point needs to be discretely mentioned in terms of the question.

A maximum of 2 marks may be given for answers which refer only to the source or in which no judgement has been made.

Possible points which may be identified in the source include:

1. Mussolini's press office issued official versions of events which all the newspapers were expected to publish without question
2. The radio and the cinema were also used to broadcast Fascist propaganda
3. News bulletins broadcast a daily diet of Mussolini's speeches and praised him as the saviour of Italy
4. The media played a crucial role in the cult of "Il Duce"

Possible points of significant omission may include:

1. Mussolini started a new calendar with Year 1 beginning in 1922
2. The regime made propagandist feature films
3. The Duce was shown as a great athlete and musician (cult of personality)
4. Brainwashing/indoctrination of young at school/textbooks or youth groups
5. The newspapers suggested that Mussolini was infallible
6. An image of youthfulness was portrayed by not referring to Mussolini's age or the fact he wore glasses/usually seen in uniform
7. It was said that Mussolini worked 16 hour days – his light was left on after he had gone to bed to maintain this fiction
8. Use of RC church to support Fascists policies eg against communism at home or in Spain

4. *Candidates can be credited in a number of ways* **up to a maximum of 4 marks.**

Candidates must make direct comparisons of the two sources, either overall or in detail. A simple comparison will indicate what points of detail or overall viewpoint they agree or disagree about and should be given **1 mark**.

A developed comparison of the points of detail or overall viewpoint should be given **2 marks**. Candidates may achieve full marks by making four simple comparisons, two developed comparisons or by a combination of these.

Possible points of comparison may include:

Overall: The sources agree that there was a limited opposition to the regime	
Source A	**Source B**
Fascist policies benefited the rich to ensure their support.	Big businessmen and landowners supported a regime which always seemed to be on their side.
The signing of the Lateran agreement in 1929 was important in winning the support of Catholics.	This new close relationship with the church reduced the threat of opposition from Catholics.
There was some opposition in the army, but this was never carried out in a coordinated way	While some army generals opposed Mussolini others liked his aggressive attitude.

Section 3, Context G, Free at Last? Civil Rights in the USA, 1918–1968

1. *Candidates can be credited in a number of ways up to a maximum of 4 marks.*

Candidates must make direct comparisons of the two sources, either overall or in detail. A simple comparison will indicate what points of detail or overall viewpoint they agree or disagree about and should be given **1 mark**.

A developed comparison of the points of detail or overall viewpoint should be given **2 marks**. Candidates may achieve full marks by making four simple comparisons, two developed comparisons or by a combination of these.

Possible points of comparison may include:

Overall: The sources agree about the poor living and working conditions of immigrants	
Source A	Source B
Immigrants from the same country usually lived in the same areas of the city	Immigrants tended to live in their own communities: in New York there was a Polish district, a Jewish district and an Italian district
These areas contained tenement slums which were damp, dark and filthy with no water supply, toilets or drains	Tenements buildings in these areas were often five or six storeys high with rooms which lacked light or sanitation
Immigrants had to take any work they could get, usually low paid jobs such as labourers or servants	Finding a well-paid, skilled job was a common problem for poorly educated immigrants

2. *Candidates can be credited in a number of ways up to a maximum of 5 marks.*

They may take different perspectives on the events and may describe a variety of different aspects of the events.

1 mark should be given for each accurate relevant key point of knowledge.

A **second mark** should be given for each point that is developed, up to a maximum of **5 marks**. Candidates may achieve full marks by providing five straightforward points, by making three developed points, or a combination of these.

Possible points of knowledge may include:
1. Legal action leading to the decision of the Supreme Court in 1954 to declare segregation in schools unconstitutional
2. Bus boycott in Montgomery
3. Little Rock, Arkansas – attempt by black students to enter Central High School
4. Sit-downs/Sit-ins eg deliberately holding up traffic/ the occupation of lunch counters and other segregated places
5. Freedom rides – travel on buses through southern states using segregated facilities at bus stations
6. Project C – sit-ins and marches in Birmingham, Alabama led by Martin Luther King
7. March on Washington

3. *Candidates can be credited in a number of ways up to a maximum of 6 marks.*

Candidates must make an overall judgement about how fully the source explains the events. **1 mark** may be given for each valid point interpreted from the source or each valid point of significant omission provided. The candidate can achieve **up to 3 marks** for their interpretation of the parts of the source they consider are relevant in terms of the proposed question where there is also at least one point of significant omission identified to imply a judgement has been made about the limitations of the source. For full marks to be given each point needs to be discretely mentioned in terms of the question.

A maximum of 2 marks may be given for answers which refer only to the source or in which no judgement has been made.

Possible points which may be identified in the source include:
1. President Truman issued orders to desegregate the US military
2. He also set up a President's Committee on civil rights in 1946 to report to him on how progress towards black civil rights could be made
3. In 1960 Congress passed a Civil Rights Act which established penalties for obstructing black voting.
4. The assassination of President Kennedy in November 1963 came at the time he was preparing a Civil Rights Bill

Possible points of significant omission may include:
1. Supreme Court decision declared that schools could no longer be segregated
2. In 1957 President Eisenhower sent in federal troops to Little Rock in Arkansas to ensure that nine black children could safely enter a recently desegregated high school
3. Federal Marshalls were sent to escort James Meredith through the gates of Mississippi University
4. Civil Rights Act passed in 1964

4. *Candidates can be credited in a number of ways up to a maximum of 5 marks.*

Candidates must show a causal relationship between events.

Up to a maximum of **5 marks in total**, **1 mark** should be given for each accurate, relevant reason, and a **second mark** should be given for reasons that are developed. Candidates may achieve full marks by providing five straightforward reasons, three developed reasons, or a combination of these.

Possible reasons may include:
1. Black Panthers gained support for their demand for the release of black prisoners
2. Black Panthers gained support due to their efforts to give practical help to poor blacks eg breakfast clubs in schools
3. Black Panthers had charismatic leaders who gained attention and popularity
4. The Black Panthers encouraged blacks to be proud of the colour of their skin and their African American culture. This appealed to many
5. Black Panthers condoned violence and this appealed to many blacks who were frustrated by the non-violent methods of the Civil Rights Movement
6. Black Panthers attracted further support after gaining the much publicised support of athletes at the Olympic Games in 1968

Section 3, Context H, Appeasement and the Road to War, 1918-1939

1. *Candidates can be credited in a number of ways up to a maximum of 5 marks.*

They may take different perspectives on the events and may describe a variety of different aspects of the events.

1 mark should be given for each accurate relevant key point of knowledge.

A second mark should be given for each point that is developed, up to a maximum of 5 marks. Candidates may achieve full marks by providing five straightforward points, by making three developed points, or a combination of these.

Possible points of knowledge may include:
1. The German army was limited to 100,000 men
2. The German army was forbidden from having tanks
3. The German army was forbidden from being situated in the Rhineland
4. The German navy was forbidden from having submarines
5. The German navy was limited to six battleships
6. Germany was forbidden from having an air force

2. *Candidates can be credited in a number of ways up to a maximum of 6 marks.*

Candidates must make an overall judgement about how fully the source explains the events. **1 mark** may be given for each valid point interpreted from the source or each valid point of significant omission provided. The candidate can achieve **up to 3 marks** for their interpretation of the parts of the source they consider are relevant in terms of the proposed question where there is also at least one point of significant omission identified to imply a judgement has been made about the limitations of the source. For full marks to be given each point needs to be discretely mentioned in terms of the question.

A maximum of 2 marks may be given for answers which refer only to the source or in which no judgement has been made.

Possible points which may be identified in the source include:
1. The USA refused to join as they were not interested in getting involved in the problems of other countries
2. Initially Russia was not invited to join, so another great country of the world was absent
3. Taking decisions was difficult as the Assembly had to be unanimous and member states often could not agree
4. A further problem was that the League did not have its own army to back up its decisions

Possible points of significant omission may include:
1. Germany was not allowed to join until 1926, so another major power was absent
2. Member countries were reluctant to agree to economic sanctions for fear of damaging their own economies
3. Member countries were reluctant to take action against a powerful member state
4. The two most powerful member countries Britain and France were reluctant to commit troops to fight for the League
5. Countries lost faith in the League with each failure

3. *Candidates can be credited in a number of ways up to a maximum of 5 marks.*

Candidates must show a causal relationship between events.

Up to a **maximum of 5 marks in total**, **1 mark** should be given for each accurate, relevant reason, and a **second mark** should be given for reasons that are developed. Candidates may achieve full marks by providing five straightforward reasons, three developed reasons, or a combination of these.

Possible reasons may include:
1. There was a belief that although Germany had broken the Treaty, they had been too severely punished at Versailles
2. It was argued that Germany had done little more than liberate her own territory
3. Many believed that the Franco-Soviet Pact had unduly provoked Hitler
4. Many within Britain saw a stronger Germany as a useful barrier against the spread of communism
5. It was hoped that a conciliatory approach might persuade Germany to re-enter the League and resume disarmament talks
6. It was felt that the relative weakness of the British armed forces restricted the opportunity for direct action
7. There was little sign that public opinion would have supported military action against Hitler

4. *Candidates can be credited in a number of ways up to a maximum of 4 marks.*

Candidates must make direct comparisons of the two sources, either overall or in detail. A simple comparison will indicate what points of detail or overall viewpoint they agree or disagree about and should be given **1 mark**.

A developed comparison of the points of detail or overall viewpoint should be given **2 marks**. Candidates may achieve full marks by making four simple comparisons, two developed comparisons or by a combination of these.

Possible points of comparison may include:

| Overall: The sources agree that Anschluss was a positive event which should be welcomed ||
Source B	Source C
The population of Austria comprised ethnic Germans, a majority of whom are enthusiastic about the Anschluss/The Austrians will not only feel at home as part of Germany/Their German brothers	That there has been no fighting is proof of the desire of the Austrian people to belong to Germany
It was a mistake of the peacemakers at Versailles to forbid the union of Austria and Germany	The union of these two countries should never have been forbidden at Versailles
They will benefit financially too from an increase in trade	Austrians will also benefit from greater markets for their raw materials and manufactured goods

Section 3, Context I, World War II, 1939-1945

1. *Candidates can be credited in a number of ways up to a maximum of 4 marks.*

Candidates must make direct comparisons of the two sources, either overall or in detail. A simple comparison will indicate what points of detail or overall viewpoint they agree or disagree about and should be given **1 mark**.

A developed comparison of the points of detail or overall viewpoint should be given **2 marks**. Candidates may achieve full marks by making four simple comparisons, two developed comparisons or by a combination of these.

Possible points of comparison may include:

Overall: The sources agree that the tactic of Blitzkrieg was effective at the beginning of the war.	
Source A	**Source B**
Blitzkrieg was a tactic based on speed and surprise	Hitler was very excited by a plan of attack that was based purely on speed and movement
It required the effective use of Stuka dive bombers	Stuka dive bombers were sent in to 'soften' up the enemy
These were supported by light tank units and infantry	Then the tanks attacked, supported by infantry

2. *Candidates can be credited in a number of ways **up to a maximum of 5 marks**.*

They may take different perspectives on the events and may describe a variety of different aspects of the events.

1 mark should be given for each accurate relevant key point of knowledge.

A second mark should be given for each point that is developed, up to a maximum of **5 marks**. Candidates may achieve full marks by providing five straightforward points, by making three developed points, or a combination of these.

Possible points of knowledge may include:
1. Citizens in the west placed under German military rule
2. Eastern European civilians more brutally governed under German civil administrations
3. Vichy regime set up in southern France where citizens lived under German controlled French Government
4. Economies controlled: industry and agriculture supervised and the people often left to go hungry
5. Workers issued with work cards and free deployment of labour was prohibited
6. In western Europe workers pressured to 'volunteer' for work in Germany/ pressure on young men to join 'crusade' against communism in East
7. Almost all food was rationed
8. Curfews in place
9. All citizens had to carry an identity card
10. Gestapo operated under Night and Fog Decree of 1941, giving them powers to seize anyone endangering German security
11. Media censorship
12. SS brutality and the Police State ruled over occupied citizens
13. Jews and other 'undesirables' deported to concentration camps mostly in the east/willing collaboration in deportation Jews eg Vichy
14. Jewish Poles dispossessed, property and belongings confiscated
15. Jews in Poland forced to live in ghettos then deported to camps in the east/examples of life in the ghettos
16. Special forces in Eastern Europe killed Jews and other undesirables in mass killings eg gypsies

3. *Candidates can be credited in a number of ways **up to a maximum of 6 marks**.*

Candidates must make an overall judgement about how fully the source explains the events. **1 mark** may be given for each valid point interpreted from the source or each valid point of significant omission provided. The candidate can achieve **up to 3 marks** for their interpretation of the parts of the source they consider are relevant in terms of the proposed question where there is also at least one point of significant omission identified to imply a judgement has been made about the limitations of the source. For full marks to be given each point needs to be discretely mentioned in terms of the question.

A maximum of 2 marks may be given for answers which refer only to the source.

Possible points which may be identified in the source include:
1. It helped Jews or Allied airmen who had crash landed in France, to escape
2. School children were recruited to help smuggle people across the borders of northern and southern France
3. The Resistance movement produced anti-German propaganda which was crucial in undermining Nazi rule
4. Nazi control was further challenged by the Resistance who worked to punish any French collaboration

Possible points of significant omission may include:
1. Key intelligence link for Allied spy networks
2. Sabotaged German military operations eg blowing up trains, convoys, ships etc
3. Targeted and killed many high ranking Nazi officials
4. Carried out acts of sabotage prior to and during the D-Day landings to help Allied establish a foothold in Normandy/pinned down vital German forces
5. Radio operators (pianists) to send messages of German activities and other communications back to Britain
6. Telephone workers sabotaged telephone lines and intercepted German military messages
7. Postal workers intercepted important military communications
8. Rail workers diverted freight shipments/caused derailments/destroyed tracks/blew up bridges
9. Created labs to manufacture explosives/stole explosives and other resources from German army

4. *Candidates can be credited in a number of ways **up to a maximum of 5 marks**.*

Candidates must show a causal relationship between events.

Up to a **maximum of 5 marks in total**, **1 mark** should be given for each accurate, relevant reason, and a **second mark** should be given for reasons that are developed. Candidates may achieve full marks by providing five straightforward reasons, three developed reasons, or a combination of these.

Possible reasons may include:
1. Russian army encircled the city by mid-April due to their success in previous battles
2. Stalin had prioritised capturing Berlin before the Allies
3. Russians advanced easily against poor German defences at the Oder River/German units chose to concentrate fighting to the west of the city so they could surrender to Allied forces rather than Russian
4. Defence of the city of Berlin relied upon disorganised/poorly armed units from the German army and Hitler Youth members/elderly men or boys
5. City of Berlin defences in panic and disarray, so easier
6. Allied aerial bombing of the city assisted the Russian army

7. Artillery barrage into the city began on April 16th and pushed back the German defences further
8. Hitler sacked commanders, created confusion
9. Loss of morale after Hitler committed suicide

Section 3, Context J, The Cold War, 1945-1989

1. *Candidates can be credited in a number of ways **up to a maximum of 5 marks**.*

Candidates must show a causal relationship between events.

Up to a **maximum of 5 marks in total**, **1 mark** should be given for each accurate, relevant reason, and a **second mark** should be given for reasons that are developed. Candidates may achieve full marks by providing five straightforward reasons, three developed reasons, or a combination of these.

Possible reasons may include:
1. The only thing that kept them together was over – the Second World War
2. Disagreements at Potsdam eg over Poland
3. The Americans had developed the atomic bomb and this angered/ worried the Soviet Union
4. Soviet troops were occupying most of Eastern Europe and this caused tension
5. Truman, the new American President was more anti-communist than Roosevelt
6. An arms race developed causing further tension
7. Different ideas – capitalism versus communism
8. The Soviets saw Marshall Aid as an American attempt to dominate Europe/Soviet satellites prevented from accepting Marshall Aid
9. Berlin Blockade, 1948-1949, deepened the divisions between East and West
10. The establishment of NATO by America and its allies in 1949 caused further division
11. Establishment of Warsaw Pact 1955 heightened tensions
12. The Soviets and the Americans involved on different sides in proxy wars eg Korea

2. *Candidates can be credited in a number of ways **up to a maximum of 6 marks**.*

Candidates must make an overall judgement about how fully the source explains the events. **1 mark** may be given for each valid point interpreted from the source or each valid point of significant omission provided. The candidate can achieve **up to 3 marks** for their interpretation of the parts of the source they consider are relevant in terms of the proposed question where there is also at least one point of significant omission identified to imply a judgement has been made about the limitations of the source. For full marks to be given each point needs to be discretely mentioned in terms of the question.

A maximum of 2 marks may be given for answers which refer only to the source or in which no judgement has been made.

Possible points which may be identified in the source include:
1. President Truman explained that America would resist the spread of Communism
2. The Americans had responded to French requests for assistance in Vietnam
3. It was clear that South Vietnam could not resist Communism without the support of American troops
4. Many in America believed war was necessary to stop the spread of Soviet influence

Possible points of significant omission may include:
1. America feared that a civil war was developing in South Vietnam.
2. America was increasingly concerned about the influence of China in south-east Asia
3. There was a widespread belief in the Domino Theory eg Thailand, Laos, Burma, Cambodia even New Zealand and Australia could fall to communism
4. There was a general concern that America was falling behind in the Cold War at this time
5. Gulf of Tonkin incident led America to become involved in a full scale war in Vietnam.

3. *Candidates can be credited in a number of ways **up to a maximum of 4 marks**.*

Candidates must make direct comparisons of the two sources, either overall or in detail. A simple comparison will indicate what points of detail or overall viewpoint they agree or disagree about and should be given **1 mark**.

A developed comparison of the points of detail or overall viewpoint should be given **2 marks**. Candidates may achieve full marks by making four simple comparisons, two developed comparisons or by a combination of these.

Possible points of comparison may include:

Overall: The sources agree that the Soviets were at fault	
Source A	Source B
The source of world trouble and tension is Moscow	We now say with confidence that this crisis was caused by Moscow.
They have rejected an all-German peace treaty	The Soviets rejected an American proposal for a peace treaty
It is they who have rejected … the rule of international law.	The Soviet domination of East Germany was a clear breach of international law

4. *Candidates can be credited in a number of ways **up to a maximum of 5 marks**.*

They may take different perspectives on the events and may describe a variety of different aspects of the events.

1 mark should be given for each accurate relevant key point of knowledge.

A second mark should be given for each point that is developed, up to a maximum of **5 marks**. Candidates may achieve full marks by providing five straightforward points, by making three developed points, or a combination of these.

Possible points of knowledge may include:
1. Cuba stayed Communist/Castro's position strengthened as Kennedy promised not to invade
2. American missiles withdrawn from Turkey/Italy
3. Kennedy greatly improved his reputation in America and the West
4. Khrushchev was able to claim he prevented America from taking over Cuba, a useful ally so close to America
5. Krushchev seemed weak as American missiles removed in secret/led directly to Krushchev's fall 2 years later
6. Led to a thaw in the Cold War
7. 'Hot line' set up between the White House and the Kremlin
8. Nuclear Test Ban Treaty signed in 1963

NATIONAL 5 HISTORY 2015

Section 1, Part A, The Wars of Independence, 1286-1328

1. *Candidates can be credited in a number of ways up to a maximum of 4 marks.*

Candidates must make direct comparisons of the two sources, either overall or in detail. A simple comparison will indicate what points of detail or overall viewpoint they agree or disagree about and should be given **1 mark**.

A developed comparison of the points of detail or overall viewpoint should be given **2 marks**. Candidates may achieve full marks by making four simple comparisons, two developed comparisons or by a combination of these.

Possible points of comparison may include:

Source A	Source B
Overall: The sources agree that Edward wanted to unite the kingdoms through marriage/the sources disagree over his methods	
His aim was to unite the kingdoms with a marriage treaty	This marriage would mean a union of the kingdoms
Edward had secretly asked the Pope's permission for the marriage before any terms had been discussed with the Scots	Edward asked for Scottish representatives to be present before any negotiations began
He plotted to arrange the marriage of his son to Scotland's infant queen, Margaret, Maid of Norway	Erik, King of Norway, father of Margaret the Maid, sent messengers to him to suggest her possible marriage with Edward's son

2. *Candidates can be credited in a number of ways up to a maximum of 5 marks.*

They may take different perspectives on the events and may describe a variety of different aspects of the events.

1 mark should be given for each accurate relevant key point of knowledge.

A second mark should be given for each point that is developed, up to a maximum of **5 marks**. Candidates may achieve full marks by providing five straightforward points, by making three developed points, or a combination of these.

Possible points of knowledge may include:
1. Edward had mustered a very large army for the invasion
2. Edward had ships waiting to enter the harbour and attack
3. Edward gave the inhabitants three days to surrender
4. the castle garrison surrendered without reprisal
5. the townspeople refused to surrender/mocked Edward's offer of surrender
6. three of Edward's ships ran aground and were burned by the townspeople
7. Edward's troops were sent in to take the town
8. there was little resistance to the attack
9. the townspeople were slaughtered/the slaughter lasted for three days

10. thirty Flemish merchants fired arrows at the English/ were burned to death in the Red Hall
11. the town was burned to the ground

3. *Candidates can be credited in a number of ways up to a maximum of 6 marks.*

Candidates must make an overall judgement about how fully the source explains the events. **1 mark** may be given for each valid point interpreted from the source or each valid point of significant omission provided. The candidate can achieve **up to 3 marks** for their interpretation of the parts of the source they consider are relevant in terms of the proposed question where there is also at least one point of significant omission identified to imply a judgement has been made about the limitations of the source. For full marks to be given each point needs to be discretely mentioned in terms of the question.

A maximum of 2 marks may be given for answers which refer only to the source.

Possible points which may be identified in the source include:
1. Bruce destroyed castles in Inverness and Nairn
2. Bruce could not spare men to defend castles from attack
3. Douglas recaptured his own castle in the south (and burned it down)
4. lack of siege engines forced Bruce to use other methods.

Possible points of significant omission may include:
1. castles that were destroyed could not later be used against him by his enemies
2. Douglas burned all the stores with the English garrisons' bodies in his castle – the 'Douglas Larder'
3. Perth castle was captured by Bruce's men wading across the river at night/scaled riverside wall at night with ladders
4. Roxburgh castle was captured by Bruce's men hiding among cattle at dusk to get close to walls/used rope ladders at night to scale walls and open gates
5. Linlithgow castle was captured by jamming the gate and portcullis with a haycart/men were hidden in the cart to fight till reinforcements arrived
6. Edinburgh castle was captured with a daring climb up the rock face/ diversionary attack on other side
7. Stirling, Bothwell and Berwick castles were recaptured later

4. *Candidates can be credited in a number of ways up to a maximum of 5 marks.*

Candidates must show a causal relationship between events.

Up to a maximum of 5 marks in total, 1 mark should be given for each accurate, relevant reason, and a second mark should be given for reasons that are developed. Candidates may achieve full marks by providing five straightforward reasons, three developed reasons, or a combination of these.

Possible reasons may include:
1. there was no battle plan as Edward did not think the Scots would fight
2. the English were overconfident due to their superior numbers
3. Edward did not take charge himself but appointed favourites to key commands, causing resentment
4. Edward ignored warnings not to attack across Bannockburn

5. marshy ground not suitable for heavy cavalry or infantry
6. there was confusion among the commanders about attacking the Scots on the first day/whether the battle was to take place that day
7. de Bohun charged Bruce without being ordered to and his defeat contributed to lowered morale among the English
8. English commanders argued among themselves and were forced to retreat on the first day of the battle by Scottish pikemen
9. Edward moved his army to the Carse during the night, so they were tired
10. the commanders did not learn from the forced retreat against the Scots pikemen on the first day of the battle so repeated the same mistake/cavalry made no headway against schiltrons
11. the English army was badly positioned
12. the English footsoldiers/archers/cavalry had no room to manoeuvre
13. huge numbers became a handicap when they attempted to retreat **across the Bannockburn**

Section 1, Part B, Mary Queen of Scots and the Scottish reformation, 1542-1587

5. *Candidates can be credited in a number of ways **up to a maximum of 5 marks**.*

They may take different perspectives on the events and may describe a variety of different aspects of the events.

1 mark should be given for each accurate relevant key point of knowledge. **A second mark** should be given for each point that is developed, up to a maximum of **5 marks**. Candidates may achieve full marks by providing five straightforward points, by making three developed points, or a combination of these.

Possible points of knowledge may include:
1. the Scots broke the Treaty of Greenwich which stated that Mary would marry Edward, Henry VIII's son
2. Henry VIII ordered the Earl of Hertford to invade Scotland and burn Edinburgh
3. the English attacked Scotland and destroyed abbeys/ towns in the south of Scotland
4. Henry VIII encouraged the assassination of Cardinal Beaton
5. Battle of Pinkie Cleugh 1547 – large Scottish army defeated
6. the Palace of Holyrood in Edinburgh was looted/large parts of Edinburgh were burned
7. the pier at Leith in Edinburgh was destroyed
8. Berwick upon Tweed was attacked and burned
9. Scots received help from the French who sent a force to Edinburgh in 1548
10. Treaty of Haddington was signed by the Scots and French which agreed Mary would marry the heir to the French throne
11. Mary was sent to France for protection

6. *Candidates can be credited in a number of ways **up to a maximum of 4 marks**.*

Candidates must make direct comparisons of the two sources, either overall or in detail. A simple comparison will indicate what points of detail or overall viewpoint they agree or disagree about and should be given **1 mark**.

A developed comparison of the points of detail or overall viewpoint should be given **2 marks**. Candidates may achieve full marks by making four simple comparisons, two developed comparisons or by a combination of these.

Possible points of comparison may include:

Source A	Source B
Overall: The sources agree that Darnley and a group of nobles entered Mary's chamber uninvited/ killed Riccio	
Suddenly, Darnley forced his way into the chamber with a large group of followers	Darnley unexpectedly appeared with a group of armed nobles, including Lord Ruthven, and burst into Mary's chamber
One of the intruders held Mary back and a pistol was pointed towards her pregnant belly	Mary, who was pregnant, could not do anything because she had been seized and had a gun pointed to her stomach
He was then dragged from the room and stabbed many times	Riccio was then pulled out of the room and stabbed over 50 times

7. *Candidates can be credited in a number of ways **up to a maximum of 5 marks**.*

Candidates must show a causal relationship between events.

Up to a **maximum of 5 marks in total**, **1 mark** should be given for each accurate, relevant reason, and a **second mark** should be given for reasons that are developed. Candidates may achieve full marks by providing five straightforward reasons, three developed reasons, or a combination of these.

Possible reasons may include:
1. Mary was implicated in the murder of her husband, Lord Darnley which put pressure on her to abdicate
2. her marriage to Bothwell cast further suspicion on Mary
3. Mary allowed Bothwell to prevent a fair investigation into the death of Darnley which angered many
4. Mary was forced to abdicate because Protestant Lords wanted her infant son on the throne
5. her half-brother Moray forced Mary to abdicate so he could become regent
6. Mary was unpopular as some objected to being ruled by a female monarch
7. military defeats forced Mary to abdicate eg Carberry Hill

8. *Candidates can be credited in a number of ways **up to a maximum of 6 marks**.*

Candidates must make an overall judgement about how fully the source explains the events. **1 mark** may be given for each valid point interpreted from the source or each valid point of significant omission provided. The candidate can achieve **up to 3 marks** for their interpretation of the parts of the source they consider are relevant in terms of the proposed question where there is also at least one point of significant omission identified to imply a judgement has been made about the limitations of the source. For full marks to be given each point needs to be discretely mentioned in terms of the question.

A maximum of 2 marks may be given for answers which refer only to the source.

Possible points which may be identified in the source include:
1. she learned that the trial would be held even in her absence
2. Mary defended herself/not allowed to call witnesses
3. Mary was not even allowed to consult any documents during her trial

4. she knew she would be found guilty because it was too great a risk to let her live

Possible points of significant omission may include:
1. Mary was arrested in September 1586 and held at Fotheringay Castle until her trial
2. Mary was implicated in a number of plots against Elizabeth eg Babington Plot, 1586
3. Mary was charged with treason
4. Mary was denied legal counsel
5. Mary claimed that she could not be accused of treason because she was not an English subject
6. Mary was convicted on 25 October 1586 and sentenced to death
7. Mary was beheaded on 8 February 1587 at Fotheringay Castle

Section 1, Part C, The Treaty of Union, 1689–1715

9. *Candidates can be credited in a number of ways **up to a maximum of 5 marks**.*

Candidates must show a causal relationship between events.

Up to a **maximum of 5 marks in total, 1 mark** should be given for each accurate, relevant reason, and a second mark should be given for reasons that are developed. Candidates may achieve full marks by providing five straightforward reasons, three developed reasons, or a combination of these.

Possible reasons may include:
1. many in Scotland were angry that the Navigation Acts prevented Scotland trading with English colonies
2. there was a feeling that the English had not done enough to help Scotland during the Ill Years of the 1690s
3. Scots were angry as they felt the Darien scheme had been sabotaged by William as it went against English interests
4. Scots' loyalties were considered suspect by the English after the Jacobite rebellion of 1689
5. Scots were angry that the English Parliament passed the succession to Sophia of Hanover without consulting the Scottish Parliament
6. the English were angry at Scottish legislation such as the Act of Security/Act Anent Peace and War
7. the English were angry over the execution of Captain Green of the Worcester

10. *Candidates can be credited in a number of ways **up to a maximum of 6 marks**.*

Candidates must make an overall judgement about how fully the source explains the events. **1 mark** may be given for each valid point interpreted from the source or each valid point of significant omission provided. The candidate can achieve **up to 3 marks** for their interpretation of the parts of the source they consider are relevant in terms of the proposed question where there is also at least one point of significant omission identified to imply a judgement has been made about the limitations of the source. For full marks to be given each point needs to be discretely mentioned in terms of the question.

A maximum of 2 marks may be given for answers which refer only to the source.

Possible points which may be identified in the source include:
1. the supporters of Union were clear that it would help Scotland to become richer in the future

2. many Protestants argued that the main advantage of Union would be securing the Protestant Succession
3. they also pointed out that the English had made it clear they would respect the independence of the Church of Scotland
4. it was also pointed out that if Union was rejected England might simply invade and take over anyway

Possible points of significant omission may include:
1. Union would guarantee the Scots access to trade with English colonies
2. Union would guarantee security against Catholic France
3. Union would see Darien investors compensated through the Equivalent
4. Union would end English piracy

11. *Candidates can be credited in a number of ways **up to a maximum of 4 marks**.*

Candidates must make direct comparisons of the two sources, either overall or in detail. A simple comparison will indicate what points of detail or overall viewpoint they agree or disagree about and should be given **1 mark**.

A developed comparison of the points of detail or overall viewpoint should be given 2 marks. Candidates may achieve full marks by making four simple comparisons, two developed comparisons or by a combination of these.

Possible points of comparison may include:

Source B	Source C
Overall: Both sources agree that most Scots opposed the Union	
Many feared that the proposed Union would lead to a rise in taxes	It was claimed that after the Union higher taxes would hit all Scots in the pocket
They argued that England was the far bigger country and so would control Scotland	Many Scots felt that the Union would not be a partnership but a takeover
Some feared for the independence of the Church of Scotland	Religion was very important to many Scots and they did not want the English to interfere in their Church

12. *Candidates can be credited in a number of ways **up to a maximum of 5 marks**.*

They may take different perspectives on the events and may describe a variety of different aspects of the events.

1 mark should be given for each accurate relevant key point of knowledge. **A second mark** should be given for each point that is developed, up to a maximum of **5 marks**. Candidates may achieve full marks by providing five straightforward points, by making three developed points, or a combination of these.

Possible points of knowledge may include:
1. there was a growth in smuggling
2. increased taxes (led to attacks on excisemen eg at Ayr in 1714)
3. the Scottish linen industry suffered because of increased taxes
4. the Scottish Privy Council was abolished in 1708
5. led to the Jacobite rebellions of 1708 and 1715
6. led to the 1712 Toleration Act which granted Episcopalians the right to worship freely in Scotland

Section 1, Part D, Migration and Empire, 1830-1939

13. *Candidates can be credited in a number of ways **up to a maximum of 6 marks.***

Candidates must make an overall judgement about how fully the source explains the events. **1 mark** may be given for each valid point interpreted from the source or each valid point of significant omission provided. The candidate can achieve **up to 3 marks** for their interpretation of the parts of the source they consider are relevant in terms of the proposed question where there is also at least one point of significant omission identified to imply a judgement has been made about the limitations of the source. For full marks to be given each point needs to be discretely mentioned in terms of the question.

A maximum of 2 marks may be given for answers which refer only to the source.

Possible points which may be identified in the source include:
1. many Scots invested money in the Empire and reinvested their profits in Scotland, adding to Scotland's wealth
2. profits were spent in other ways on luxury houses and impressive public buildings which changed the appearance of Scottish cities
3. profits from trade with the Empire were also used to develop chemical industries and textiles, creating even more jobs
4. the Empire provided markets for Scottish coal/employed thousands of miners

Possible points of significant omission may include:
1. Clyde shipyards produced much of the shipping needed to trade goods and carry passengers to the Empire
2. thousands of railway locomotives were produced in Scotland and exported to India, Canada, New Zealand etc
3. raw materials produced in the Empire were brought to Scotland for processing eg jute to Dundee, sugar to Greenock, cotton to Paisley
4. cheap food imports from the Empire eg wheat/Canada, lamb/Australia affected Scots farmers
5. Glasgow thought of itself as the Second City of the Empire/Scotland was known as the 'Workshop of the Empire'
6. provided Scots with jobs abroad as administrators, diplomats, soldiers etc.
7. provided Scots with the opportunity to emigrate abroad to the Empire e.g. Canada, Australia etc.

14. *Candidates can be credited in a number of ways **up to a maximum of 5 marks.***

Candidates must show a causal relationship between events.

Up to a **maximum of 5 marks in total**, **1 mark** should be given for each accurate, relevant reason, and a **second mark** should be given for reasons that are developed. Candidates may achieve full marks by providing five straightforward reasons, three developed reasons, or a combination of these.

Possible reasons may include:
1. many small farms/smallholdings disappeared as landowners created large farms, leaving tenants without a livelihood
2. new larger farms were too expensive for most tenant farmers to rent/buy
3. increased mechanisation in agriculture meant fewer workers were needed
4. skilled craftsmen such as weavers lost their livelihoods when more factories were built
5. trade depressions put many out of work and encouraged them to seek work abroad
6. family, relations wrote letters home telling of better wages, living standards etc.
7. wages in Scotland were low/wages in USA and Canada were higher
8. living conditions in Scottish cities were poor with much overcrowding
9. faster Atlantic crossings on steamships enabled more temporary emigration especially for skilled workers
10. skilled Scottish workers eg engineers/fishermen/stonemasons were in great demand in the colonies
11. countries such as Australia and Canada advertised heavily for Scottish immigrants/sent agents to give talks on emigration
12. cheap or free land was offered in Canada, Australia and New Zealand
13. government schemes encouraged emigration with cheap fares to boost numbers of British settlers in Empire countries

15. *Candidates can be credited in a number of ways **up to a maximum of 5 marks.***

They may take different perspectives on the events and may describe a variety of different aspects of the events.

1 mark should be given for each accurate relevant key point of knowledge. **A second mark** should be given for each point that is developed, up to a maximum of **5 marks**. Candidates may achieve full marks by providing five straightforward points, by making three developed points, or a combination of these.

Possible points of knowledge may include:
1. gave new settlements/towns Scottish names eg Hamilton, Glendale
2. settled in groups together/helped other Scots immigrants to settle
3. built churches and continued to worship in their traditional ways eg Presbyterian Churches in Australia
4. continued to place emphasis on education/built schools and founded universities
5. continued to speak Gaelic/taught Gaelic to their children
6. formed Caledonian societies/St Andrews societies/Masonic Lodges
7. organised Burns Suppers/ate traditional foods (e.g. haggis)
8. played bagpipes/sang Scottish songs/taught Highland dancing/organised ceilidhs
9. celebrated Tartan Day (Australia)/wore tartan/created new local tartans
10. established Highland Games eg Grandfather Mountain, Maryborough
11. founded golf clubs
12. kept traditions such as Hogmanay/New year's Day holiday
13. researched their ancestry
14. produced magazines with Scottish content
15. Heritage retained Scots martial traditions eg Canadian Scots regiments in WW1

16. *Candidates can be credited in a number of ways **up to a maximum of 4 marks.***

Candidates must make direct comparisons of the two sources, either overall or in detail. A simple comparison will indicate what points of detail or overall viewpoint they agree or disagree about and should be given **1 mark.**

A developed comparison of the points of detail or overall viewpoint should be given **2 marks**. Candidates may achieve full marks by making four simple comparisons, two developed comparisons or by a combination of these.

Possible points of comparison may include:

Source A	Source B
Overall: The sources agree that Scots made a positive contribution to the development of Australia	
Thomas Mitchell from Stirling was the first European to explore the rich lands of Victoria for new settlement	The Scottish explorer John McDouall Stuart was the first European to cross Australia
Scottish Australia Company was formed in Aberdeen to encourage Scottish investment to businesses in Australia	Glasgow investors formed the influential New Zealand and Australian Land Company to encourage the wool export trade
Fife-born Sir Peter Russell gave £100,000 to the University of Sydney to develop the study of engineering	Francis Ormond from Aberdeen gave large sums for setting up the Working Men's Technical College in Melbourne to support education

Section 1, Part E, The Era of the Great War, 1910-1928

17. *Candidates can be credited in a number of ways up to a maximum of 6 marks.*

Candidates must make an overall judgement about how fully the source explains the events. **1 mark** may be given for each valid point interpreted from the source or each valid point of significant omission provided. The candidate can achieve **up to 3 marks** for their interpretation of the parts of the source they consider are relevant in terms of the proposed question where there is also at least one point of significant omission identified to imply a judgement has been made about the limitations of the source. For full marks to be given each point needs to be discretely mentioned in terms of the question.

A maximum of 2 marks may be given for answers which refer only to the source.

Possible points which may be identified in the source include:

1. the sudden appearance of the new weapon stunned their German opponents
2. early tanks were very slow moving.
3. they often broke down
4. tanks often became stuck in the heavy mud of no man's land.

Possible points of significant omission may include:

1. they destroyed enemy machine guns/enemy pill boxes (concrete emplacements)
2. were a great life-saver of infantry/gave protection to advancing troops crossing no-man's land
3. raised British morale at crucial period in war.
4. were more effective than an artillery bombardment/ allowed element of surprise/short bombardment
5. cross-country mobility allowed them to go over rough ground/no-man's land
6. smashed gaps in the barbed-wire
7. able to cross enemy trenches
8. their 6 pounder guns and machine-guns could clear enemy troops out of their trenches
9. their armour meant bullets couldn't stop them
10. could only be stopped by a direct shell hit
11. some initial success at Cambrai
12. their advance was blocked by wide ditches, rivers, canals etc
13. land captured by tanks often lost when Germans counterattacked/tanks could capture land but not hold it.
14. massed tank attacks in 1917 & 1918 helped break German morale and win war

18. *Candidates can be credited in a number of ways up to a maximum of 4 marks.*

Candidates must make direct comparisons of the two sources, either overall or in detail. A simple comparison will indicate what points of detail or overall viewpoint they agree or disagree about and should be given **1 mark**.

A developed comparison of the points of detail or overall viewpoint should be given **2 marks**. Candidates may achieve full marks by making four simple comparisons, two developed comparisons or by a combination of these.

Possible points of comparison may include:

Source B	Source C
Overall: The sources agree the conditions in the trenches were terrible.	
poor men in trenches standing in very deep mud	soldiers had to make their way sometimes through very heavy mud
water is often up to their waists	thirty yards of waterlogged trench/ chest-deep in water in some places
shells burst all round and shook the place	the duckboard track was constantly shelled, and in places a hundred yards of it had been blown to smithereens

19. *Candidates can be credited in a number of ways up to a maximum of 5 marks.*

Candidates must show a causal relationship between events.

Up to a **maximum of 5 marks in total, 1 mark** should be given for each accurate, relevant reason, and a **second mark** should be given for reasons that are developed. Candidates may achieve full marks by providing five straightforward reasons, three developed reasons, or a combination of these.

Possible reasons may include:

1. people were unhappy that they could not strike for better working conditions/pay
2. people were upset with censorship of the press/the censorship of private correspondence related to the war
3. people disliked the treatment of/restriction of movement of foreign nationals/many were interned
4. pub owners were unhappy with restrictions on alcohol/ limitation of pub opening hours/watering down of alcohol/the effect on their ability to make a living
5. blackouts made it dangerous to get around at night
6. pigeon fanciers resented the complication of having to have a licence to keep their birds/other seemingly trivial restrictions annoyed people (e. g. not being able to fly kites/buy binoculars)

7. people could be fined/arrested/imprisoned for breaking the terms of DORA
8. some resented the restrictions of their civil liberties
9. government took control of land to turn it over to food production, which landowners
10. people resented restrictions on movement around railways and docks
11. other government restrictions were resented (redirection of labour, leaving certificates, conscription, rationing)

20. *Candidates can be credited in a number of ways* **up to a maximum of 5 marks.**

They may take different perspectives on the events and may describe a variety of different aspects of the events.

1 mark should be given for each accurate relevant key point of knowledge. **A second mark** should be given for each point that is developed, up to a maximum of **5 marks.** Candidates may achieve full marks by providing five straightforward points, by making three developed points, or a combination of these.

Possible points of knowledge may include:
1. foreign competition affected industries (such as coal, iron, steel, jute and shipbuilding)
2. downturn in demand affected industries (such as shipbuilding, iron, steel and jute)
3. poor industrial relations was a difficulty
4. High unemployment in certain industries/areas
5. shortages of skilled manpower/materials also led to problems
6. the collapse of foreign markets for herring greatly affected the industry
7. much of the fishing fleet needed to be replaced/compensation was inadequate
8. the price of goods collapsed (the government removed the guaranteed price for herring in 1920/food prices fell)
9. coal industry in decline due to competition from electricity
10. Lack of government investment
11. Technology was outdated and needed to be improved

Section 2, Part A, The Creation of the Medieval Kingdoms, 1066–1406

21. *Candidates can be credited in a number of ways* **up to a maximum of 5 marks.**

They may take different perspectives on the events and may describe a variety of different aspects of the events.

1 mark should be given for each accurate relevant key point of knowledge. **A second mark** should be given for each point that is developed, up to a maximum of **5 marks.** Candidates may achieve full marks by providing five straightforward points, by making three developed points, or a combination of these.

Possible points of knowledge may include:
1. barons took an oath of fealty/promised to be loyal and serve the king
2. barons provided knights for the king's army
3. barons were an important part of the feudal system eg gave land to knights/peasants
4. barons protected those who lived on their land
5. barons were members of the king's council/helped him govern the country
6. barons helped enforce law and order at local level
7. trusted barons became sheriffs and collected fines and taxes for the king
8. barons paid extra tax during times of war

22. *Candidates can be credited in a number of ways* **up to a maximum of 5 marks.**

Candidates must show a causal relationship between events.

Up to a **maximum of 5 marks in total, 1 mark** should be given for each accurate, relevant reason, and a **second mark** should be given for reasons that are developed. Candidates may achieve full marks by providing five straightforward reasons, three developed reasons, or a combination of these.

Possible reasons may include:
1. Henry felt betrayed by the behaviour of his former close friend eg Becket resigned as chancellor
2. Becket disagreed with Henry over the issue of Criminous Clerks
3. Becket refused to sign the Constitution of Clarendon
4. Henry kept Becket imprisoned for 3 days until the document was signed
5. Becket failed to appear at the Northampton Trial
6. Henry charged Becket with contempt of court
7. Henry humiliated Becket and confiscated his lands/Henry accused him of fraud
8. Becket fled to France without the King's permission
9. Becket appealed to the Pope/continued to defend the rights of the Church
10. Henry refused to give Becket the royal kiss when they met in France
11. Henry asked the Archbishop of York, instead of Becket, to crown his son
12. Becket excommunicated the Archbishop of York and the bishops involved in the coronation

23. *Candidates can be credited in a number of ways* **up to a maximum of 5 marks.**

Candidates must make an overall judgement about how fully the source explains the events. **1 mark** may be given for each valid point interpreted from the source or each valid point of significant omission provided. The candidate can achieve **up to 3 marks** for their interpretation of the parts of the source they consider are relevant in terms of the proposed question where there is also at least one point of significant omission identified to imply a judgement has been made about the limitations of the source. For full marks to be given each point needs to be discretely mentioned in terms of the question.

A maximum of 2 marks may be given for answers which refer only to the source.

Possible points which may be identified in the source include:
1. monks were expected to carry out hard physical labour in the field or herb garden
2. well-educated monks studied the bible/spent hours copying and illuminating books
3. monks supported their local community by collecting alms and caring for the poor
4. monks provided the only medical help available at the time, looking after the sick in the monastery's infirmary.

Possible points of significant omission may include:
1. monks prayed for the souls of the dead
2. monks educated boys/prepared them for a career in the Church
3. monks looked after pilgrims who stayed at the monastery
4. monks were involved in politics eg wrote charters
5. monks ran monastic farms/reared sheep
6. monks were involved in the fishing industry eg built harbour at Arbroath

24. *Candidates can be credited in a number of ways up to a maximum of 5 marks.*

Candidates must make a judgement about the usefulness of the source and support this by making evaluative comments on identified aspects of the source.

1 mark should be given for each relevant comment made, up to a **maximum of 5 marks in total.**
- A maximum of 4 marks can be given for evaluative comments relating to the author, type of source, purpose and timing.
- A maximum of 2 marks may be given for comments relating to the content of the source.
- A maximum of 2 marks may be given for comments relating to points of significant omission.

Examples of aspects of the source and relevant comments:

Aspect of the source	Possible comment
Author: Doctor	Useful because he was an eyewitness/expert to the symptoms of the Black Death
Type of Source: Book	Useful because it will have been well researched
Purpose: To inform	Useful because it gives a detailed description of how terrible the symptoms of the Black Death were
Timing: 1350	Useful because it was written at the time of the Black Death

Content	Possible comment
The first sign of death was a swelling called a buboe under the armpit or in the groin	Useful because it gives accurate details of the symptoms of the Black Death
Soon after, the victim began to vomit and developed a fever	Useful because it gives accurate details of the symptoms of the Black Death
This was followed by the appearance of black and purple spots on the arms or thighs	Useful because it provides accurate information on what happened next

Possible points of significant omission may include:
1. victims suffered terrible headaches
2. victims suffered spasms

Section 2, Part B, War of the Three Kingdoms, 1603-1651

25. *Candidates can be credited in a number of ways up to a maximum of 5 marks.*

They may take different perspectives on the events and may describe a variety of different aspects of the events.

1 mark should be given for each accurate relevant key point of knowledge. **A second mark** should be given for each point that is developed, up to a maximum of **5 marks.** Candidates may achieve full marks by providing five straightforward points, by making three developed points, or a combination of these.

Possible points of knowledge may include:
1. no new institutions or government structures were put in place (except that, when parliament met, a royal 'commissioner' represented the King)

2. a postal service was established between Edinburgh and London to keep the King in touch with his government in Edinburgh (the origins of the Royal Mail)
3. James declared himself to be 'King of Great Britain', although for legal reasons, the separate kingdoms of Scotland and England continued to exist
4. King was based in London so rarely visited Scotland after his coronation
5. Scotland was to be ruled by a Privy Council
6. Privy Council ensured the King's will was followed in Scotland
7. Parliament was brought under strict royal control
8. Parliament was run by a small committee called the Committee of Articles (Lords of the Articles)
9. Committee/Lords of the Articles could only suggest new laws for Scotland
10. the King chose the Lords and bishops to become part of the Committee/Lords of the Articles

26. *Candidates can be credited in a number of ways up to a maximum of 5 marks.*

Candidates must make a judgement about the usefulness of the source and support this by making evaluative comments on identified aspects of the source.

1 mark should be given for each relevant comment made, up to a **maximum of 5 marks in total.**
- A maximum of **4 marks** can be given for evaluative comments relating to the author, type of source, purpose and timing.
- A maximum of **2 marks** may be given for comments relating to the content of the source.
- A maximum of **2 marks** may be given for comments relating to points of significant omission.

Examples of aspects of the source and relevant comments:

Aspect of the source	Possible comment
Author: King James VI and I	Useful because it is written by King James himself who had a strong personal belief in the Divine Right of Kings/eyewitness
Type of Source: Book	Useful because it has been researched (written specifically to outline the King's beliefs in Divine Right)
Purpose: To inform	Less useful because it is a biased view
Timing: 1598	Useful because it is written at the time when the King was asserting his belief in the Divine Right of Kings

Content	Possible comment
The power of the monarchy is the supreme authority on Earth	Useful because it accurately outlines the power of the King as being the highest power on earth
it is treason for a King's subjects to challenge what a King may or may not do	Useful because it accurately states that the King's authority cannot be challenged
King is not obliged to follow that law unless he sees fit to do so	Useful because it accurately illustrates the belief that the King is above earthly law

Possible points of significant omission may include:

1. Even if a king behaved badly no one could criticise him, only God could punish him
2. God bestows on a king the right to rule
3. The king is not subject to the will of his people, the aristocracy, or any other estate of the realm, including (in the view of some, especially in Protestant countries) the Church

27. *Candidates can be credited in a number of ways up to a maximum of 5 marks.*

Candidates must show a causal relationship between events.

Up to a **maximum of 5 marks in total, 1 mark** should be given for each accurate, relevant reason, and a **second mark** should be given for reasons that are developed. Candidates may achieve full marks by providing five straightforward reasons, three developed reasons, or a combination of these.

Possible reasons may include:

1. the General Assembly was not allowed to meet which caused resentment
2. resentment at Charles' money raising methods (e.g. Ship Money)
3. Scottish nobles resented Charles' Act of Revocation whereby church lands which had been alienated since 1540 had to be returned to the Crown
4. Charles' coronation in Edinburgh was a High Church ceremony based on Anglican forms and Scottish Presbyterians were suspicious of Anglican ideas
5. Charles demanded that Scottish Ministers accept and use the new English Prayer Book which caused a great deal of resentment and some riots in Edinburgh
6. Scottish clergy opposed Laud's Canons and their requirement to wear gowns and surplices because it seemed too Catholic
7. Bishops were to be introduced into the Scottish Church which was resented by the Scots
8. rejection of the Canons was included in the National Covenant for the Defence of True Religion in 1638 and was signed by thousands because they wanted to protect Scottish religious practices

28. *Candidates can be credited in a number of ways up to a maximum of 5 marks.*

Candidates must make an overall judgement about how fully the source explains the events. **1 mark** may be given for each valid point interpreted from the source or each valid point of significant omission provided. The candidate can achieve **up to 3 marks** for their interpretation of the parts of the source they consider are relevant in terms of the proposed question where there is also at least one point of significant omission identified to imply a judgement has been made about the limitations of the source. For full marks to be given each point needs to be discretely mentioned in terms of the question.

A maximum of 2 marks may be given for answers which refer only to the source.

Possible points which may be identified in the source include:

1. the demands in the Nineteen Proposals divided Parliament (between those who supported the Nineteen Proposals and those who thought Parliament had gone too far)
2. Parliament and Charles then began to raise their own armies
3. People were then forced to choose sides

Possible points of significant omission may include:

1. the King dissolved the parliament in 1640 (Short Parliament) after only 3 weeks
2. activities of the Long Parliament angered the King (e.g. arrest and imprisonment of Archbishop Laud/arrest and imprisonment of Strafford)
3. The Grand Remonstrance in November 1641 divided the House of Commons
4. rumours over the causes of the Irish rebellion in November 1641 angered Protestants who thought the King was behind it
5. attempted arrest of 5 Members of Parliament in January 1642 angered Parliament
6. Parliaments decision to throw Bishops out of the House of Lords in February 1642 divided the House of Commons
7. Parliament took control of the army in March 1642 without the Kings consent

Section 2, Part C, The Atlantic Slave Trade, 1770-1807

29. *Candidates can be credited in a number of ways up to a maximum of 5 marks.*

They may take different perspectives on the events and may describe a variety of different aspects of the events.

1 mark should be given for each accurate relevant key point of knowledge. **A second mark** should be given for each point that is developed, up to a maximum of **5 marks.** Candidates may achieve full marks by providing five straightforward points, by making three developed points, or a combination of these.

Possible points of knowledge may include:

1. ships sailed from Europe to Africa carrying manufactured goods.
2. ships often departed from/arrived at British ports such as Bristol, Liverpool, occasionally Glasgow.
3. manufactured goods eg guns, alcohol, glass beads, pots and pans were exchanged for slaves.
4. slaves were held in slave factories on the west coast of Africa.
5. slave ships left West Africa carrying slaves to West Indies and the Americas (the Middle Passage).
6. slaves were packed on to ships to maximise profits.
7. conditions on the middle passage were very poor and slaves often died from disease or mistreatment.
8. slaves were usually sold by auction upon arrival in West Indies/America.
9. profits from slave auctions were then invested in sugar, coffee, cotton, tobacco.
10. ships carrying tobacco, sugar, molasses, cotton would sail back across the Atlantic (the Home Run).
11. cotton, tobacco, sugar, coffee could be sold on return to Britain for a large profit.

30. *Candidates can be credited in a number of ways up to a maximum of 5 marks.*

Candidates must make an overall judgement about how fully the source explains the events. **1 mark** may be given for each valid point interpreted from the source or each valid point of significant omission provided. The candidate can achieve **up to 3 marks** for their interpretation of the parts of the source they consider are relevant in terms of the proposed question where there is also at least one point of significant omission identified to imply a judgement has been made about the limitations of the source. For full marks to be given each point needs to be discretely mentioned in terms of the question.

A maximum of 2 marks may be given for answers which refer only to the source.

Possible points which may be identified in the source include:

1. the slave trade had raised Liverpool from a struggling port to one of the richest and most prosperous trading centres in the world
2. the slave trade provided work in almost every industry in the town
3. slave cotton provided work for the mills of Lancashire
4. merchants made huge profits importing sugar from the Caribbean

Possible points of significant omission may include:

1. the importation of tobacco was a big part of Glasgow's economy
2. the economy of Glasgow later shifted to the processing of sugar imported from the West Indies
3. jobs were provided in many industries: shipbuilding, rope making, dock work, banking, finance, sailors
4. profits from the slave trade were invested in British Industry
5. wealthy colonial families built huge mansions in many British cities.
6. the profits from the slave trade were invested in the development of British towns and cities
7. many important civic buildings in British cities were constructed using the profits of the slave trade

31. *Candidates can be credited in a number of ways **up to a maximum of 5 marks**.*

Candidates must make a judgement about the usefulness of the source and support this by making evaluative comments on identified aspects of the source.

1 mark should be given for each relevant comment made, **up to a maximum of 5 marks in total.**

A maximum of **4 marks** can be given for evaluative comments relating to the author, type of source, purpose and timing.

A maximum of **2 marks** may be given for comments relating to the content of the source.

A maximum of **2 marks** may be given for comments relating to points of significant omission.

Examples of aspects of the source and relevant comments:

Aspect of the source	Possible comment
Author: Written by a modern historian	Useful because he would have carried out research/ studied the topic
Type of Source: a history book	Useful as it is likely to contain relevant and accurate information
Purpose: to inform people about the impact of the slave trade on the Caribbean island of Barbados	Less useful as it only informs us about one of the Caribbean islands.
Timing: 1987	Useful because it is a secondary source, written a long time after the end of the slave trade/slavery in the Caribbean with the benefit of hindsight.

Content	Possible comment
the Caribbean island of Barbados was transformed by slave trade/ small farms replaced by large plantations	Useful because it accurately describes the changes brought to Barbados by the slave trade
The beautiful wilderness was slowly but surely cleared of its native people and its vegetation	Useful because it accurately shows the damage to the island and its native people
Plantations were the work place and final resting place of armies of African slaves	Useful because it accurately shows the scale of the suffering involved in the slave trade

Possible points of significant omission may include:

1. many other Caribbean islands such as Jamaica were also affected in a similar way
2. many of the native people were killed by the white settlers, or died from disease
3. as well as plantations, factories were also set up on the islands to refine the sugar

32. *Candidates can be credited in a number of ways **up to a maximum of 5 marks**.*

Candidates must show a causal relationship between events.

Up to a **maximum of 5 marks in total, 1 mark** should be given for each accurate, relevant reason, and a **second mark** should be given for reasons that are developed. Candidates may achieve full marks by providing five straightforward reasons, three developed reasons, or a combination of these.

Possible reasons may include:

1. life on the plantations was controlled by very strict laws or codes
2. many of the islands were small and there was little hope of fleeing the island
3. it was difficult for slaves with basic weapons to fight back against plantation owners who had guns
4. the brutal treatment of captured slaves acted as a powerful deterrent to other slaves
5. captured slaves would often be put to death/subject to horrific punishments/mutilation
6. plantation owners offered large rewards for the capture of escaped slaves
7. escaped slaves could easily be identified by brandings or lack of legal papers
8. plantation owners used bounty hunters/bloodhounds to track down runaway slaves

Section 2, Part D, Changing Britain, 1760-1900

33. *Candidates can be credited in a number of ways **up to a maximum of 5 marks**.*

Candidates must make an overall judgement about how fully the source explains the events. **1 mark** may be given for each valid point interpreted from the source or each valid point of significant omission provided. The candidate can achieve **up to 3 marks** for their interpretation of the parts of the source they consider are relevant in terms of the proposed question where there is also at least one point of significant omission identified to imply a judgement has been made about the limitations of the source. For full marks to be given each point needs to be discretely mentioned in terms of the question.

A maximum of 2 marks may be given for answers which refer only to the source.

Possible points which may be identified in the source include:

1. spinning improved by the invention of the Spinning Jenny/could spin eight threads at once
2. Arkwright's Water Frame used water power and made much better thread than the Spinning Jenny
3. steam engine was easy to use in factories
4. steam engine meant that factories did not have to be built near fast-running water for power supply

Possible points of significant omission may include:

1. Crompton's Mule combined ideas of Spinning Jenny and Water Frame/made high quality thread
2. Arkwright developed Carding Engine in 1770s
3. flax spinner developed in 1780s
4. weaving greatly improved by invention of the Power Loom (in 1785)
5. Power Loom now meant that weaving as well as spinning could be done in factories.
6. many handloom weavers were made unemployed when weaving was mechanised/wages of workers fell
7. machine/cylinder printing used to print patterns on to finished cloth
8. technological inventions meant that one person or even a child could now do the work of many people
9. technology meant that there were huge numbers of textile mills built in Britain

34. *Candidates can be credited in a number of ways **up to a maximum of 5 marks.***

They may take different perspectives on the events and may describe a variety of different aspects of the events.

1 mark should be given for each accurate relevant key point of knowledge. **A second mark** should be given for each point that is developed, up to a maximum of **5 marks**. Candidates may achieve full marks by providing five straightforward points, by making three developed points, or a combination of these.

Possible points of knowledge may include:

1. young children worked as trappers/opening and closing trap doors (to help circulate air around the mine)
2. women and teenagers worked as putters/drawers/pushing or pulling carts of coal along
3. dangerous as carts could run over fingers/toes/knock workers over
4. women worked as bearers/carried coal to the surface in baskets on their backs
5. dangerous as ladders slippery/coal could fall out of baskets/baskets very heavy
6. men worked as hewers cutting coal by hand with picks and shovels
7. danger of cave-ins
8. danger of flooding
9. danger of explosions (explosive gasses/fire damp)
10. danger of suffocation (suffocating gasses/choke damp)
11. lack of adequate ventilation
12. risks of falls down the shaft
13. safety lamps were available, but lighting was poor
14. long working hours
15. it was very hot in the mines

35. *Candidates can be credited in a number of ways **up to a maximum of 5 marks.***

Candidates must make a judgement about the usefulness of the source and support this by making evaluative comments on identified aspects of the source.

1 mark should be given for each relevant comment made, up to a maximum of **5 marks in total.**

A maximum of 4 marks can be given for evaluative comments relating to the author, type of source, purpose and timing.

A maximum of 2 marks may be given for comments relating to the content of the source.

A maximum of 2 marks may be given for comments relating to points of significant omission.

Examples of aspects of the source and relevant comments:

Aspect of the source	Possible comment
Author: Railway inspector	Useful as eyewitness experience of working on the railways
Type of Source: Book	Useful because it will have been well researched/based on expert knowledge
Purpose: To inform readers of changes in railway travel	Useful as it is balanced/an honest personal reflection
Timing: 1870	Useful because it was written at the time of improvements in railway travel

Content	Possible comment
Third-class carriages were often little different from basic cattle trucks	Useful as it is accurate, third class carriages were little more than boxes.
For a considerable time they were completely open and had no seats	Useful as it is accurate/third-class carriages were open/had no roof
First and second class carriages were covered and had seating/the luggage of the passengers was packed on top of the carriages	Useful as it is accurate/second and first-class carriages did have roofs/luggage was stored on top

Possible points of significant omission may include:

1. carriages modelled on stage-coaches
2. third-class carriages were covered by law after the 1844 Railway Act
3. parliamentary trains/cheap fares introduced after the 1844 Railway Act
4. later corridors added to trains
5. later additions included sleeping and buffet cars
6. railway travel considerably cheaper/more comfortable than road travel
7. platforms made train travel safer
8. continuous brakes/brakes on carriages made train travel safer
9. improved signalling made train travel safer
10. as railway network developed it was possible to travel to nearly every town or city by train/made leisure trips/holidays easier
11. rail travel faster than other forms of transport

36. *Candidates can be credited in a number of ways **up to a maximum of 5 marks.***

Candidates must show a causal relationship between events.

Up to a **maximum of 5 marks in total, 1 mark** should be given for each accurate, relevant reason, and a **second mark** should be given for reasons that are developed. Candidates may achieve full marks by providing five straightforward reasons, three developed reasons, or a combination of these.

Possible reasons may include:

1. immunisation and vaccination campaigns led to decline of killer diseases such as smallpox/made compulsory 1853
2. anaesthetics improved surgical survival rates
3. antiseptics reduced deaths from infection
4. more fresh food was available due to railways so diet improved/ people more resistant to disease
5. improved working conditions led to fewer accidents
6. Public Health Acts gave local authorities the powers to improve social conditions
7. clean water supplies meant the eradication of water borne diseases e.g. Cholera
8. new reservoirs built in the countryside to supply large towns/cities meant improved hygiene
9. town councils took responsibility for piping fresh water supplies which enabled people to keep clean
10. cleaner streets reduced the spread of vermin
11. improved sewerage systems/proper drainage reduced spread of germs/diseases
12. impact of Housing Acts/destruction of slum properties provided better standards of housing so reducing overcrowding and the spread of disease
13. flushing toilets improved sanitation
14. more hospitals helped to treat more people/reduce spread of disease
15. wash houses and public baths introduced in 1878 which improved personal hygiene
16. cheaper soap available improving hygiene
17. cheap cotton clothing was easier to wash which improved personal hygiene
18. improved food standards reduced illness caused by adulterated food
19. by 1900 milk could be sterilised which reduced risk of illness caused by contaminated milk

Section 2, Part E, The Making of Modern Britain, 1880-1951

37. *Candidates can be credited in a number of ways **up to a maximum of 5 marks**.*

They may take different perspectives on the events and may describe a variety of different aspects of the events.

1 mark should be given for each accurate relevant key point of knowledge. **A second** mark should be given for each point that is developed, up to a maximum of **5 marks**. Candidates may achieve full marks by providing five straightforward points, by making three developed points, or a combination of these.

Possible points of knowledge may include:

1. School Medical Inspections were introduced in 1907
2. local councils received grants to provide medical treatment for the poor (school clinics were introduced in 1912)
3. Liberals introduced national insurance for sickness/ National Insurance Act (Part 1)
4. contributory scheme/workers, employers and state paid into the scheme
5. government tried to sell the scheme with the slogan '9d for 4d'
6. compulsory for all workers who earned under £160 per year
7. contributions were recorded by stamps on cards

8. insured workers received benefits when they were off sick (10 shillings per week for 26 weeks/5 shillings a week after that until fit to return to work)
9. free medical treatment and medicine for insured workers
10. sanatorium treatment for those suffering from TB
11. National Insurance covered wage-earners, but not their families
12. (Workmen's Compensation Act) provided compensation for workers injured or made ill through work
13. workers entitled to half of their salary until they were fit to return to work

38. *Candidates can be credited in a number of ways **up to a maximum of 5 marks**.*

Candidates must make a judgement about the usefulness of the source and support this by making evaluative comments on identified aspects of the source.

1 mark should be given for each relevant comment made, up to a **maximum of 5 marks in total**.

A maximum of **4 marks** can be given for evaluative comments relating to the author, type of source, purpose and timing.

A maximum of **2 marks** may be given for comments relating to the content of the source.

A maximum of **2 marks** may be given for comments relating to points of significant omission.

Examples of aspects of the source and relevant comments:

Aspect of the source	Possible comment
Author: Book based on author's own life/autobiographical	Useful as eyewitness account
Type of Source: Book	Useful because it will have been well researched/based on personal experience
Purpose: To inform readers of the benefits of pensions	Useful as it is an honest personal reflection
Timing: Published in 1939, over 30 years after the events it describes	Less useful as details may have been forgotten/author may selectively remember the facts or useful because it has the benefit of hindsight

Content	Possible comment
Pensions transformed the life of the old	Useful as it is accurate that pensions did make a real difference to many/Less useful as an exaggeration. Pensions helped those who were entitled, but limited.
Pensioners were relieved of anxiety and were suddenly rich	Useful as it is accurate that pensions did relieve anxiety for many of the elderly poor/ Less useful as exaggeration Pension amount was very small.
Pensioners were grateful/ tears of gratitude/God bless that Lord George	Useful as it is accurate that pensioners were grateful/ pensions helped to keep some of the elderly poor out of the workhouse

Possible points of significant omission may include:
1. amount of pensions – between 1s and 5s on a sliding scale/7s 6d for a married couple
2. who was entitled to pensions – over 70s
3. pensions were non-contributory
4. collection at the Post Office removed the stigma of Poor Relief
5. exemptions – those who had been in prison within last ten years/those who had habitually failed to work
6. pensions were not intended to provide subsistence
7. pensions did keep many of the elderly poor out of the workhouse

39. *Candidates can be credited in a number of ways up to a maximum of 5 marks.*

Candidates must make an overall judgement about how fully the source explains the events. **1 mark** may be given for each valid point interpreted from the source or each valid point of significant omission provided. The candidate can achieve **up to 3 marks** for their interpretation of the parts of the source they consider are relevant in terms of the proposed question where there is also at least one point of significant omission identified to imply a judgement has been made about the limitations of the source. For full marks to be given each point needs to be discretely mentioned in terms of the question.

A maximum of 2 marks may be given for answers which refer only to the source.

Possible points which may be identified in the source include:
1. tackling one of the five giants wouldn't do much good; the government would have to tackle them all
2. there should be a welfare system that would look after people from the 'cradle to the grave'
3. there should be a comprehensive social security system, providing benefits for the unemployed, the sick, the elderly and widows
4. advised the government to adopt a policy of full employment

Possible points of significant omission may include:
1. explanation of what the 'five giants' were
2. National Health Service to tackle disease
3. family allowances to tackle poverty/want
4. System of national insurance to tackle want
5. standard weekly national insurance payments were to be made by all workers
6. payments to be made at a standard rate, without a means test
7. unemployment benefit to be paid for an indefinite period
8. Reform of the education system/raising of school leaving age to tackle ignorance
9. House-building/slum clearance to tackle squalor

40. *Candidates can be credited in a number of ways up to a maximum of 5 marks.*

Candidates must show a causal relationship between events.

Up to a **maximum of 5 marks in total, 1 mark** should be given for each accurate, relevant reason, and a second mark should be given for reasons that are developed. Candidates may achieve full marks by providing five straightforward reasons, three developed reasons, or a combination of these.

Possible reasons may include:
1. by time of 1951 election still a shortage of (750,000) homes/(750,000) fewer houses than households

2. massive destruction/bombing of Second World War had created a huge housing shortage
3. great deal of slum housing still existed
4. post-war marriage and baby boom added to pressure for housing
5. shortage of building materials
6. shortage of skilled labour
7. Bevan given Ministry of Health and Housing – too much/should have been a separate Ministry of Housing
8. Bevan emphasised quality over quantity/insisted on a high standard for council houses
9. government faced financial restraints/had to prioritise
10. government faced many social problems/scale of problem meant that it would take more than one term to tackle
11. provision of prefab houses as a temporary solution to the housing shortage
12. New towns planned but not built by 1951 (12 planned in Scotland, only 4 built)
13. New towns isolated/lacked proper amenities/destroyed previous communities

Section 3, Part A, The Cross and the Crescent; the Crusades, 1071-1192

41. *Candidates can be credited in a number of ways up to a maximum of 8 marks.*

Candidates must use knowledge to present a balanced assessment of the influence of different possible factors and come to a reasoned conclusion. **Up to 5 marks** are allocated for relevant points of knowledge used to address the question. **1 mark** should be given for each relevant, factual key point of knowledge used to support a factor. **If only one factor is presented, a maximum of 3 marks should be given for relevant points of knowledge.**

Possible factors may include:	Relevant, factual, key points of knowledge to support this factor may include:
Religious	1. the Pope stated that it was the duty of every Christian to help their brothers in the east 2. wanted to protect Christian churches and shrines which had been damaged or destroyed 3. wanted to re-open pilgrim routes to Jerusalem
Political	4. wanted to heal the schism/unite the Christian Churches 5. wanted to increase his own power/ become head of a united Church 6. wanted to demonstrate power of the Church to European rulers eg Dispute with the Holy Roman Emperor
Economic	7. wanted to re-open trade routes with the east 8. wanted to make money from pilgrims again

| Threat of Islam | 9. wanted to stop the spread of Islam in Europe eg Muslims had already conquered part of Spain |
| Other factors | 10. Any other valid point |

Up to 3 marks should be given for presenting the answer in a structured way, leading to a conclusion which addresses the question, as follows:

1 mark for the answer being presented in a structured way, with knowledge being organised in support of different factors.

1 mark given for a conclusion with a valid judgement or overall summary.

1 mark given for a reason being provided in support of the judgement.

42. *Candidates can be credited in a number of ways **up to a maximum of 6 marks**.*

Candidates must show a causal relationship between events.

Up to a **maximum of 6 marks in total, 1 mark** should be given for each accurate, relevant reason, and a **second mark** should be given for reasons that are developed. Candidates may achieve full marks by providing six straightforward reasons, three developed reasons, or a combination of these.

Possible reasons may include:
1. Crusaders were divided eg Guy de Lusignan and Reynald of Chatillon hated each other
2. Crusaders had different ideologies towards the Muslims eg the Hawks and the Doves
3. death of Baldwin IV meant that Jerusalem did not have a strong ruler
4. King Guy made a tactical error by leaving Jerusalem with the Crusader army
5. Crusaders were defeated at the Battle of Hattin
6. Crusaders lacked resources to defend Jerusalem once army defeated
7. Muslims were united under Saladin's leadership making them stronger
8. Saladin's army outnumbered the Crusaders.

43. *Candidates can be credited in a number of ways **up to a maximum of 6 marks**.*

Candidates must make a judgement about the usefulness of the source and support this by making evaluative comments on identified aspects of the source.

1 mark should be given for each relevant comment made, up to a **maximum of 6 marks in total**.
- A maximum of 4 marks can be given for evaluative comments relating to the author, type of source, purpose and timing.
- A maximum of 2 marks may be given for comments relating to the content of the source.
- A maximum of 2 marks may be given for comments relating to points of significant omission.

Examples of aspects of the source and relevant comments:

Aspect of the source	Possible comment
Author: Crusader	Useful because he was an eyewitness to events

Type of Source: Chronicle	Useful because it was a well-researched record of events
Purpose: To persuade people that Richard's actions were justifiable	Less useful as clearly biased/author may have exaggerated when describing Saladin's behaviour
Timing: 1191	Useful because it was at the time of the Third Crusade

Content	Possible comment
Saladin did not pay the ransom agreed for the Muslim hostages/did not return the True Cross to the Crusaders	Useful because it provides accurate details of the negotiations between Richard and Saladin
Saladin attempted to trick King Richard, sending him gifts and treasures/he hoped that Richard would release the Muslims for free	Less useful because it may have exaggerated Saladin's responsibility for the massacre
The next morning the king ordered the Muslims to be led out of the city and beheaded	Useful because it provides accurate details of the massacre

Possible points of significant omission may include:
1. nearly 3,000 Muslim men, women and children were killed
2. some Muslims were beaten
3. some Muslims were killed with an axe or a lance

Section 3, Part B, "Tea and Freedom": the American Revolution, 1774-1783

44. *Candidates can be credited in a number of ways **up to a maximum of 6 marks**.*

Candidates must show a causal relationship between events.

Up to a **maximum of 6 marks in total, 1 mark** should be given for each accurate, relevant reason, and a **second mark** should be given for reasons that are developed. Candidates may achieve full marks by providing five straightforward reasons, three developed reasons, or a combination of these.

Possible reasons may include:
1. the colonists were unhappy with the imposition of laws and taxes which were seen as unjust
2. the passing of the Stamp Act and Townshend Act in 1760s had been very unpopular measures
3. the colonists resented being taxed without representation
4. events such as the Boston Massacre and the Boston Tea Party led to an increase in anti-British feeling among colonists
5. boycott of British goods added to tension
6. the continuing presence of British soldiers in the colonies had caused tension
7. the colonists were further angered by the passing of The Quartering Act
8. some colonists were frustrated that the British were stopping them from moving west
9. some colonists felt that the policies of the British government were damaging trade

10. the First Continental Congress in 1774 had created a feeling of anti – British unity among the leaders of the colonies
11. the colonists started to establish their own armed forces following the First Continental Congress in 1774/ Continental Congress declared to be traitors by British Crown meant no going back
12. clashes between British forces and colonists at Lexington and Concord in 1775 led to the outbreak of war

45. *Candidates can be credited in a number of ways up to a maximum of 6 marks.*

Candidates must make a judgement about the usefulness of the source and support this by making evaluative comments on identified aspects of the source.

1 mark should be given for each relevant comment made, up to a **maximum of 6 marks in total.**

A maximum of **4 marks** can be given for evaluative comments relating to the author, type of source, purpose and timing.

A maximum of **2 marks** may be given for comments relating to the content of the source.

A maximum of **2 marks** may be given for comments relating to points of significant omission.

Examples of aspects of the source and relevant comments:

Aspect of the source	Possible comment
Author: Army surgeon	Useful as he is an eyewitness
Type of Source: A diary	Useful as it is likely to give an honest/ accurate description of the condition of the American army/less useful as it only gives information about the American army.
Purpose: To record the difficulties being faced by the soldiers during the winter of 1777	Useful because it provides a detailed/ balanced description of the conditions
Timing: 1777	Useful as it is taken from 1777, during the course of the war

Content	Possible comment
The army now begins to grow tired of the continued difficulties they have faced in this winter campaign.	Useful as it gives an accurate and detailed insight into difficulties faced by the colonial army
Poor food, tough living conditions, cold weather, sickness, fatigue, nasty clothes, nasty cookery, the Devil's in it!	Useful as it gives accurate and detailed information on the conditions faced by the American army.
Our men still show a great spirit and morale that is unexpected from such young soldiers.	Useful as it gives an accurate insight into why the Americans were eventually able to win the war.

Possible points of significant omission may include:
1. the American army had suffered a series of setbacks during the winter of 1777 – 1778
2. the Americans had difficulty holding on to their recruits and many would return home after a short period of service

3. conditions were also very difficult for the British as it was difficult to supply an army that was fighting so far from home
4. American soldiers were acclimatised, British found climate difficult

46. *Candidates can be credited in a number of ways up to a maximum of 8 marks.*

Candidates must use knowledge to present a balanced assessment of the influence of different possible factors and come to a reasoned conclusion. **Up to 5 marks** are allocated for relevant points of knowledge used to address the question. **1 mark** should be given for each relevant, factual key point of knowledge used to support a factor. **If only one factor is presented, a maximum of 3 marks should be given for relevant points of knowledge.**

Possible factors may include:	Relevant, factual, key points of knowledge to support this factor may include:
Foreign intervention	1. France provided the colonists with finance 2. France provided the colonists with military assistance – soldiers, gunpowder etc 3. the French attacked British colonies in the Caribbean and elsewhere 4. the French harassed British shipping in the Atlantic 5. Foreign intervention caused Britain to lose its control of the seas 6. Foreign intervention made it more difficult for Britain to reinforce and supply its forces in America 7. Spain distracted Britain by attacking Gibraltar 8. a Franco-Spanish force threatened Britain with invasion in 1779
American strengths:	9. George Washington held the American army together and emerged as a great leader 10. the colonists had greater forces/ American colonies were relatively wealthy and could support an army 11. the colonists were able to call on minutemen when required 12. the colonists knew the terrain better/used to the climate 13. the colonists often used guerrilla tactics against the British

British weakness:	14. the British were poorly led
	15. the British made tactical errors eg Yorktown, Saratoga
	16. the British army was small in number/ British army had a large empire to protect as well as fight the colonists and had to rely on mercenary forces
	17. the British soldiers were not properly trained/ equipped to cope with terrain and conditions
	18. diseases like smallpox affected British much more than Americans.
	19. the British never had a clear strategy for winning the war
	20. the British were weakened by their reliance on supplies from overseas
	21. the British Parliament was not united behind the war effort
	22. unlike Americans British had no allies to assist them
Other factors	23. Any other valid point

Up to 3 marks should be given for presenting the answer in a structured way, leading to a conclusion which addresses the question, as follows:

1 mark for the answer being presented in a structured way, with knowledge being organised in support of different factors.

1 mark given for a conclusion with a valid judgement or overall summary.

1 mark given for a reason being provided in support of the judgement.

Section 3, Part C, USA 1850-1880

47. *Candidates can be credited in a number of ways **up to a maximum of 6 marks**.*

Candidates must show a causal relationship between events.

Up to a **maximum of 6 marks in total, 1 mark** should be given for each accurate, relevant reason, and a **second mark** should be given for reasons that are developed. Candidates may achieve full marks by providing six straightforward reasons, three developed reasons, or a combination of these.

Possible reasons may include:
1. the migration of the buffalo was disturbed (homesteaders/railways)
2. settlers were killing the buffalo
3. settlers spread disease such as cholera among tribes
4. Native Americans were being forced off their traditional/sacred lands

5. Native Americans were signing treaties with the US Government (such as Laramie and Medicine Creek) which were broken
6. Native Americans felt lied to by the US Government
7. Native Americans felt cheated – food was of poor quality or money promised was not paid
8. army attacks such as Sand Creek or Washita River continued to cause resentment
9. Native Americans were being forced to live on reservations which they resented

48. *Candidates can be credited in a number of ways **up to a maximum of 8 marks**.*

Candidates must use knowledge to present a balanced assessment of the influence of different possible factors and come to a reasoned conclusion. **Up to 5 marks** are allocated for relevant points of knowledge used to address the question. **1 mark** should be given for each relevant, factual key point of knowledge used to support a factor. **If only one factor is presented, a maximum of 3 marks should be given for relevant points of knowledge.**

Possible factors may include:	Relevant, factual, key points of knowledge to support this factor may include:
Lincoln's election	1. southerners feared he would abolish slavery
	2. some Southern States had not carried his name on ballot papers which angered Republican supporters in the North
	3. south Carolina seceded from Union as a result of Lincoln's election/other states followed
	4. rise of the Republican party seen as representing Northern interests which upset the South
Issue of Slavery	5. South feared economic impact of abolition e.g. loss of cheap labour
	6. abolitionist activities caused tension between North and South ('Uncle Tom's Cabin'/ Underground Railroad)
	7. compromise of 1850 had allowed California to be a free state/it also saw the introduction of Fugitive Slave Law – this caused more hostility in the North
	8. raid on Harpers Ferry by John Brown had worried Southern States
	9. Dred Scott case concerned many anti-slavery supporters, it allowed the existence of slavery in the Northern States
	10. Kansas Nebraska Act allowed popular sovereignty. This led to violence between pro and anti-slavery supporters which heightened tension

Attack on Fort Sumter	11. the fort was besieged by Confederate troops
	12. food supply to the fort was cut off
	13. the commander of the fort was warned of an attack
	14. the fort was attacked by Confederate troops
Other factors	15. Any other valid point

49. *Candidates can be credited in a number of ways **up to a maximum of 6 marks**.*

Candidates must make a judgement about the usefulness of the source and support this by making evaluative comments on identified aspects of the source.

1 mark should be given for each relevant comment made, up to a **maximum of 6 marks in total.**

A maximum of **4 marks** can be given for evaluative comments relating to the author, type of source, purpose and timing.

A maximum of **2 marks** may be given for comments relating to the content of the source.

A maximum of **2 marks** may be given for comments relating to points of significant omission.

Examples of aspects of the source and relevant comments:

Aspect of the source	Possible comment
Author: Officer of the Freedman's Bureau	Useful because he was an eyewitness/expertise
Type of Source: Report	Useful because reports have usually been well researched
Purpose: To inform	Useful because it provides a detailed account of the effects of Reconstruction/less useful because it is one-sided
Timing: 1866.	Useful because it was written shortly after the end of the Civil War

Content	Possible comment
The freed slaves in Texas have been terrorised by attacks from the desperate men of the local area.	Useful as it is accurate because many attacks did take place on freed slaves after 1865
The murderers dislike the fact that they no longer have control over their former slaves.	Useful as it is accurate because attacks by Southern Whites were an attempt to keep control over the freed slaves
Many of the freedmen are unhappy with their freedom and would prefer to be slaves as it offered them some protection	Useful as it is accurate because some freed slaves did not see a major improvement in their lives after 1865

Possible points of significant omission may include:
1. no mention of the work of the Freedman's Bureau – education/advice
2. no mention of the changes that took place involving freed slaves eg ability to vote
3. led to other ways to keep control over freed slaves e.g. Jim Crow Laws
4. the violence of the Ku Klux Klan towards the freed slaves e.g. lynchings
5. sharecropping was disadvantageous to blacks in the South

Section 3, Part D, Hitler and Nazi Germany, 1919-1939

50. *Candidates can be credited in a number of ways **up to a maximum of 6 marks**.*

Candidates must show a causal relationship between events.

Up to a **maximum of 6 marks in total, 1 mark** should be given for each accurate, relevant reason, and a **second mark** should be given for reasons that are developed. Candidates may achieve full marks by providing six straightforward reasons, three developed reasons, or a combination of these.

Possible reasons may include:
1. some people felt coalition governments were weak/parties seemed too busy arguing to solve the country's problems
2. many Germans didn't like democracy/longed for the return of the strong leadership of the Kaiser
3. frequent changes of government made it difficult to follow consistent policies
4. appeared to be unable to solve the country's economic problems such as war debt/hyper-inflation
5. six governments in six years in the mid-1920s created an appearance of a weak government
6. it seemed incapable of maintaining order/stopping frequent outbreaks of violence/political assassinations
7. criticised by nationalists for giving in to foreign powers
8. criticised for allowing the French invasion of the Ruhr
9. associated with Germany's defeat in the First World War
10. blamed the Weimar Government for accepting the Treaty of Versailles

51. *Candidates can be credited in a number of ways **up to a maximum of 8 marks**.*

Candidates must use knowledge to present a balanced assessment of the influence of different possible factors and come to a reasoned conclusion. **Up to 5 marks** are allocated for relevant points of knowledge used to address the question. **1 mark** should be given for each relevant, factual key point of knowledge used to support a factor. **If only one factor is presented, a maximum of 3 marks should be given for relevant points of knowledge.**

Possible factors may include:	Relevant, factual, key points of knowledge to support this factor may include:
Social policies	1. Nazi youth policy encouraged loyalty 2. Nazi education policy brainwashed the young 3. Nazi policy towards the Jews – first isolate, then persecute and finally destroy created a fear of similar treatment 4. Nazi family policy – Kinder, Kirche, Kuche won support/ from tranditionalists 5. subsidised holidays/leisure activities of the Kraft durch Freude programme were popular 6. a Concordat with the Catholic Church was reached/a Reichsbishop was appointed as head of the Protestant churches which limited possible opposition from the churches 7. creation of the national community (*Volksgemeinschaft*) created a sense of national purpose
Economic policies	8. Nazi economic policy/ German labour Front attempted to deal with economic ills affecting Germany, especially unemployment and won support 9. Nazis began a massive programme of public works; work of Hjalmar Schacht providing jobs, which won support
Propaganda	10. use of Nuremburg Rallies inspired loyalty 11. use of radio ensued that the Nazi message was widely spread 12. Cult of the Leader: the Hitler Myth ensured that Hitler remained personally very popular 13. use of the Cinema: Triumph of the Will etc spread the Nazi message widely 14. Nazi propaganda effectively spread the Nazi message

Establishment of totalitarian state	15. political parties outlawed; non-Nazi members of the civil service were dismissed, crushing possible opposition 16. Nazis never quite able to silence opposition to the regime 17. speed of takeover of power and ruthlessness of the regime made opposition largely ineffective 18. anti-Nazi judges were dismissed and replaced with those favourable to the Nazis ensuring the support of the legal system 19. Acts Hostile to the National Community (1935) – all-embracing law which allowed the Nazis to persecute opponents in a 'legal' way
Fear and state terrorism	20. the use of fear/terror through the Nazi police state; role of the Gestapo made opposition unlikely/ impossible 21. the use of the SS created a climate of fear and enforced loyalty 22. a) concentration camps were set up
Crushing of opposition	22. b) opponents liable to severe penalties, as were their families which added to the climate of fear and enforced loyalty 23. opponents never able to establish a single organisation to channel their resistance – role of the Gestapo, paid informers 24. opposition lacked cohesion and a national leader; also lacked armed supporters 25. lack of cooperation between socialists and communists
Other factors	26. any other relevant points

Up to 3 marks should be given for presenting the answer in a structured way, leading to a conclusion which addresses the question, as follows:

1 mark for the answer being presented in a structured way, with knowledge being organised in support of different factors.

1 mark given for a conclusion with a valid judgement or overall summary.

1 mark given for a reason being provided in support of the judgement.

52. *Candidates can be credited in a number of ways up to a maximum of 6 marks.*

Candidates must make a judgement about the usefulness of the source and support this by making evaluative comments on identified aspects of the source.

1 mark should be given for each relevant comment made, up to a **maximum of 6 marks in total**.
- A maximum of **4 marks** can be given for evaluative comments relating to the author, type of source, purpose and timing.
- A maximum of **2 marks** may be given for comments relating to the content of the source.
- A maximum of **2 marks** may be given for comments relating to points of significant omission.

Examples of aspects of the source and relevant comments:

Aspect of the source	Possible comment
Author Historian	Useful because author is an expert who will have researched the topic
Type of Source Textbook	Useful because the information would be informative/factual
Purpose To inform	Useful because the historian provides a detailed account of the discrimination faced by Jews in Nazi Germany
Timing 2013	Useful because it is a secondary source with the benefit of hindsight

Content	Possible comment
On buses and park benches, Jews had to sit on seats marked for them.	Useful because it gives accurate and relevant examples of how Jews were segregated
Jewish children were ridiculed by teachers	Useful because it gives accurate and relevant examples of how Jewish children were discriminated against in schools
Bullying of Jews in the playground by other pupils went unpunished.	Useful because it gives accurate and relevant examples of how Jewish children were intimidated in schools

Possible points of significant omission may include:
1. violence against Jews (eg Kristallnacht)
2. from 1933 Anti-Jewish Laws/boycott of Jewish shops/ doctors/lawyers/ lecturers dismissed
3. Law for the Restoration of the Professional Civil Service banned Jews from government jobs
4. 1935: Jews forbidden to join the Army; restrictions on opportunities for employment/education; Civil Liberties restricted; Anti-Jewish signs displayed in shops/ restaurants/cafes
5. 1935 Nuremburg Laws for the Protection of German Blood and Honour: ban on marriage between Jews and non-Jews
6. sexual relations between Jews and non-Jews outside marriage – criminal/prison offence
7. 1935 National Law of Citizenship meant Jews lost citizenship – no vote/ rights
8. 1938 only Aryan doctors were allowed to treat Aryan patients

Section 3, Part E, Red Flag: Lenin and the Russian Revolution, 1894-1921

53. *Candidates can be credited in a number of ways up to a maximum of 6 marks.*

Candidates must show a causal relationship between events.

Up to a **maximum of 6 marks in total**, **1 mark** should be given for each accurate, relevant reason, and a **second mark** should be given for reasons that are developed. Candidates may achieve full marks by providing six straightforward reasons, three developed reasons, or a combination of these.

Possible reasons may include:
1. the Fundamental Laws gave the Tsar autocratic power
2. the nobility controlled the peasants on their estates
3. Civil Service enforced the Tsar's decisions
4. the Secret Police (Okhrana) arrested opponents and exiled them to Siberia
5. the Okhrana had spies everywhere listening for criticism of the Tsar
6. censorship used to restrict opposition
7. army used to crush opponents
8. Orthodox Church taught people to obey Tsar
9. Government Minister was put in charge of church and he passed on the Tsar's instructions to the Bishops

54. *Candidates can be credited in a number of ways up to a maximum of 8 marks.*

Candidates must use knowledge to present a balanced assessment of the influence of different possible factors and come to a reasoned conclusion. **Up to 5 marks** are allocated for relevant points of knowledge used to address the question. **1 mark** should be given for each relevant, factual key point of knowledge used to support a factor. **If only one factor is presented, a maximum of 3 marks should be given for relevant points of knowledge.**

Possible factors may include:	Relevant, factual, key points of knowledge to support this factor may include:
Problems caused by the First World War	1. defeats in 1914 at Tannenburg/Masurian Lakes reduced public confidence 2. Tsar became Commander in Chief so could now be blamed for defeats 3. Tsar blamed for the shortages of weapons 4. high casualty rates made the Tsar even more unpopular 5. shortages of food/ fuel in Petrograd led to widespread discontent 6. rising prices due to inflation/food prices were rising faster than wages and this upset the Russian people 7. growing political opposition/due to the continuation of the war

Dislike of the Royal Family	8. Tsarina was seen as a German spy who could not be trusted 9. she replaced ministers regularly who disagreed with her which caused confusion – "Ministerial Leapfrog"
Rasputin	10. people resented his sinister influence over the Tsarina 11. brought his friends into important positions which was not popular 12. seen as drunkard and people disapproved of his corrupt influence
Other factors	13. Any other relevant point

Up to 3 marks should be given for presenting the answer in a structured way, leading to a conclusion which addresses the question, as follows:

1 mark for the answer being presented in a structured way, with knowledge being organised in support of different factors.

1 mark given for a conclusion with a valid judgement or overall summary.

1 mark given for a reason being provided in support of the judgement.

55. *Candidates can be credited in a number of ways **up to a maximum of 6 marks.***

Candidates must make a judgement about the usefulness of the source and support this by making evaluative comments on identified aspects of the source.

1 mark should be given for each relevant comment made, up to a **maximum of 6 marks in total.**
- A maximum of **4 marks** can be given for evaluative comments relating to the author, type of source, purpose and timing.
- A maximum of **2 marks** may be given for comments relating to the content of the source.
- A maximum of **2 marks** may be given for comments relating to points of significant omission.

Examples of aspects of the source and relevant comments:

Aspect of the source	Possible comment
Author: British Ambassador	Useful because he was an eyewitness
Type of Source: Diary	Useful because it will usually give an honest opinion
Purpose: To record	Less useful because it gives his biased opinions on the Russian Government
Timing: 24 October 1917	Useful because it is from the time of the Bolshevik seizure of power

Content	Possible comment
I heard this morning that the Bolsheviks would overthrow the Government in the course of the next few days because they had captured enough weapons	Useful because it accurately shows the Bolsheviks were well armed
I was not convinced that the Government had enough force behind them to deal with the situation	Useful because it accurately shows how weak the Government was
I told him that I could not understand how the Government could allow Trotsky to go on encouraging the population to murder and steal	Useful because it accurately shows that the Government had little control of Petrograd

Possible points of significant omission may include:
1. no mention of the reasons why Provisional Government was unpopular eg continuing the war, land problem, high food price and shortages
2. Bolshevik promises of peace, bread and land gained support
3. no mention of Military Revolutionary Council or its influence over army units
4. Red Guards provided Bolsheviks with a disciplined army
5. no mention of the lack of military support for the Government

Section 3, Part F, Mussolini and Fascist Italy, 1919-1939

56. *Candidates can be credited in a number of ways **up to a maximum of 8 marks.***

Candidates must use knowledge to present a balanced assessment of the influence of different possible factors and come to a reasoned conclusion. **Up to 5 marks** are allocated for relevant points of knowledge used to address the question. **1 mark** should be given for each relevant, factual key point of knowledge used to support a factor. **If only one factor is presented, a maximum of 3 marks should be given for relevant points of knowledge.**

Possible factors may include:	Relevant, factual, key points of knowledge to support this factor may include:
Widespread appeal	1. by 1921 fascism was anti-communist/ anti-trade union/ anti-socialist/ nationalist and thus became attractive to the middle and upper classes 2. Fascism became conservative/appealed to family values/supported church/ monarchy 3. the Fascists were able to exploit the anger of various different sections of Italian society at the post war peace settlement eg the failure to give Fiume to the Italians
The personal appeal of Mussolini	4. Mussolini attracted many with his oratory 5. Fascist propaganda presented Mussolini as a strong man who could save Italy 6. Mussolini was able to exploit his own humble background to present himself as a man of the people

Fascist opponents were weak	7. parliamentary government was weak – informal 'liberal' coalitions 8. Mussolini's political opponents were divided and this weakened them 9. the King gave in to Fascist pressure during the March on Rome/he failed to call Mussolini's bluff
Use of violence	10. Mussolini's Blackshirts terrorised the cities and provinces 11. destruction of opposition press severely weakened them 12. the murder of Matteotti intimidated potential opponents
Other factors	13. Any other valid reason

Up to 3 marks should be given for presenting the answer in a structured way, leading to a conclusion which addresses the question, as follows:

1 mark for the answer being presented in a structured way, with knowledge being organised in support of different factors.

1 mark given for a conclusion with a valid judgement or overall summary.

1 mark given for a reason being provided in support of the judgement.

57. *Candidates can be credited in a number of ways* **up to a maximum of 6 marks.**

Candidates must make a judgement about the usefulness of the source and support this by making evaluative comments on identified aspects of the source.

1 mark should be given for each relevant comment made, up to **a maximum of 6 marks in total.**
- A maximum of **4 marks** can be given for evaluative comments relating to the author, type of source, purpose and timing.
- A maximum of **2 marks** may be given for comments relating to the content of the source.
- A maximum of **2 marks** may be given for comments relating to points of significant omission.

Examples of aspects of the source and relevant comments:

Aspect of the source	Possible comment
Author: Historian	Useful because he is well informed/an expert
Type of Source: Book	Useful because it will have been well researched
Purpose: To inform	Useful because it contains details of aspects of life in Fascist Italy
Timing: 2006	Useful because it will have been written with the benefit of hindsight

Content	Possible comment
The Battle for Grain began in 1925 and was a major attempt to promote Fascist power and national self-sufficiency	Useful because it is accurate, the Fascist regime constantly sought propaganda opportunities
The government tried to boost grain production by giving farmers grants so that they could buy tractors, fertiliser and any other machinery necessary for wheat production	Useful because it is accurate, the Fascists were willing to intervene directly in the economy when they felt this was necessary
Farmers were also guaranteed a high price for the grain they produced	Useful because it is accurate, the Fascists were willing to intervene directly in the economy when they felt this was necessary

Possible points of significant omission may include:
1. initially, under de Stefani, economic policy limited spending in order to control inflation.
2. the currency was revalued in the "battle for the lira."
3. tariffs were placed on many foreign imports.
4. corporations composed of workers, bosses and Fascist trade unions were set up in each sector of the economy.
5. public works schemes were used to build motorways.

58. *Candidates can be credited in a number of ways* **up to a maximum of 6 marks.**

Candidates must show a causal relationship between events.

Up to a **maximum of 6 marks in total**, **1 mark** should be given for each accurate, relevant reason, and a **second mark** should be given for reasons that are developed. Candidates may achieve full marks by providing six straightforward reasons, three developed reasons, or a combination of these.

Possible reasons may include:
1. many opponents of the regime were murdered which removed potential rivals
2. some opponents were sent to concentration camps which scared people
3. opponents were denied a platform for their views as political activity outside of the Fascist Party was banned
4. censorship made it difficult to oppose Mussolini
5. the banning of trade unions removed another potential source of opposition
6. opponents were spied upon by the Secret Police
7. the rewards given to loyal journalists and academics discouraged opposition
8. the Lateran Agreements neutralised opposition from the Catholic Church

Section 3, Context G, Free at Last? Civil Rights in the USA, 1918-1968

59. *Candidates can be credited in a number of ways* **up to a maximum of 8 marks.**

Candidates must use knowledge to present a balanced assessment of the influence of different possible factors and come to a reasoned conclusion. **Up to 5 marks** are allocated for relevant points of knowledge used to address the question. **1 mark** should be given for each relevant, factual key point of knowledge used to support a factor. **If only one factor is presented, a maximum of 3 marks should be given for relevant points of knowledge.**

Possible factors may include:	Relevant, factual, key points of knowledge to support this factor may include:
Fear of white violence	1. lynching of black Americans was commonplace in the South 2. black Americans were beaten/crippled to punish them and to intimidate others 3. the Ku Klux Klan bombed churches, schools and other meeting places /burned crosses to intimidate black Americans 4. masked Klansmen marched through the streets of towns and cities carrying posters threatening black Americans with punishment and warning others to leave town 5. black American businesses were destroyed to ensure black Americans would not prosper
Segregation	6. Southern states enforced segregation of the races through Jim Crow laws 7. the Jim Crow laws affected all areas of life – education, entertainment, housing, travel, health, leisure, marriage, work 8. typically, facilities for blacks were far inferior to those for whites
Political Disenfranchisement	9. Southern states had restricted voting rights for blacks through literacy tests, poll taxes and Grandfather Clauses
Sharecropping	10. many blacks were poor sharecroppers heavily in debt to white landowners for farming equipment and seeds for planting 11. the boll weevil damaged crops throughout the South between 1910 and 1920 - as a result, there was less demand for agricultural workers, leaving many blacks unemployed

Employment Opportunities	12. in the South blacks suffered from discrimination in jobs and were only employed in low paid unskilled work. 13. during the First World War workers were in great demand in Northern factories and steel works. 14. agents from various industrial sectors arrived in the South, enticing black men and women to migrate North by paying their travel expenses. 15. wages in the Northern factories were typically double those received by most black workers in the South.
Other pull factors	16. publications (such as the Chicago Defender) published train schedules and lists of jobs to persuade Southern blacks to migrate North. 17. other publications (such as the Pittsburgh Courier and the Amsterdam News) published editorials and cartoons showing the promise of moving from the South to the North. 18. these promises included better education for children, the right to vote, access to various types of employment and improved housing conditions
Other factors	19. any other relevant points

Up to 3 marks should be given for presenting the answer in a structured way, leading to a conclusion which addresses the question, as follows:

1 mark for the answer being presented in a structured way, with knowledge being organised in support of different factors.

1 mark given for a conclusion with a valid judgement or overall summary.

1 mark given for a reason being provided in support of the judgement.

60. *Candidates can be credited in a number of ways **up to a maximum of 6 marks**.*

Candidates must show a causal relationship between events.

Up to a **maximum of 6 marks in total, 1 mark** should be given for each accurate, relevant reason, and a **second mark** should be given for reasons that are developed. Candidates may achieve full marks by providing six straightforward reasons, three developed reasons, or a combination of these.

Possible reasons may include:
1. it proved that blacks had economic power and could use it to end segregation/the bus company had no choice but to desegregate the buses as they were losing so much money
2. it gave other blacks the confidence and determination to campaign for civil rights/proved that non-violent protest could work (other bus boycotts followed in over 20 of the Southern states)
3. non-violence became a useful and popular tactic in the civil rights campaign
4. it generated a lot of publicity and support/funding for the Civil Rights Movement, particularly in the North
5. it led to a district court ruling that segregation on the buses in Montgomery was unconstitutional /this was later supported by the Supreme Court
6. it brought Martin Luther King to the forefront of the Civil Rights Movement
7. it led to the setting up of the Southern Christian Leadership Conference (SCLC) – which was to become involved in many of the most famous protests of the 1960s

61. *Candidates can be credited in a number of ways up to a maximum of 6 marks.*

Candidates must make a judgement about the usefulness of the source and support this by making evaluative comments on identified aspects of the source.

1 mark should be given for each relevant comment made, up to a **maximum of 6 marks in total.**
- A maximum of **4 marks** can be given for evaluative comments relating to the author, type of source, purpose and timing.
- A maximum of **2 marks** may be given for comments relating to the content of the source.
- A maximum of **2 marks** may be given for comments relating to points of significant omission.

Examples of aspects of the source and relevant comments:

Aspect of the source	Possible comment
Author: Malcolm X	More useful as it will give an insight to the beliefs of Malcom X at first hand
Type of Source: Speech	May be less useful as it may not include all of his beliefs/could be tailored to a particular audience
Purpose: To persuade	More useful as it will explain the beliefs of Malcolm X/ gives several reasons to support the Nation of Islam
Timing: December 1962	More useful as by this time Malcolm X had emerged as a leading public figure in the Black Power movement/less useful as does not reflect his later beliefs

Content	Possible comment
The teaching of the Honourable Elijah Muhammad is making our people, for the first time, proud to be black, and that is most important	More useful as it accurately reflects Malcom X's support for the Nation of Islam/ belief in the need for black Americans to celebrate their black heritage and culture
I just wanted to point out that whites are a race of devils	More useful as it accurately reflects Malcolm X's belief that whites were evil
If we separate then we have a chance for salvation	More useful as it accurately reflects Malcolm X's belief in the need for black Americans to separate themselves from white Americans

Possible points of significant omission may include:
1. Malcolm X also disagreed with the methods of Martin Luther King - he criticised his non-violent tactics and argued that for black Americans "non-violence is another word for defenceless."
2. Malcolm X later renounced his support for Elijah Muhammad and the Nation of Islam
3. Malcolm X later adopted a more moderate view of white Americans

Section 3, Part H, Appeasement and the Road to War, 1918-1939

62. *Candidates can be credited in a number of ways up to a maximum of 6 marks.*

Candidates must show a causal relationship between events.

Up to a **maximum of 6 marks in total, 1 mark** should be given for each accurate, relevant reason, and a **second mark** should be given for reasons that are developed. Candidates may achieve full marks by providing six straightforward reasons, three developed reasons, or a combination of these.

Possible reasons may include:
1. Hitler wanted to restore German national pride
2. Hitler hated the Treaty of Versailles and was determined to break the military restrictions it imposed on Germany
3. the Treaty of Versailles was loathed by most Germans and Hitler believed that by rearming he could strengthen his support amongst the German people
4. Hitler was a militarist and believed in a country having strong armed forces
5. Hitler also knew that recruiting men into the army would reduce unemployment, further increasing his popularity amongst the German people
6. Hitler believed it was Germany's right to have an army of equal size to the other major powers in Europe
7. Hitler believed that Germany would have to rearm to achieve lebensraum - the policy required land to be taken from other countries and armed conflict was likely
8. Hitler believed that a stronger army was required to resist the Communist threat from Soviet Russia
9. Hitler was encouraged by the lack of firm action against him by Britain and France

63. *Candidates can be credited in a number of ways up to a maximum of 8 marks.*

Candidates must use knowledge to present a balanced assessment of the influence of different possible factors and come to a reasoned conclusion. **Up to 5 marks** are allocated for relevant points of knowledge used to address the question. **1 mark** should be given for each relevant, factual key point of knowledge used to support a factor. **If only one factor is presented, a maximum of 3 marks should be given for relevant points of knowledge.**

Possible factors may include:	Relevant, factual, key points of knowledge to support this factor may include:
Public opinion	1. majority of the public were still fearful of war after the huge losses suffered during World War One 2. public fears of war were further heightened by novels and films giving terrifying portrayals of the devastation that bombers would bring in any modern war/these fears were further heightened by newsreel footage of the Nazi bombing of Guernica in the Spanish Civil War 3. public concerns over the cost of rearmament (welfare vs warfare) 4. there was a significant pacifist movement in the 1930s which was strongly against war 5. the problems of Czechoslovakia seemed remote to the majority of the public who cared little about a problem in a country far away inhabited by 'people of whom we know nothing'
German demands	6. Chamberlain believed that Hitler had a genuine grievance over the Sudetenland/Versailles was unjust and Germans should have some form of self-determination 7. Chamberlain felt Hitler had only limited demands/was a man he could do business with
Military reasons	8. Britain's air preparations were inadequate, with insufficient fighter planes, radar systems or anti-aircraft artillery 9. Britain's military chiefs stressed Britain's military weakness and the need to avoid a major war with Germany, Italy and Japan at the same time 10. the Munich agreement allowed Chamberlain to 'buy time' to rearm 11. ten year rule to avoid conflict
Lack of allies	12. France was unwilling to support conflict over the Sudetenland 13. USA was isolationist 14. Chamberlain did not trust Soviet Russia
Concerns over Empire	15. Australia, Canada and South Africa would not be easily convinced to support conflict over Czechoslovakia. 16. Empire was unwilling to fight eg disturbances in India
Other factors	17. Any other valid point

Up to 3 marks should be given for presenting the answer in a structured way, leading to a conclusion which addresses the question, as follows:

1 mark for the answer being presented in a structured way, with knowledge being organised in support of different factors.

1 mark given for a conclusion with a valid judgement or overall summary.

1 mark given for a reason being provided in support of the judgement.

64. *Candidates can be credited in a number of ways up to a maximum of 6 marks.*

Candidates must make a judgement about the usefulness of the source and support this by making evaluative comments on identified aspects of the source.

1 mark should be given for each relevant comment made, up to a **maximum of 6 marks in total.**

- A maximum of **4 marks** can be given for evaluative comments relating to the author, type of source, purpose and timing.
- A maximum of **2 marks** may be given for comments relating to the content of the source.
- A maximum of **2 marks** may be given for comments relating to points of significant omission.

Examples of aspects of the source and relevant comments:

Aspect of the source	Possible comment
Author: Historian	More useful as he is well informed/expert
Type of Source: Book	More useful as it will have been well-researched
Purpose: To inform	More useful as it is likely to be a balanced/comprehensive account of the events leading up to the outbreak of war in 1939
Timing: Published in 1989	More useful as written with the benefit of hindsight

Content	Possible comment
On 15th March 1939, German troops marched in to Prague and within two days Czechoslovakia ceased to exist.	More useful as accurately reflects the destruction of Czechoslovakia as a nation state.
On 29th March the British government gave Poland a guarantee to protect it against any threat to its independence.	More useful as accurately reflects Britain's issue of the 'Polish Guarantee'.
On 22nd May Hitler and Mussolini strengthened the ties between their two countries by signing an agreement which required them to help each other in time of war.	More useful as accurately reflects the signing of the 'Pact of Steel' between Germany and Italy.

Possible points of significant omission may include:
1. the day after entering Prague, Hitler declared Bohemia and Moravia as a 'Protectorate' of Germany
2. Slovakia remained independent but had to sign a treaty accepting German protection
3. Ruthenia was given to Hungary
4. France joined Britain in the 'Polish Guarantee'
5. just days following the 'Polish Guarantee', Hitler gave secret orders for the German army to be ready to invade Poland by 1st September
6. in August, Germany and the Soviet Union signed the Nazi-Soviet Pact whereby they agreed not to attack each other and to divide Poland
7. on 1st September, German forces attacked Poland
8. both Britain and France issued ultimatums to Hitler to withdraw German forces from Poland or face war
9. Hitler did not respond to the ultimatums and on 3rd September Britain and France declared war on Germany

Section 3, Part I, World War II, 1939-1945

65. *Candidates can be credited in a number of ways **up to a maximum of 6 marks**.*

Candidates must make a judgement about the usefulness of the source and support this by making evaluative comments on identified aspects of the source.

1 mark should be given for each relevant comment made, up to a **maximum of 6 marks in total.**
- A maximum of **4 marks** can be given for evaluative comments relating to the author, type of source, purpose and timing.

- A maximum of **2 marks** may be given for comments relating to the content of the source.
- A maximum of **2 marks** may be given for comments relating to points of significant omission.

Examples of aspects of the source and relevant comments:

Aspect of the source	Possible comment
Author: Sailor	Useful because the sailor was an eyewitness
Type of Source: Interview	Useful because it provides honest personal opinions
Purpose: To inform	Useful because it gives a balanced account of the events
Timing: May 1940	Useful because it is from the time of the evacuation from Dunkirk

Content	Possible comment
Soldiers coming back without equipment	Useful because it is accurate - the army at Dunkirk had to leave a lot of equipment behind
Began to think it was the end of our way of life	Useful because it is accurate that many people did see it as a defeat
We knew we had the Navy, and that we could fight/however we didn't know what our soldiers would be able to do if Jerry invaded, because they had nothing	Useful because although it is accurate that some people wanted to fight, others were worried that they could not continue the war

Possible points of significant omission may include:
1. British military had been pushed back to the beaches of Dunkirk by the advancing German army
2. British government requested all available civilian boats to travel across the Channel to evacuate the stranded British army
3. over 300,000 British and French soldiers rescued

66. *Candidates can be credited in a number of ways **up to a maximum of 6 marks**.*

Candidates must show a causal relationship between events.

Up to a **maximum of 6 marks in total**, **1 mark** should be given for each accurate, relevant reason, and a **second mark** should be given for reasons that are developed. Candidates may achieve full marks by providing six straightforward reasons, three developed reasons, or a combination of these.

Possible reasons may include:
1. Japanese were angered at the US economic restrictions placed on them after their expansion into French Indochina/Chinese mainland
2. Japanese were confident in their military superiority over the US
3. Pearl Harbour was chosen because the entire US fleet was based there
4. Japanese wanted to extend their influence into South East Asia/needed to knock out the US Pacific fleet in order to gain control of the Pacific
5. Japanese hoped to crush US morale by destroying its prestigious naval fleet
6. Japan hoped to destroy the US naval fleet in order to gain breathing space – aircraft carriers were a particular target

7. Japanese confident of the support of Hitler/Pact with Germany

67. *Candidates can be credited in a number of ways up to a maximum of 8 marks.*

Candidates must use knowledge to present a balanced assessment of the influence of different possible factors and come to a reasoned conclusion. **Up to 5 marks** are allocated for relevant points of knowledge used to address the question. **1 mark** should be given for each relevant, factual key point of knowledge used to support a factor. **If only one factor is presented, a maximum of 3 marks should be given for relevant points of knowledge.**

Possible factors may include:	Relevant, factual, key points of knowledge to support this factor may include:
Effective Allied planning	1. deception plans led German intelligence to believe an attack would target Calais 2. use of dummy staging areas in Dover fooled the Germans 3. lessons learned after the failure of Dieppe invasion in 1942 4. Allies took advantage of bad weather to surprise the Germans
Allied resources	5. Allied superiority in men and equipment 6. use of Mulberry harbours 7. use of Pluto – pipeline transporting fuel across the Channel 8. gaining of naval and air superiority during the invasion 9. paratroopers landed the night before to secure bridges and roads near Normandy landing sites
Failure of German counter-attack	10. Communication problems caused German commanders to fail to react to the assault 11. German High Command remained fixated on the Calais area even after the attack on Normandy had started 12. German troops of poorer quality
Other factors	13. Any other valid point

Up to 3 marks should be given for presenting the answer in a structured way, leading to a conclusion which addresses the question, as follows:

1 mark for the answer being presented in a structured way, with knowledge being organised in support of different factors.

1 mark given for a conclusion with a valid judgement or overall summary.

1 mark given for a reason being provided in support of the judgement.

Section 3, Part J, The Cold War, 1945-1989

68. *Candidates can be credited in a number of ways up to a maximum of 8 marks.*

Candidates must use knowledge to present a balanced assessment of the influence of different possible factors and come to a reasoned conclusion. **Up to 5 marks** are allocated for relevant points of knowledge used to address the question. **1 mark** should be given for each relevant, factual key point of knowledge used to support a factor. **If only one factor is presented, a maximum of 3 marks should be given for relevant points of knowledge.**

Possible factors may include:	Relevant, factual, key points of knowledge to support this factor may include:
Difference in political beliefs	1. a clash of political beliefs led to division - Capitalism v Communism 2. a multi-party system operated in the West, while the Soviet Union and its satellites were one party states which led to tension 3. the Soviets claimed that Western societies were run by the rich, while the Americans claimed the Eastern bloc countries were totalitarian dictatorships which led to mistrust
Military reasons	4. the Soviets were angry that the Americans had not shared nuclear technology with them 5. the Soviets believed the atom bomb was used against Japan so that America could bully other countries 6. suspicions were raised as each side raced to develop new technology, eg the H Bomb 7. NATO vs Warsaw Pact
The Berlin Blockade	8. tensions rose in Berlin as the wartime alliance between the Americans and the Soviets broke down 9. the Soviets closed routes into West Berlin in an attempt to force the Western powers to leave which upset the West 10. the Berlin airlift showed the determination of the Western powers to keep hold of West Berlin which annoyed the Soviets 11. the Blockade cemented division by leading to the creation of West and East Germany

Soviet actions in Eastern Europe	12. Soviet troops occupied most of Eastern Europe and this caused tension
	13. the Americans believed the Soviets had violated the Yalta agreement which annoyed the US
	14. the Soviets claimed control of Eastern Europe was vital to stop future attacks on their homeland and resented Western interference
Other factors	15. Any other valid point

Up to 3 marks should be given for presenting the answer in a structured way, leading to a conclusion which addresses the question, as follows:

1 mark for the answer being presented in a structured way, with knowledge being organised in support of different factors.

1 mark given for a conclusion with a valid judgement or overall summary.

1 mark given for a reason being provided in support of the judgement.

69. *Candidates can be credited in a number of ways **up to a maximum of 6 marks.***

Candidates must make a judgement about the usefulness of the source and support this by making evaluative comments on identified aspects of the source.

1 mark should be given for each relevant comment made, up to a **maximum of 6 marks in total.**
- A maximum of **4 marks** can be given for evaluative comments relating to the author, type of source, purpose and timing.
- A maximum of **2 marks** may be given for comments relating to the content of the source.
- A maximum of **2 marks** may be given for comments relating to points of significant omission.

Examples of aspects of the source and relevant comments:

Aspect of the source	Possible comment
Author: Journalist	useful because he was an eyewitness
Type of Source: Newspaper	more useful as it should accurately reflect opinion at the time/less useful because it only gives British view
Purpose: To inform/persuade	More useful as it gives a detailed account of events during the Hungarian revolution in 1956/ less useful as he may exaggerate the level of support for the revolution
Timing: 23 October 1956	useful because it dates from the time of the Hungarian revolution

Content	Possible comment
Rebellion against their Soviet masters/Send the Red Army home	more useful as it is accurate, Soviet occupation was deeply unpopular
We want free and secret elections	more useful as it is accurate, people were tired of Communist/ one party rule
Demanding the sacking of the present government	more useful as it is accurate, the old regime was associated with corruption

Possible points of significant omission may include:
1. the Hungarian secret police were hated
2. many wanted repression of the Catholic Church to end
3. central control had stifled economic growth
4. Krushchev's move away from Stalinism led Hungarians to believe the Soviets would allow them to exercise more independence
5. many in Hungary believed the Americans would give support to their revolution

70. *Candidates can be credited in a number of ways **up to a maximum of 6 marks.***

Candidates must show a causal relationship between events.

Up to a **maximum of 6 marks in total**, **1 mark** should be given for each accurate, relevant reason, and a **second mark** should be given for reasons that are developed. Candidates may achieve full marks by providing six straightforward reasons, three developed reasons, or a combination of these.

Possible reasons may include:
1. America was trying to supply a war 8,000 miles from home which made it very difficult for them
2. the Vietcong were able to make use of local knowledge/ familiarity with the terrain which gave them a clear advantage
3. many Vietnamese gave shelter to the Vietcong/it was very difficult for the Americans to identify the enemy
4. the Vietcong were highly motivated as they were fighting to drive out invaders from their country
5. the morale of US soldiers was very low and this reduced their combat effectiveness
6. most Vietnamese wanted to see the defeat of the US and the corrupt South Vietnamese regime
7. the brutality of the Americans (eg My Lai Massacre) alienated the Vietnamese

NATIONAL 5 HISTORY 2016

Section 1, Context A, The Wars of Independence, 1286-1328

1. *Candidates can be credited in a number of ways up to a maximum of 6 marks.*

Candidates must show a causal relationship between events.

Up to a maximum of **6 marks** in total, **1 mark** should be given for each accurate, relevant reason, and a **second mark** should be given for reasons that are developed. Candidates may achieve full marks by providing six straightforward reasons, three developed reasons, or a combination of these.

Possible reasons may include:

1. he was inexperienced in Scottish affairs/he was essentially an English noble
2. had to accept Edward as Overlord of Scotland/he had paid homage to Edward which made him unpopular
3. Edward insisted on treating him like an English noble/not as a king
4. Edward undermined him by summoning him to appear at court/before his parliament
5. Edward undermined his authority by hearing Scottish legal cases
6. Edward forced him to appoint an Englishman as his Chancellor, further humiliating him
7. not supported by the Scottish nobles/the twelve Guardians challenged his authority
8. made an Alliance with France which provoked Edward and other Scottish nobles loyal to him
9. the powerful Bruce family resented his kingship and did not support him
10. his army was defeated by Edward at Dunbar
11. he was publicly stripped of his kingship by Edward/taken from Scotland to the Tower of London as Edward's prisoner

2. *Candidates can be credited in a number of ways up to a maximum of 6 marks.*

Candidates must make a judgement about the usefulness of the source and support this by making evaluative comments on identified aspects of the source.

1 mark should be given for each relevant comment made, up to a **maximum of 6 marks in total**.

- A maximum of **4 marks** can be given for evaluative comments relating to the author, type of source, purpose and timing.
- A maximum of **2 marks** may be given for comments relating to the content of the source.
- A maximum of **2 marks** may be given for comments relating to points of significant omission.
- Examples of aspects of the source and relevant comments:

Examples of aspects of the source and relevant comments:

Aspect of the source	Possible comment
Author: Wallace and Murray (Moray)	Useful as it is a first-hand account
Type of Source: Letter	Useful as it is an official document
Purpose: To persuade	Less useful as it exaggerates the level of stability in Scotland
Timing: 1297	Useful as it is from the time when Wallace was Guardian

Content	Possible comment
The kingdom has been freed by war from the power of the English	Useful as it accurately states (the hope that) Scotland is free again
Merchants...may safely trade their goods to all ports in the kingdom of Scotland	Useful as it accurately states (the hope that) Scotland is open for business again
Our merchants will bring their trade to you	Useful as it accurately shows Scots looking out to Europe as they did before war

Possible points of significant omission may include:
1. Wallace made Guardian because of victory at Stirling Bridge
2. only a temporary respite for Scotland
3. Wallace resigned as Guardian after his defeat at Falkirk
4. Wallace went to Europe to negotiate Balliol's release
5. Wallace needed to trade for iron for the army

3. *Candidates can be credited in a number of ways up to a maximum of 8 marks.*

Candidates must use knowledge to present a balanced assessment of the influence of different possible factors and come to a reasoned conclusion. Up to **5 marks** are allocated for relevant points of knowledge used to support factors (but one mark should be deducted if the process is not clear in at least two factors).

1 mark should be given for each relevant, factual key point of knowledge used to support a factor. If only one factor is presented, a maximum of 3 marks should be given for relevant points of knowledge.

Possible factors may include:	Relevant, factual, key points of knowledge to support this factor may include:
Defeated Scottish enemies	1. Had killed his main rival – John Comyn 2. Had destroyed the Comyns in the north 3. Had defeated the MacDougalls at the Pass of Brander 4. He defeated the Earl of Buchan at Inverurie
Defeated English opponents	5. Successfully used guerrilla tactics to defeat English forces 6. Defeated English troops at Loudoun Hill 7. Won back control of Scottish castles from the English 8. Destroyed captured castles to prevent their use against him in the future
Defeated Edward II	9. Defeated superior English army at Bannockburn 10. Humiliated Edward II by Bannockburn defeat and by raiding into Northumbria
Some opposition remained	11. Edward II still would not accept Bruce as king/still claimed to be overlord 12. Failed to convince the Pope to lift his excommunication 13. Forced nobles to choose between their Scottish or English lands/titles – alienated some nobles by this (eg Edward) Balliol/Soules – created the "Disinherited" 14. English had captured and imprisoned Bruce's family
	15. Any other valid point.

Up to 3 marks should be given for presenting the answer in a structured way, leading to a conclusion which addresses the question, as follows:

1 mark for the answer being presented in a structured way, with knowledge being organised in support of different factors.

1 mark for a conclusion with a valid judgement or overall summary.

1 mark for a reason being provided in support of the judgement.

Section 1, Context B, Mary Queen of Scots, and the Scottish Reformation, 1542–1587

4. *Candidates can be credited in a number of ways up to a maximum of 6 marks.*

Candidates must show a causal relationship between events.

Up to a maximum of 6 marks in total, 1 mark should be given for each accurate, relevant reason, and a second mark should be given for reasons that are developed. Candidates may achieve full marks by providing six straightforward reasons, three developed reasons, or a combination of these.

Possible reasons may include:
1. some Scots began to question the teachings of the Catholic Church
2. resentment at churchmen who were wealthy while everyone else worked hard
3. criticisms of the wealth of the Church in Scotland and its concerns with money (eg Pluralism)
4. shortages of parish priests and poor quality of rest drew criticism
5. criticisms of the lack of spirituality among some members of the Catholic Church (eg monks and nuns not leading holy lives)
6. criticisms of abuse of responsibilities by some members of the Church (eg local priests charging money for important ceremonies such as christenings and funerals/ or employing others to perform ceremonies for them)
7. resentment of French Catholic influence on Scotland/ resentment at Mary of Guise who had persecuted Protestants
8. Protestant Lords of the Congregation used Protestant religion to attack French influence
9. presence of Protestant preachers from England widespread (eg John Knox)
10. criticism of the severity of treatment of some Protestant preachers (eg Wishart who was burned at the stake for being a heretic in 1546)
11. Protestantism was appealing to many as the style of worship meant people could be more involved/ congregation allowed to sing psalms and say prayers
12. English translations of the New Testament were being distributed in Scotland during the period of the 'Rough Wooing'/the Good and Godly Ballads spread Protestant ideas
13. resentment over money spent to decorate Roman Catholic churches

5. *Candidates can be credited in a number of ways up to a maximum of 8 marks.*

Candidates must use knowledge to present a balanced assessment of the influence of different possible factors and come to a reasoned conclusion. **Up to 5 marks** are allocated for relevant points of knowledge used to support factors (but one mark should be deducted if the process is not clear in at least two factors). **1 mark** should be given for each relevant, factual key point of knowledge used to support a factor. **If only one factor is presented, a maximum of 3 marks should be given for relevant points of knowledge.**

Possible factors may include:	Relevant, factual, key points of knowledge to support this factor may include:
Mary's marriage to Darnley	1. Darnley was unpopular with many Scots/Mary ignored warnings about him 2. Darnley discredited Mary with his behaviour (eg excessive drinking/gambling) 3. Darnley insulted James Stewart and most of the important Scottish nobles which lost Mary support 4. Most of Mary's trusted officials resigned and rebelled against him (Chaseabout Raid), which weakened her Government 5. Darnley was involved in the murder of Riccio which reflected badly on Mary 6. Darnley was murdered and Mary was assumed to be involved/led to Mary's imprisonment and abdication
Mary's relationship with Bothwell	7. Mary was blamed for having a relationship with Bothwell before Darnley's murder 8. Mary married Bothwell who was assumed to be Darnley's murderer which made her a co-conspirator 9. Mary allowed Bothwell to prevent a fair inquiry into Darnley's death
Religious reasons	10. Many Scots did not want to have a Catholic as a ruler 11. Protestants did not trust her for being pro-French 12. Attitude of Knox and the Kirk who criticised Mary 13. Bothwell was a Protestant and the marriage turned some Catholics against her
Other factors	14. any other valid point

Up to 3 marks should be given for presenting the answer in a structured way, leading to a conclusion which addresses the question, as follows:

1 mark for the answer being presented in a structured way, with knowledge being organised in support of different factors.

1 mark for a conclusion with a valid judgement or overall summary.

1 mark for a reason being provided in support of the judgement.

6. *Candidates can be credited in a number of ways up to a maximum of 6 marks.*

Candidates must make a judgement about the usefulness of the source and support this by making evaluative comments on identified aspects of the source.

1 mark should be given for each relevant comment made, up to a maximum of **6 marks** in total.

A maximum of **4 marks** can be given for evaluative comments relating to the author, type of source, purpose and timing.

A maximum of **2 marks** may be given for comments relating to the content of the source.

A maximum of **2 marks** may be given for comments relating to points of significant omission.

Examples of aspects of the source and relevant comments:

Aspect of the source	Possible comment
Author: Mary Queen of Scots	Useful as it is a first-hand account (directly implicates her as co-operating with the plotters)
Type of Source: Letter	Useful as personal/secret communication so may be less guarded
Purpose: To persuade	Useful as it shows Mary was directly involved in plotting to escape
Timing: 1586	Useful as it is from the time leading up to Mary's execution

Content	Possible comment
When everything is prepared and the forces are ready both in this country and abroad, then you must set the six gentlemen to work	Useful as it accurately shows Mary's knowledge of the plot
Give orders that when the act is done, they get me away from here	Useful as accurately shows Mary giving orders to be released from her captivity/may refer to plans to kill Elizabeth
At the same time get all your forces into battle order to protect me while we wait for help from abroad	Useful as accurately indicates Mary's intent to seek foreign assistance

Possible points of significant omission may include:
1. Sir Francis Walsingham added an extra section where he forged Mary's request for the names of the men who would kill Elizabeth
2. English Parliament had already voted that Mary would be executed should there be any more plots against Elizabeth discovered
3. Mary was denied legal counsel at her trial

Section 1, Context C, The Treaty of Union, 1689-1715

7. *Candidates can be credited in a number of ways **up to a maximum of 8 marks**.*

Candidates must use knowledge to present a balanced assessment of the influence of different possible factors and come to a reasoned conclusion. **Up to 5 marks** are allocated for relevant points of knowledge used to support factors (but one mark should be deducted if the process is not clear in at least two factors). **1 mark** should be given for each relevant, factual key point of knowledge used to support a factor. **If only one factor is presented, a maximum of 3 marks should be given for relevant points of knowledge.**

Possible factors may include:	Relevant, factual, key points of knowledge to support this factor may include:
Anger over the Darien Scheme	1. King William wanted to remain on good terms with the Spanish and so deliberately sabotaged the colony 2. English officials prevented investment in the Darien Scheme 3. English colonies, including Jamaica, Barbados and New York, were forbidden by William to offer assistance to Scots at Darien 4. William worried that success for Darien would encourage independence for the American colonies 5. A huge number of Scots had invested in the Darien Scheme 6. many Scots believed that only the successful establishment of colonies could make Scotland a prosperous nation
Anger over the poor state of the Scottish economy strained relations	7. many in Scotland were angry that the Navigation Acts prevented Scotland trading with English colonies 8. there was a feeling that the English had not done enough to help Scotland during the "ill years" of the 1690s 9. the Worcester Incident where some of the English crew were hanged
Many Scots were unhappy over the operation of the Union of Crowns	10. belief that since the Union of Crowns Scotland had been unable to operate independently 11. William took little interest in Scotland. 12. Darien had shown Scotland had a King who acted against her interests 13. Anne declared herself to be "entirely English" 14. Scottish trade had been disrupted by England's wars and there was no recompense in the peace treaties
Problems arose over the succession	15. Scots were angry that the English Parliament passed the succession to Sophia of Hanover without consulting them 16. Scots reacted by passing the Act of Security which annoyed the English
Other factors	17. any other valid point

Up to 3 marks should be given for presenting the answer in a structured way, leading to a conclusion which addresses the question, as follows:

1 mark for the answer being presented in a structured way, with knowledge being organised in support of different factors.

1 mark for a conclusion with a valid judgement or overall summary.

1 mark for a reason being provided in support of the judgement.

8. *Candidates can be credited in a number of ways **up to a maximum of 6 marks**.*

Candidates must make a judgement about the usefulness of the source and support this by making evaluative comments on identified aspects of the source.

1 mark should be given for each relevant comment made, up to a **maximum of 6 marks in total**.

- A maximum of **4 marks** can be given for evaluative comments relating to the author, type of source, purpose and timing.
- A maximum of **2 marks** may be given for comments relating to the content of the source.
- A maximum of **2 marks** may be given for comments relating to points of significant omission.

Examples of aspects of the source and relevant comments:

Aspect of the source	Possible comment
Author: Stirling town council	Useful as it is a first-hand account of the concerns of a royal burgh/ typical of the concerns of other burghs
Type of Source: A petition	Useful as it shows that many people opposed the Union
Purpose: To persuade	Useful as the majority of petitions were against the Union
Timing: November 1706	Useful as it is written at the time of Union

Content	Possible comment
Union will bring a high burden of taxation upon this land	Useful as it accurately reflects a widespread concern
The English may discourage our trade (if they think it will be in competition with their own)	Useful as it accurately states a common view expressed by those who were anti-Treaty
The Union will ruin our industry, our religion, laws and liberties	Useful as it accurately states a common view expressed by those who were anti-Treaty

Possible points of significant omission may include:
1. Scotland had always been an independent nation and its identity would be subsumed if there was a new united Parliament/a dislike of merging with 'The Auld Enemy'
2. there were already fears that English foreign policy was operating against Scottish interests, eg anger in Scotland over failure of English to consult before entry into Spanish War of Succession
3. public opinion in Scotland was against a union
4. some Scots would have preferred a Federal Union
5. Episcopalians in Scotland opposed union as it would secure the Hanoverian succession and only a return to the Stuart dynasty could restore episcopacy to the Scottish church/Union guaranteed the position of the Presbyterian Church

9. *Candidates can be credited in a number of ways **up to a maximum of 6 marks**.*

Candidates must show a causal relationship between events.

Up to a **maximum of 6 marks in total**, **1 mark** should be given for each accurate, relevant reason, and a **second mark** should be given for reasons that are developed. Candidates may achieve full marks by providing six straightforward reasons, three developed reasons, or a combination of these.

Possible reasons may include:
1. Act of Security for the Kirk was vital in securing Presbyterian support for Union (in the aftermath of its passage Presbyterian ministers preached in favour of Union)

2. fear of English invasion if Union was rejected (during the Union negotiations English troops were stationed on the border with Scotland)
3. opponents of Union were unable to unite because of their differences (eg Catholics and extreme Presbyterians hated each other)
4. the Duke of Hamilton proved to be a very ineffective leader of the anti-Union cause
5. many Scots were worried that the Aliens Act would come into effect if they voted against Union. Scots would have lost land which they owned in England
6. many Scots were attracted by the possibility of trade with England's colonies (the Scots economy had gone through a very bad time in the 1690s and the prospect of full access to England's colonies seemed too good an opportunity to miss)
7. many were attracted by the prospect of compensation for Darien
8. the role of the Squadrone Volante was vital in ensuring Union was accepted (some motivated by their moderate Presbyterianism, others by belief they would control distribution of the Equivalent)
9. some Scottish nobles were offered English titles (which meant an automatic seat in the House of Lords) if they voted for Union
10. other inducements (money, trading privileges) were offered to others in the Scottish Parliament in return for their vote
11. fear of withdrawal of royal favour (and even loss of expenses claims and salary) if they did not vote for Union

Section 1, Context D, Migration and Empire, 1830–1939

10. *Candidates can be credited in a number of ways **up to a maximum of 8 marks**.*

Candidates must use knowledge to present a balanced assessment of the influence of different possible factors and come to a reasoned conclusion. **Up to 5 marks** are allocated for relevant points of knowledge used to support factors (but one mark should be deducted if the process is not clear in at least two factors). **1 mark** should be given for each relevant, factual key point of knowledge used to support a factor.
If only one factor is presented, a maximum of 3 marks should be given for relevant points of knowledge

Possible factors may include:	Relevant, factual, key points of knowledge to support this factor may include:
Clearances	1. many landlords no longer lived in the Highlands and needed additional income to fund their new lifestyles 2. landlords would make more money letting land to sheep farmers/ creating hunting estates 3. tenants had no security of tenure so could easily be evicted/made homeless 4. whole districts were brutally cleared (eg Strathconon in 1850, South Uist and Barra in 1851, Knoydart in 1853) 5. some landlords assisted tenants by paying their passage if they agreed to leave 6. forced clearances ended after Crofters' Holdings Act 1886

Difficulties of earning a living	7. collapse of kelp industry/fall in demand for black cattle
	8. overpopulation led to subdivision of holdings/not enough land to support a family or pay rent
	9. poor stony soils – primitive equipment (cas chrom)/poor climate – short growing season
	10. failure of potato crop in 1846 – blight and famine
	11. loss of market for herring after Russian Revolution
	12. few employment opportunities for ambitious young people/limited number of professional posts for well educated
	13. deer forests and shooting estates employed few people
	14. little land made available to returning servicemen after the war
Poor standard of living	15. 19th century blackhouses shared with animals/blackhouses often had no chimneys/roofs leaked
	16. houses often lacked basic amenities (eg bathrooms/toilets, electricity in 1920s and 30s)
	17. limited access to medical care/shops/entertainment
Pull factors	18. the promise of cheap land
	19. employment opportunities/higher wages
	20. encouragement from relatives/friends
Other factors	21. any other valid point

Up to 3 marks should be given for presenting the answer in a structured way, leading to a conclusion which addresses the question, as follows:

1 mark for the answer being presented in a structured way, with knowledge being organised in support of different factors.

1 mark for a conclusion with a valid judgement or overall summary.

1 mark for a reason being provided in support of the judgement.

11. *Candidates can be credited in a number of ways **up to a maximum of 6 marks**.*

Candidates must show a causal relationship between events.

Up to a **maximum of 6 marks in total**, **1 mark** should be given for each accurate, relevant reason, and a **second mark** should be given for reasons that are developed. Candidates may achieve full marks by providing six straightforward reasons, three developed reasons, or a combination of these.

Possible reasons may include:

1. close to Ireland so only a short journey – important for people with little money to have only a short time when they could not earn
2. fares to Scotland from Ireland were very cheap so it was a more affordable destination/adverts encouraged immigration
3. Catholic Church offered assistance with finding jobs and housing
4. Scotland was involved early in the Industrial Revolution so there was a wide range of jobs available (eg coal mines, textile factories, sugar refineries, construction, railway building etc which used existing skills or were suitable for unskilled workers)
5. some jobs (eg coal mining, had tied housing available to workers/housing available in growing towns and cities)
6. wages in Scotland were consistently higher than they were in Ireland
7. it became cheaper for migrants from Europe to sail to America from Glasgow instead of direct from Europe; many stayed in Scotland rather than move on
8. there were existing communities of Jews, Irish, Italians which made it easy for others to settle in/Protestant Irish found it very easy to settle in Scottish society
9. Italians were able to set up small family businesses such as cafes and fish and chip shops all over Scotland, as few others were doing this and the Scots enjoyed the products
10. Scotland did not persecute religious minorities which made it attractive to Jewish immigrants fleeing from Russia

12. *Candidates can be credited in a number of ways **up to a maximum of 6 marks**.*

Candidates must make a judgement about the usefulness of the source and support this by making evaluative comments on identified aspects of the source.

1 mark should be given for each relevant comment made, up to a **maximum of 6 marks in total**.

- A maximum of 4 marks can be given for evaluative comments relating to the author, type of source, purpose and timing.
- A maximum of 2 marks may be given for comments relating to the content of the source.
- A maximum of 2 marks may be given for comments relating to points of significant omission.

Examples of aspects of the source and relevant comments:

Aspect of the source	Possible comment
Author: Scottish emigrant	Useful as he experienced emigration for himself
Type of Source: Song	Less useful as it may be exaggerated for emotional effect
Purpose: To inform	Less useful as his feelings may not be representative of others' experiences/useful because many immigrants shared these feelings
Timing: 1920s	Useful as at a time after the war when many Scots emigrated to Canada

Content	Possible comment
I see only bleak empty prairie, There's no sound of waves breaking on the shore/ The winter night is long for me.	Useful as it accurately states new physical environment very unfamiliar for many emigrants/were unused to long Canadian winter
In the evening darkness My spirit sinks with homesickness	Useful as it accurately states many Scots experienced homesickness
No ceilidh on the prairie	Useful as it accurately states what many immigrants felt or less useful as may be a purely personal response to the situation/ feeling of isolation/loneliness

Possible points of significant omission may include:

1. many Scots successfully formed close-knit communities
2. many Scots were attracted by the grants of prairie land and prospered there
3. many Scots kept their traditions going with Caledonian societies, Burns Clubs, Highland dancing, pipe bands, etc.
4. many Scots became very successful in Canada and other new countries (eg Andrew Carnegie, John A MacDonald, Robert Dunsmuir)
5. some Scots did not settle and returned to Scotland
6. some Scots prospered and returned wealthy to Scotland

Section 1, Context E, The Era of the Great War, 1900-1928

13. *Candidates can be credited in a number of ways up to a maximum of 6 marks.*

Candidates must show a causal relationship between events.

Up to a **maximum of 6 marks in total**, **1 mark** should be given for each accurate, relevant reason, and a **second mark** should be given for reasons that are developed. Candidates may achieve full marks by providing six straightforward reasons, three developed reasons, or a combination of these.

Possible reasons may include:

Patriotism/Martial Tradition

1. Patriotic appeal of slogans/people were carried away by a wave of patriotism
2. Scotland already had a proud military/martial tradition

Xenophobia

3. Scots affected by stories of spies and "Belgian Atrocities" of German Army

Local Loyalties

4. the Cameronians recruited largely from Glasgow and Lanarkshire. The Royal Scots tended to attract men from Edinburgh
5. after 13 Hearts players signed up, 600 Hearts supporters in six days also joined the 16th Royal Scots which became known as McCrae's Battalion

Adventure

6. opportunity to see new places and countries and perform heroic deeds – and/or quite possibly to leave behind a boring or difficult job
7. the attraction of setting out on this great adventure with your friends was possible by the formation of "pals" battalions'

Peer Pressure

8. peer pressure from family, friends and wider society/ sense of duty
9. women were encouraged to press men into service eg white feather campaign

Economic Necessity

10. fear of unemployment was probably an important factor in joining up/recruitment in high unemployment areas more successful than in low
11. Earl of Wemyss threatened to dismiss any employee who failed to join up

Propaganda

Posters/Newspapers/Government propaganda

14. *Candidates can be credited in a number of ways up to a maximum of 8 marks.*

Candidates must use knowledge to present a balanced assessment of the influence of different possible factors and come to a reasoned conclusion. **Up to 5 marks** are allocated for relevant points of knowledge used to support factors (but one mark should be deducted if the process is not clear in at least two factors). **1 mark** should be given for each relevant, factual key point of knowledge used to support a factor. **If only one factor is presented, a maximum of 3 marks should be given for relevant points of knowledge.**

Possible factors may include:	Relevant, factual, key points of knowledge to support this factor may include:
Food Shortages	1. Voluntary rationing had little impact/posters discouraged people from wasting food 2. People started to keep an allotment to grow food 3. The contribution of the Women's Land Army 4. Conscientious Objectors were used to produce food 5. Parks and tennis courts turned into vegetable plots 6. Rationing introduced for certain foodstuff from 1917 7. Substitute foods were used/ standard loaves made using powdered potato flour and beans 8. Rationing had some health benefits
	9. Game such as rabbit was eaten-especially by country dwellers 10. Black market existed for those who could afford it 11. People had to queue for some foods/on occasion food lorries hijacked
DORA	12. Blackouts 13. Restrictions to pub opening hours/ watering down of alcohol 14. Censorship 15. Conscription
Loss of loved ones	16. Mourning huge numbers of soldiers killed
Changing role of women	17. Women became head of household 18. Difficulties experienced balancing work with looking after the children 19. More women working than ever before 20. Details about Land Army/Munitions factories/nursing etc 21. Experienced more freedom/equality
Other factors	22. any other valid point (including more details of DORA restrictions)

Up to 3 marks should be given for presenting the answer in a structured way, leading to a conclusion which addresses the question, as follows:

1 mark for the answer being presented in a structured way, with knowledge being organised in support of different factors.

1 mark for a conclusion with a valid judgement or overall summary.

1 mark for a reason being provided in support of the judgement.

15. *Candidates can be credited in a number of ways* **up to a maximum of 6 marks.**

Candidates must make a judgement about the usefulness of the source and support this by making evaluative comments on identified aspects of the source.

1 mark should be given for each relevant comment made, up to a **maximum of 6 marks in total.**

- A maximum of **4 marks** can be given for evaluative comments relating to the author, type of source, purpose and timing.
- A maximum of **2 marks** may be given for comments relating to the content of the source.
- A maximum of **2 marks** may be given for comments relating to points of significant omission.

Examples of aspects of the source and relevant comments:

Aspect of the source	Possible comment
Author: Historian John Kerr	Useful as he is a well-informed expert/will have researched the issue (using a variety of primary sources)
Type of Source: Book	Useful because it is a factual viewpoint on the extension on the right to vote
Purpose: To inform	Useful as it is balanced/no evidence of historical bias
Timing: 2010	Useful as it is a secondary source written with the benefit of hindsight

Content	Possible comment
The 1918 Representation of the People Act gave some women over 30 the vote in national elections	Useful as it accurately states that the franchise was restricted to "some" women.
They had to be either: householders or the wives of householders, occupiers of property with an annual rent of £5, graduates of British universities	Useful as it accurately explains the qualifications required for women to get the vote.
The electorate increased to about 21 million, of which 8.4 million were women	Useful as it accurately gives the statistical evidence of the increase in the franchise.

Possible points of significant omission may include:
1. it gave the right to vote to all men over 21
2. women still did not have the vote on the same terms as men
3. 19 if they had been on active service in the armed forces
4. women now made up 40% of the total voters

Section 2, Context A, The Creation of the Medieval Kingdoms, 1066–1406

16. *Candidates can be credited in a number of ways* **up to a maximum of 5 marks.**

Candidates must show a causal relationship between events.

Up to a **maximum of 5 marks in total, 1 mark** should be given for each accurate, relevant reason, and a **second mark** should be given for reasons that are developed. Candidates

may achieve full marks by providing five straightforward reasons, three developed reasons, or a combination of these.

Possible reasons may include:
1. William was related to Edward the Confessor through marriage
2. William claimed Edward had promised him the throne
3. William had supported Edward during rebellion in England/had supplied Edward with soldiers to put down the revolt
4. Harold Godwinson had sworn an oath to accept William as the rightful heir
5. Harold had seized the throne/broken his oath/this made him unworthy to be king
6. William had also received the support of the Pope before his invasion
7. William felt God was on his side after his victory at Hastings

17. *Candidates can be credited in a number of ways* **up to a maximum of 4 marks.**

Candidates must make direct comparisons of the two sources, either overall or in detail. A simple comparison will indicate what points of detail or overall viewpoint they agree or disagree about and should be given **1 mark.**

A developed comparison of the points of detail or overall viewpoint should be given **2 marks.** Candidates may achieve full marks by making four simple comparisons, two developed comparisons or by a combination of these.

Possible points of comparison may include:

Overall: The sources agree about the way William dealt with rebellion	
Source A	Source B
Every home and farmland was burnt and all livestock destroyed	Crops were set on fire, herds of animals were slaughtered and supplies of food ruined
So many people were massacred that their bodies filled the streets	Hundreds of people were slaughtered
The few who had survived now faced starvation	Whole families died of hunger

18. *Candidates can be credited in a number of ways* **up to a maximum of 5 marks.**

They may take different perspectives on the events and may describe a variety of different aspects of the events.

1 mark should be given for each accurate relevant key point of knowledge.

A second mark should be given for each point that is developed, up to a maximum of **5 marks.** Candidates may achieve full marks by providing five straightforward points, by making three developed points, or a combination of these.

Possible points of knowledge may include:
1. Henry knocked down any castles built illegally by the barons
2. Henry sent the barons' armies home
3. Henry introduced the exchequer (eg Nigel of Ely)
4. Henry introduced new laws to deal with crime (eg The Assize of Clarendon/Northampton)
5. Henry introduced new laws to deal with land (eg The Novel Disseisin)
6. Henry introduced the jury system/trial by ordeal
7. Henry sacked corrupt sheriffs
8. Henry prevented barons from becoming sheriffs

9. Henry introduced key officials (eg Justices in Eyre)
10. Henry appointed his sons to control other parts of his kingdom

19. *Candidates can be credited in a number of ways **up to a maximum of 6 marks.***

Candidates must make an overall judgement about how fully the source explains the events. **1 mark** may be given for each valid point from the source or each valid point of significant omission provided.

A maximum of 2 marks may be given for answers in which no judgement has been made or which refer only to the source.

Possible points which may be identified in the source include:
1. offered support and comfort in difficult times/ encouraged people not to give up
2. taught people how to be good Christians
3. heard confessions/issued penance
4. controlled the way people behaved

Possible points of significant omission may include:
5. carried out key ceremonies (eg baptism/marriage/funeral)
6. performed last rites for the dying
7. kept tithes for villages in case of harvest failure
8. identified holidays
9. educated boys/trained them for a career in the Church
10. was part of the feudal system/owed service to the king
11. was active politically (eg clergy often acted as advisors to the king)
12. employed large number of people from the community

Section 2, Context B, War of the Three Kingdoms, 1603-1651

20. *Candidates can be credited in a number of ways **up to a maximum of 4 marks.***

Candidates must make direct comparisons of the two sources, either overall or in detail. A simple comparison will indicate what points of detail or overall viewpoint they agree or disagree about and should be given **1 mark**.

A developed comparison of the points of detail or overall viewpoint should be given **2 marks**. Candidates may achieve full marks by making four simple comparisons, two developed comparisons or by a combination of these.

Possible points of comparison may include:	
Overall: The sources agree that the reign of Charles was unpopular	
Source A	**Source B**
The reign of Charles I began with an unpopular friendship with the Duke of Buckingham/Buckingham was assassinated in 1628	Charles also angered many by having favourites at court, particularly the Duke of Buckingham/In 1628 Buckingham was assassinated
There was ongoing tension with Parliament over money (made worse by the costs of war abroad)	Charles also angered many with the methods he used to raise money
Religious tensions led to further resentment of Charles I as he preferred Anglican forms of worship which made Puritans suspicious	Charles I was a very religious man who enjoyed Anglican church services full of ritual, and this led to clashes with Puritans who preferred plain and simple services

21. *Candidates can be credited in a number of ways **up to a maximum of 5 marks.***

Candidates must show a causal relationship between events.

Up to a **maximum of 5 marks in total**, **1 mark** should be given for each accurate, relevant reason, and a **second mark** should be given for reasons that are developed. Candidates may achieve full marks by providing five straightforward reasons, three developed reasons, or a combination of these.

Possible reasons may include:
1. ship money – only to be collected in times of war and from coastal areas – Charles began to collect it from inland areas, in times of peace and on a yearly basis
2. forest fines imposed on people living in areas that had been forests in the distant past (14th century)
3. distraint of Knighthood fines – fining people if they did not accept knighthoods (Knights had to provide loans to the Crown)
4. nuisances – in London people who had built outside of the original walls were forced to buy a licence to 'commit a nuisance'
5. monopolies – reappeared in different forms, the most resented being the soap monopoly
6. Court of Wards – the much disliked Court of Wards doubled its income (to £76,000)
7. plantations – 1632 City of London was fined for failing to push forward the plantation of Ulster (finding Protestant families to take over land in Ireland)
8. customs farmers – customs farmers gave the Crown a larger sum in exchange for the right to collect the customs, these extra dues were passed on to the merchants to pay
9. many disliked new taxation caused by King and court's love of luxury (eg banquets, clothes, foreign dynastic wars)

22. *Candidates can be credited in a number of ways **up to a maximum of 5 marks.***

They may take different perspectives on the events and may describe a variety of different aspects of the events.

1 mark should be given for each accurate relevant key point of knowledge.

A second mark should be given for each point that is developed, up to a maximum of **5 marks**. Candidates may achieve full marks by providing five straightforward points, by making three developed points, or a combination of these.

Possible points of knowledge may include:
1. riot in St. Giles Cathedral saw men and women assault the Dean of St. Giles whilst reading from the New Prayer Book
2. other potential violence in the north as Bishop of Brechin threatened his congregation with two loaded pistols as he read from the new service
3. emergency body was formed to organise opposition to the New Prayer Book – "The Tables" members were chosen from the Scottish Parliament
4. Petitions organised and sent to Charles
5. National Covenant for the Defence of True religion was drawn up in 1638
6. General Assembly of the Kirk banned the New Prayer Book in 1638
7. Charles decided to use force against the Scots in 1638 (First Bishops' War), caused further opposition

23. *Candidates can be credited in a number of ways **up to a maximum of 6 marks.***

Candidates must make an overall judgement about how fully the source explains the events. **1 mark** may be given for each valid point interpreted from the source or each valid point of significant omission provided

A maximum of 2 marks may be given for answers in which no judgement has been made or which refer only to the source.

Possible points which may be identified in the source include:

1. the King ordered his army to occupy the high ridge on Edgehill, hoping that the Parliamentarian army would be forced to attack uphill
2. Parliament arranged their army on flat ground
3. Essex decided to wait for the King to make the first move
4. Essex's decision to wait forced the King to take action/ the King moved his army down off the ridge and attacked

Possible points of significant omission may include:

5. Royalist cavalry on the right wing charged into Parliamentarian cavalry causing them to flee
6. Royalist cavalry pursued the Parliamentarians to village of Kineton/3 miles away
7. Royalist left wing cavalry scattered by right wing of Parliamentarian army
8. Parliamentarians now had the only effective cavalry left on the field
9. Royalist cavalry drifted back from Kineton to find the situation had altered greatly
10. night came and exhausted soldiers stopped fighting
11. 3000 men had died, many wounded or fled
12. battle ended in a draw – both sides moved towards London the next day
13. Charles' army was prevented from capturing London

Section 2, Context C, The Atlantic Slave Trade, 1770-1807

24. *Candidates can be credited in a number of ways up to a maximum of 6 marks.*

Candidates must make an overall judgement about how fully the source explains the events. **1 mark** may be given for each valid point interpreted from the source or each valid point of significant omission provided.

A maximum of 2 marks may be given for answers in which no judgement has been made or which refer only to the source.

Possible points which may be identified in the source include:

1. slaves were often tightly packed below deck for the journey across the Atlantic ocean
2. conditions below deck were horrendous and slaves were denied basic sanitation
3. disease was common/and many died (from conditions such as dysentery)
4. the food was unfamiliar and many slaves simply refused to eat

Possible points of significant omission may include:

5. slaves were sometimes held below deck using a loose pack system/men usually kept shackled
6. lack of fresh air – slaves held for long periods below deck/terrible smell below deck
7. floor in hold became covered in blood, mucus, vomit and faeces
8. some slaves had to be force fed to keep them alive
9. crew were often cruel towards slaves
10. female slaves often suffered sexual abuse from crew
11. slaves taken above deck and whipped to make them exercise/made to dance

25. *Candidates can be credited in a number of ways up to a maximum of 5 marks.*

Candidates must show a causal relationship between events.

Up to a **maximum of 5 marks in total**, **1 mark** should be given for each accurate, relevant reason, and a **second mark** should be given for reasons that are developed. Candidates may achieve full marks by providing five straightforward reasons, three developed reasons, or a combination of these.

Possible reasons may include:

1. the slave trade brought great wealth to British cities
2. the slave trade provided employment for many people (eg jobs for sailors, dock workers, rope makers)
3. manufactured goods made in Britain were traded in Africa or exported to the plantations
4. the slave trade provided a boost to shipbuilding/led to expansion of docks
5. the port cities (eg Liverpool or Glasgow) grew in size and power through its involvement in the transportation of slaves
6. Glasgow made great profits from the trade in tobacco and sugar
7. many great buildings were built from the profits of the slave trade
8. led to the growth of banking and insurance industries (eg in London)
9. Bristol became wealthy through its involvement in the sugar trade
10. British cotton mills relied on supplies of slave produced cotton

26. *Candidates can be credited in a number of ways up to a maximum of 4 marks.*

Candidates must make direct comparisons of the two sources, either overall or in detail. A simple comparison will indicate what points of detail or overall viewpoint they agree or disagree about and should be given **1 mark**.

A developed comparison of the points of detail or overall viewpoint should be given **2 marks**. Candidates may achieve full marks by making four simple comparisons, two developed comparisons or by a combination of these.

Possible points of comparison may include:

Source B	Source C
Overall: The sources agree about resistance on the plantations.	
They sabotaged their owners by working slowly and inefficiently	The mildest forms of resistance were doing a job slowly or badly.
They were harshly punished for such behaviour/ whipping, slaves had their ears, noses and limbs cut off	The punishments for slaves who resisted were very harsh/ punishments such as hanging, mutilation or lashing were common
Many slaves attempted to run away	Slaves ran away when they saw a chance

27. *Candidates can be credited in a number of ways up to a maximum of 5 marks.*

Candidates must show a causal relationship between events.

Up to a **maximum of 5 marks in total**, **1 mark** should be given for each accurate, relevant reason, and a **second mark** should be given for reasons that are developed. Candidates may achieve full marks by providing five straightforward reasons, three developed reasons, or a combination of these.

Possible reasons may include:

1. abolitionists formed The Society for the Abolition of the Slave Trade to campaign against the Slave Trade
2. Thomas Clarkson visited ports such as Liverpool and Bristol to collect evidence/collected artefacts such as manacles and thumbscrews to show people the horrors of the trade
3. Equiano highlighted his experience of slavery
4. a diagram of a slave ship, the Brookes, was also published/other pamphlets and posters were produced
5. the society produced evidence that hundreds of British seamen involved in the trade died every year
6. William Wilberforce tried to influence the prime minister and Prince of Wales to support the abolition of the slave trade/MPs were routinely petitioned
7. Wilberforce presented a bill to Parliament on numerous occasions to end the slave trade
8. John Newton, a former slave ship captain, preached against slavery
9. Newton wrote the hymn "Amazing Grace"
10. Granville Sharp challenged slavery in the courts
11. anti-slavery petitions were signed
12. Wedgwood produced goods with the slogan "Am I not a man and a brother?"
13. people boycotted goods such as sugar

Section 2, Context D, Changing Britain, 1760-1914

28. *Candidates can be credited in a number of ways **up to a maximum of 4 marks**.*

Candidates must make direct comparisons of the two sources, either overall or in detail. A simple comparison will indicate what points of detail or overall viewpoint they agree or disagree about and should be given **1 mark**.

A developed comparison of the points of detail or overall viewpoint should be given **2 marks**. Candidates may achieve full marks by making four simple comparisons, two developed comparisons or by a combination of these.

Possible points of comparison may include:	
Overall: Sources mostly agree about the events of the massacre	
Source B	**Source C**
People had gathered from all over Lancashire in St Peter's Fields	I saw a large crowd that had gathered from miles around and was moving towards St Peter's Fields
The magistrates wrongly believed that people had been marching and drilling like soldiers in preparation	(I laughed at the fears of the magistrates as) the so-called "marching" protest was actually a procession of men with their wives, sisters and children
11 people were killed and hundreds injured	I could see that many people had been hurt/I will always be haunted by the sight of those trampled bodies.

29. *Candidates can be credited in a number of ways **up to a maximum of 5 marks**.*

Candidates must show a causal relationship between events.

Up to a **maximum of 5 marks in total**, **1 mark** should be given for each accurate, relevant reason, and a **second mark**

should be given for reasons that are developed. Candidates may achieve full marks by providing five straightforward reasons, three developed reasons, or a combination of these.

Possible reasons may include:

1. hot temperatures led to exhaustion/poor health/made accidents more likely
2. long hours (12 to 18 hour days) led to exhaustion/poor health/made accidents more likely
3. few breaks led to exhaustion/made accidents more likely
4. lack of ventilation made it hard to breathe
5. harmful dust particles and fibres in the air led to a high rate of lung disease (TB)
6. noise of machinery often damaged hearing
7. open lavatory buckets smelly and unhygienic
8. machines were not fenced, so accidents were frequent
9. workers often had to work and eat during short breaks which led to accidents being more likely
10. children often had to climb beneath machinery to clean, causing accidents
11. child workers prone to rickets due to lack of sunlight and poor quality of food
12. workers became deformed/stomach pains due to long hours bending over machines
13. varicose veins common from workers spending long hours on feet
14. workers were often badly treated or beaten by overseers
15. before 1830s no laws to regulate working conditions/protect health
16. difficult to enforce laws passed/not enough factory inspectors

30. *Candidates can be credited in a number of ways **up to a maximum of 6 marks**.*

Candidates must make an overall judgement about how fully the source explains the events. **1 mark** may be given for each valid point interpreted from the source or each valid point of significant omission provided.

A maximum of 2 marks may be given for answers in which no judgement has been made or which refer only to the source.

Possible points which may be identified in the source include:

1. even the most remote country areas were brought into contact with towns and cities
2. industries benefited greatly from being able to transport their raw materials and goods quickly/cheaply
3. farmers were able to sell their fresh produce over greater distances
4. faster travel meant that people could live further from their jobs/towns spread as suburbs were built

Possible points of significant omission may include:

5. many jobs created (eg to build or run the railways)
6. daily national newspapers now possible
7. improved postal services
8. cheap fares/day trips and holidays for working class possible
9. Parliamentary trains meant railway travel was accessible to all
10. MPs could travel quickly between constituencies and London
11. political parties able to campaign nationwide
12. enabled growth of trade union movement
13. standardised time across Britain (GMT/Railway time)
14. enabled national sporting leagues to develop
15. perishable foods more widely available, so diet improved

31. *Candidates can be credited in a number of ways up to a maximum of 5 marks.*

They may take different perspectives on the events and may describe a variety of different aspects of the events.

1 mark should be given for each accurate relevant key point of knowledge.

A second mark should be given for each point that is developed, up to a maximum of **5 marks**. Candidates may achieve full marks by providing five straightforward points, by making three developed points, or a combination of these.

Possible points of knowledge may include:

1832 Reform Act:

1. seats were distributed more fairly (eg industrial towns gained MPs)
2. pocket/rotten boroughs lost their MPs
3. boroughs with less than 4,000 inhabitants lost one MP each
4. more seats were awarded to the counties
5. Scotland was awarded extra seats/Ireland was given extra seats
6. some people lost the right to vote (eg working men in 'potwalloper' burghs)
7. 1 in 6 adult men now had the vote/1 in 8 in Scotland, 1 in 5 in England.
8. electorate increased by about 60%/from 435,000 to 652,000
9. in Scotland the electorate increased from 4,500 to 65,000
10. in burghs the franchise was standardised/all male householders paying £10 per annum rent got the vote
11. in counties the franchise was extended to 40 shilling (£2) freeholders/ £10 copyholders/£50 tenants
12. this meant that middle-class men now had the vote (eg small landowners, tenant farmers and shopkeepers)
13. voter registration introduced/duration of polling limited to two days

1867 Reform Act:

14. enfranchised 1.25 million men/effectively doubled the electorate/1 in 3 men now had vote
15. all male householders/lodgers in burghs who paid rent of £10 per annum got the vote (enfranchised skilled working men in towns)
16. business owners who paid rates of £12 per annum got the vote
17. seats were redistributed from small towns to the growing industrial towns or counties(eg Liverpool got an extra MP/Edinburgh from two to four MPs)
18. the University of London was also given a seat/two seats given to Scottish universities

Section 2, Context E, The Making of Modern Britain, 1880–1951

32. *Candidates can be credited in a number of ways up to a maximum of 5 marks.*

They may take different perspectives on the events and may describe a variety of different aspects of the events.

1 mark should be given for each accurate relevant key point of knowledge. **A second mark** should be given for each point that is developed, up to a maximum of **5 marks**. Candidates may achieve full marks by providing five straightforward points, by making three developed points, or a combination of these.

Possible points of knowledge may include:

1. poor housing (eg dampness, vermin, shared outside toilets)
2. poor health/lack of affordable health-care.
3. overcrowding – often leading to health problems (eg TB)
4. malnutrition led to health problems (eg Rickets)
5. low wages/few benefits
6. Unemployment/employment often cyclical or seasonal
7. dependence on charity/voluntary organisations (eg no pensions until 1908)
8. fear/stigma of workhouse/poorhouse (splitting up of families in workhouse)
9. destitution/homelessness
10. high death rates – especially of young children/ vulnerable people
11. lack of sympathy – due to laissez-faire attitudes
12. lack of education
13. excessive drunkenness/gambling

33. *Candidates can be credited in a number of ways up to a maximum of 6 marks.*

Candidates must make an overall judgement about how fully the source explains the events. **1 mark** may be given for each valid point interpreted from the source or each valid point of significant omission provided.

A maximum of 2 marks may be given for answers in which no judgement has been made or which refer only to the source.

Possible points which may be identified in the source include:

1. other parties were afraid that they might lose votes to Labour if they did not show that they wanted to help the poor
2. most working class men now had the vote, so it was possible that they could vote for Labour
3. Trade unions put pressure on the Liberals and Conservatives, to do more to help the poor
4. society was beginning to accept that some people became poor through no fault of their own

Possible points of significant omission may include:

5. Booth's survey revealed high levels of poverty in London.
6. Rowntree's survey revealed that the problem was not confined to London — provincial cities like York affected too.
7. concerns over fitness of recruits during Boer War led to desire to improve health by tackling poverty.
8. concerns over national efficiency/worries about Britain's future workforce led to desire to tackle poverty and poor health
9. other countries beginning to challenge Britain's position (eg Germany and the USA)
10. "New Liberals" accepted that government had to intervene more in the lives of the people to help the poor
11. politicians such as David Lloyd George came from a working class background and had genuine concern for the poor
12. the Germans had introduced some welfare reforms already and the "German Model" was studied and copied by the British/David Lloyd George had visited Germany for this purpose

34. *Candidates can be credited in a number of ways up to a maximum of 5 marks.*

Candidates must show a causal relationship between events.

Up to a maximum of **5 marks** in total, **1 mark** should be given for each accurate, relevant reason, and **a second mark** should be given for reasons that are developed. Candidates may achieve full marks by providing five straightforward reasons, three developed reasons, or a combination of these.

Possible reasons may include:
1. Liberals had no overall plan for social reform
2. reforms were selective/only helped some groups/ deserving poor
3. benefit levels were ungenerous/often below subsistence level (eg pensions)
4. many of the reforms were voluntary/optional/control given to local authorities (eg school meals only made compulsory in 1914)
5. unemployment benefit only paid for short-term (15 weeks), so did not tackle long-term unemployment
6. unemployment insurance only for certain trades
7. problems with pensions (eg payable at 70 – well above average life-expectancy)
8. medical inspections did not provide treatment (until 1912 when school clinics introduced)
9. health insurance did not cover most hospital treatment
10. families of workers not covered by health insurance
11. housing not tackled at all
12. Education barely tackled (apart from some scholarships in 1907/8 Education Act)

35. *Candidates can be credited in a number of ways* **up to a maximum of 4 marks.**

Candidates must make direct comparisons of the two sources, either overall or in detail. A simple comparison will indicate what points of detail or overall viewpoint they agree or disagree about and should be given **1 mark.**

A developed comparison of the points of detail or overall viewpoint should be given **2 marks.** Candidates may achieve full marks by making four simple comparisons, two developed comparisons or by a combination of these

Possible points of comparison may include:	
Overall: The Sources disagree about the success of the Labour reforms	
Source B	**Source C**
Their record of success is difficult to argue with	Their reputation ... is not entirely deserved
The National Health Service was the greatest achievement of the Labour welfare state, giving free medical and dental treatment to all	By 1951, charges had to be introduced (for some dentaled treatment, spectacles and prescriptions) meaning that the NHS was not an entirely free service.
Considerable progress was made in tackling the housing shortage/between 1948 and 1951, around 200,000 homes were built per year	Labour's record on house building is poor (when compared to that of the previous governments of the 1930s)

Section 3, Context A, The Cross and the Crescent; the Crusades, 1071-1192

36. Candidates can be credited in a number of ways **up to a maximum of 5 marks.**

They may take different perspectives on the events and may describe a variety of different aspects of the events.

1 mark should be given for each accurate relevant key point of knowledge. **A second mark** should be given for each point that is developed, up to a maximum of **5 marks.** Candidates may achieve full marks by providing five straightforward points, by making three developed points, or a combination of these.

Possible points of knowledge may include:
1. knights were expected to fight for the king
2. knights were expected to carry out castle guard duty
3. knights were expected to fight for the Church/protect the clergy
4. orders of knights protected pilgrims (eg the Knights Templar)
5. knights were expected to protect the weak and vulnerable in society (eg elderly, children)
6. knights were part of the feudal system providing land for peasants to cultivate
7. knights enforced law and order/were members of a jury in some countries
8. knights were expected to be role models/to live by the Code of Chivalry

37. *Candidates can be credited in a number of ways* **up to a maximum of 5 marks.**

Candidates must show a causal relationship between events.

Up to a **maximum of 5 marks in total**, **1 mark** should be given for each accurate, relevant reason, and a **second mark** should be given for reasons that are developed. Candidates may achieve full marks by providing five straightforward reasons, three developed reasons, or a combination of these.

Possible reasons may include:
1. Peter the Hermit was a poor military leader
2. belief in the righteousness of their cause made them overconfident
3. the peasants were not trained soldiers/accompanied by wives, children, even the elderly
4. the peasants had few weapons
5. the peasants ran out of supplies/money whilst travelling across Europe
6. the peasants were ill-disciplined on their journey (eg treatment of the Jews making communities unwilling to help them)
7. the peasants ignored Emperor Alexius' advice to wait for the main Crusader army
8. the peasants split into different groups and elected their own leaders/Peter the Hermit was cast aside
9. peasants were lured into an ambush by spies
10. the peasants were defeated by Muslim forces/most were killed/supplies lost

38. *Candidates can be credited in a number of ways* **up to a maximum of 5 marks.**

Candidates must make an overall judgement about how fully the source explains the events. **1 mark** may be given for each valid point interpreted from the source or each valid point of significant omission provided

A maximum of 2 marks may be given for answers in which no judgement has been made or which refer only to the source.

Possible points which may be identified in the source include:
1. Muslim communities did not attack Crusaders/gave them money to keep the peace
2. refused to join together and thought only of their own land
3. Seljuk Turks had been defeated by Egyptian forces and lost the city
4. Egyptians asked for help but no Muslim armies came to their aid

Possible points of significant omission may include:
5. the Crusaders captured Nicaea because Kilij Arslan was away fighting other Muslims (eg The Danishmends)

6. at Antioch the Crusaders bribed a Muslim who let them into the city eg Firouz
7. Kerbogha arrived late to Antioch because he spent time trying to protect his own land first (eg attacked Edessa)
8. Muslim forces refused to attack together at Antioch (eg Ridwan of Aleppo/Duqaq of Damascus)
9. Kerbogha's men fled the battlefield at Antioch
10. Turks did not attempt to recapture Jerusalem because they had land disputes to settle with other Muslim groups elsewhere.

39. *Candidates can be credited in a number of ways up to a maximum of 5 marks.*

Candidates must make a judgement about the usefulness of the source and support this by making evaluative comments on identified aspects of the source.

1 mark should be given for each relevant comment made, up to a **maximum of 5 marks in total.**
- A maximum of **4 marks** can be given for evaluative comments relating to the author, type of source, purpose and timing.
- A maximum of **2 marks** may be given for comments relating to the content of the source.
- A maximum of **2 marks** may be given for comments relating to points of significant omission.

Examples of aspects of the source and relevant comments:

Aspect of the source	Possible comment
Author: A Crusader	Useful because he has first-hand experience/eyewitness
Type of Source: Chronicle	Useful because it was a well-researched record of events in the East
Purpose: To record/blame King Guy for the defeat	Useful because it provides a detailed account of the battle/less useful as it may be biased
Timing: 1187	Useful because it was written at the time of the Battle of Hattin

Content	Possible comment
Crusaders constantly attacked by Saladin's army	Useful because it accurately explains why the Crusaders tired
King Guy made a terrible mistake and made camp near Hattin	Useful because it accurately describes the error made by the Crusaders
Saladin's army surrounded the Crusaders' camp and slaughtered nearly all those inside	Useful because it accurately describes what happened in the battle.

Possible points of significant omission may include:
1. Saladin's army set fire to the grass around the Crusaders' camp
2. not all Crusaders agreed with the march to Tiberias (eg Roland of Tripoli)
3. Saladin's army captured some Crusaders as prisoners
4. Saladin's army captured a shard of the True Cross
5. Saladin spared the life of King Guy and some other Christian lords
6. repeated charges by mounted Crusaders against Muslim lines failed

Section 3, Context B, "Tea and Freedom": the American Revolution, 1774-83

40. *Candidates can be credited in a number of ways up to a maximum of 5 marks.*

Candidates must show a causal relationship between events.

Up to a **maximum of 5 marks in total**, **1 mark** should be given for each accurate, relevant reason, and a **second mark** should be given for reasons that are developed. Candidates may achieve full marks by providing five straightforward reasons, three developed reasons, or a combination of these.

Possible reasons may include:
1. the colonists were unhappy with the imposition of laws and taxes which were seen as unjust (eg the passing of the Stamp Act and Townshend Act in the 1760s had been very unpopular measures)
2. they resented being taxed without representation in the British parliament
3. events such as the Boston Tea Party led to an increase in anti-British feeling among colonists/unhappiness at high-handed actions of British government
4. the colonists were unhappy with the continuing presence of British soldiers in the colonies
5. some colonists were frustrated that the British were stopping them from moving West
6. some colonists felt that the policies of the British government were damaging trade

41. *Candidates can be credited in a number of ways up to a maximum of 5 marks.*

They may take different perspectives on the events and may describe a variety of different aspects of the events.

1 mark should be given for each accurate relevant key point of knowledge.

A second mark should be given for each point that is developed, up to a maximum of **5 marks**. Candidates may achieve full marks by providing five straightforward points, by making three developed points, or a combination of these.

Possible points of knowledge may include:
1. Colonists secured high ground at Bunker Hill overlooking British forces
2. British Navy opened fire on the colonists' position (but shells fell short)
3. Prescott told the colonists, "Don't fire until you see the whites of their eyes!" (to save much needed ammunition)
4. British charged the hill three times before the colonists were driven away/ran out of ammunition
5. British soldiers were exposed to American musket fire as they made their way up the hill
6. Bright uniforms of British soldiers made them easy targets
7. British suffered around 1,000 casualties (226 killed, 828 wounded)
8. Colonists suffered less than half of British casualties (around 100-400 killed and 300 wounded)
9. British were victorious/Colonists achieved confidence boost for future battles against British forces

42. *Candidates can be credited in a number of ways up to a maximum of 5 marks.*

Candidates must make an overall judgement about how fully the source explains the events. **1 mark** may be given for each valid point interpreted from the source or each valid point of significant omission provided.

A maximum of **2 marks** may be given for answers in which no judgement has been made or which refer only to the source.

Possible points which may be identified in the source include:
1. British soldiers were dispatched to seize the supplies
2. when the British arrived at Lexington they were confronted by a group of minutemen
3. shots were fired and several colonists were killed
4. the British then marched on to Concord where they destroyed any remaining supplies.

Possible points of significant omission may include:
1. the Sons of Liberty had discovered that the British were planning to march on to Concord.
2. Paul Revere and other riders sounded the alarm
3. church bells roused the minutemen from their beds.
4. the British soldiers were attacked by angry colonists as they tried to make their way back to Boston.
5. many British soldiers were killed and injured.
6. Colonists in Massachusetts continued to attack the British forces.

43. *Candidates can be credited in a number of ways **up to a maximum of 5 marks**.*

Candidates must make a judgement about the usefulness of the source and support this by making evaluative comments on identified aspects of the source.

1 mark should be given for each relevant comment made, up to a **maximum of 5 marks in total**.
- A maximum of **4 marks** can be given for evaluative comments relating to the author, type of source, purpose and timing.
- A maximum of **2 marks** may be given for comments relating to the content of the source.
- A maximum of **2 marks** may be given for comments relating to points of significant omission.

Examples of aspects of the source and relevant comments:

Aspect of the source	Possible comment
Author: American army officer	Useful as he is an eyewitness/first-hand experience
Type of Source: Diary entry	Useful as it is more likely to reveal his true opinion/feelings
Purpose: To record	Useful as it is a private record and is less likely to be biased on the poor condition of the American army
Timing: 1777	Useful because it was written during the Wars of Independence

Content	Possible comment
The army now continues to grow sickly from the exhaustion they have suffered in this campaign	Useful as it accurately shows the true condition of the army
Poor food/cold weather/nasty clothes/nasty cooking	Useful as it accurately shows the extent of suffering of the army
The men still show a spirit	Useful as it accurately shows that the morale of the American army remained high

Possible points of significant omission may include:
1. the American forces had endured a number of military setbacks in 1777
2. the Army was small in number/lacked experienced leadership/few professional soldiers
3. Washington used the difficult winter of 1777 to train and discipline his soldiers into a much more effective force

Section 3, Context C, USA 1850-1880

44. *Candidates can be credited in a number of ways **up to a maximum of 5 marks**.*

They may take different perspectives on the events and may describe a variety of different aspects of the events.

1 mark should be given for each accurate relevant key point of knowledge.

A second mark should be given for each point that is developed, up to a maximum of **5 marks**. Candidates may achieve full marks by providing five straightforward points, by making three developed points, or a combination of these.

Possible points of knowledge may include:
1. problems of trying to cross mountains and rivers
2. difficulties with wagons (eg broken wheels)
3. had to be timed to complete journey before winter struck
4. dangers of weather – possibility of being stuck in snow
5. had to cross deserts and plains/lack of water
6. navigating the terrain was challenging
7. problems of supplies lasting for the whole journey/lack of fuel in treeless plains
8. threats of attack from Native Americans
9. problems of disease (eg cholera killed many)
10. attacks by wild animals

45. *Candidates can be credited in a number of ways **up to a maximum of 5 marks**.*

Candidates must show a causal relationship between events.

Up to a **maximum of 5 marks in total**, **1 mark** should be given for each accurate, relevant reason, and a **second mark** should be given for reasons that are developed. Candidates may achieve full marks by providing five straightforward reasons, three developed reasons, or a combination of these.

Possible reasons may include:
1. failure to resolve slavery as an issue between the states
2. failure to resolve disputes over tariffs
3. growth of abolitionism in North
4. Dred Scott Case upset Northern States and abolitionists
5. Kansas – Nebraska Act led to "Bleeding Kansas"
6. growing tension between North and South (eg incidents such as John Brown/Harpers Ferry)
7. south felt it was being blocked from expansion in new western territories
8. growing industry/wealth and immigrant population of North was at odds with plantation life of South
9. growth of Republican Party which favoured Northern interests/North increasingly dominating politics
10. south felt it was being marginalised/losing influence election of Lincoln in 1860 angered Southern states who saw it as an attack upon them

46. *Candidates can be credited in a number of ways **up to a maximum of 5 marks**.*

Candidates must make a judgement about the usefulness of the source and support this by making evaluative comments on identified aspects of the source.

1 mark should be given for each relevant comment made, up to a **maximum of 5 marks in total**.

- A maximum of 4 marks can be given for evaluative comments relating to the author, type of source, purpose and timing.
- A maximum of 2 marks may be given for comments relating to the content of the source.
- A maximum of 2 marks may be given for comments relating to points of significant omission.

Examples of aspects of the source and relevant comments:

Aspect of the source	Possible comment
Author: George Fitzhugh	Useful as he was an eyewitness/ first-hand experience
Type of Source: Letter	Useful as it gives his own honest opinion
Purpose: To persuade	Less useful as it presents a biased view of slavery
Timing: 1857	Useful as it was written at the time when slavery existed

Content	Possible comment
The children, the aged and the sick do not work at all	Less useful as not true of all plantations
They have all the comforts and necessaries of life provided for them such as food and housing	Less useful as false impression given is of caring owners
The slave men and boys do not work more than nine hours a day in good weather/the slave women do little hard work	Less useful as slaves worked very long hours in all weathers

Possible points of significant omission may include:
1. no mention of punishments
2. no mention of particular mistreatment of female slaves
3. no mention of splitting of slave families
4. no mention of slaves as property
5. no mention of slaves running away
6. no mention of Abolitionist viewpoints

47. *Candidates can be credited in a number of ways up to a maximum of 5 marks.*

Candidates must make an overall judgement about how fully the source explains the events. **1 mark** may be given for each valid point interpreted from the source or each valid point of significant omission provided.

A maximum of 2 marks may be given for answers in which no judgement has been made or which refer only to the source.

Possible points which may be identified in the source include:
1. slaves were made free in 1865
2. the right of citizenship granted in the Fourteenth Amendment is practically a mockery/is ignored
3. the right to vote, provided for in the Fifteenth Amendment, is under attack/is ignored
4. the old ruling class is victorious today/the newly freed slaves are little better off than they were before

Possible points of significant omission may include:
5. Carpetbaggers and Scalawags exploited opportunities in South
6. Freedman's Bureau helped freed slaves with their needs (eg jobs)
7. Sharecroppers little better off after 1865
8. Black Codes restricted the rights of black Americans eg could not leave employment without permission
9. KKK and other groups used violence to attack freed slaves
10. Jim Crow Laws began to be passed after 1877 (eg separate facilities)

Section 3, Context D, Hitler and Nazi Germany, 1919–1939

48. *Candidates can be credited in a number of ways up to a maximum of 5 marks.*

Candidates must show a causal relationship between events.

Up to a **maximum of 5 marks in total**, **1 mark** should be given for each accurate, relevant reason, and a **second mark** should be given for reasons that are developed. Candidates may achieve full marks by providing five straightforward reasons, three developed reasons, or a combination of these.

Possible reasons may include:
1. Germany got no say in the Treaty/called it a "DIKTAT" a dictated peace
2. Germany blamed for starting the war (War Guilt Clause)
3. felt it humiliated Germany/was unacceptable/too harsh
4. Germans resented having to pay reparations
5. with the Kaiser gone Germans did not believe they should be punished
6. not based on Wilson's 14 points eg no self determination
7. Germany lost land eg people living under foreign rule
8. loss of colonies felt to be unfair
9. Armed forces reduced increasing unemployment/leaving them vulnerable to attack

49. *Candidates can be credited in a number of ways up to a maximum of 5 marks.*

They may take different perspectives on the events and may describe a variety of different aspects of the events.

1 mark should be given for each accurate relevant key point of knowledge. **A second mark** should be given for each point that is developed, up to a maximum of **5 marks**. Candidates may achieve full marks by providing five straightforward points, by making three developed points, or a combination of these.

Possible points of knowledge may include:
1. Anti-Jewish propaganda: blamed for World War One/ Communism/economic ruin/contaminating the "Master Race"
2. Jews were often abused or beaten up in the streets
3. Anti-Semitic education: pupils taught to be hostile to Jews; teachers humiliated Jewish children
4. from 1933 Anti-Jewish Laws/boycott of Jewish shops/ doctors/lawyers/ lecturers dismissed
5. Law for the Restoration of the Professional Civil Service banned Jews from government jobs
6. 1935: Jews forbidden to join the Army; restrictions on opportunities for employment, education; Civil Liberties restricted; Anti-Jewish signs displayed in shops/ restaurants/cafes

7. 1935 Nuremburg Laws for protection of German blood and honour (eg ban on marriage between Jews and non-Jews)
8. Sexual relations between Jews and non-Jews outside marriage – criminal offence
9. 1935 National Law of Citizenship meant Jews lost citizenship – no vote/rights
10. 1938 Government contracts only for Aryan firms
11. 1938 only Aryan doctors were allowed to treat Aryan patients
12. 1938 all Jews had to take new first name: Israel and Sarah: adding to signatures/passport stamped with letter "J"
13. 1938 Kristallnacht – massive anti-Semitic campaign: Jewish homes/shops/synagogues destroyed; 100 killed/2000 arrested
14. Many Jews sent to concentration camps/murdered

50. *Candidates can be credited in a number of ways* **up to a maximum of 5 marks.**

Candidates must make a judgement about the usefulness of the source and support this by making evaluative comments on identified aspects of the source.

1 mark should be given for each relevant comment made, up to a **maximum of 5 marks in total**.
- A maximum of **4 marks** can be given for evaluative comments relating to the author, type of source, purpose and timing.
- A maximum of **2 marks** may be given for comments relating to the content of the source.
- A maximum of **2 marks** may be given for comments relating to points of significant omission.

Examples of aspects of the source and relevant comments:

Aspect of the source	Possible comment
Author: Ernst Thalmann	Useful as it is from someone who has first-hand experience of Nazi intimidation
Type of Source: Diary	Useful as it is an honest personal account
Purpose: To inform	Useful as it provides a balanced (and detailed) account of the use of intimidation by the Nazis
Timing: 1933	Useful as it is from the time that the Nazis were routinely intimidating their opponents

Content	Possible comment
Every cruel method of blackmail was used against me	Useful as it accurately describes how the Nazis threatened prisoners families to extract confessions
I was then assaulted and in the process had four teeth knocked out/a Gestapo officer with a whip in his hand then beat me with measured strokes	Useful as it accurately describes methods used by Gestapo
They tried hypnosis which was also ineffective	Useful as it accurately describes methods used by Gestapo

Possible points of significant omission may include:
1. the SS also very intimidating
2. fear of concentration camps intimidating

3. use of Gestapo informers/other spying systems intimidated people public executions acted as a warning to others
4. public executions acted as a warning to others

51. *Candidates can be credited in a number of ways* **up to a maximum of 5 marks.**

Candidates must make an overall judgement about how fully the source explains the events. **1 mark** may be given for each valid point interpreted from the source or each valid point of significant omission provided.

A maximum of 2 marks may be given for answers in which no judgement has been made or which refer only to the source.

Possible points which may be identified in the source include:
1. boys learned military skills such as practising with weapons
2. to toughen them up, they were taken on cross country hikes and runs
3. boys were also tested on their knowledge of Nazism
4. however they did not all enjoy the endless marching

Possible points of significant omission may include:
5. details on "military athletics" (Wehrsport) (eg bayonet drill, grenade throwing, trench digging, map reading, gas defence, use of dugouts, how to get under barbed wire and pistol shooting)
6. compulsory gymnastics/other sporting activities like football/handball
7. competitive boxing matches (where the rules were not as important as beating your opponent)
8. camping trips
9. played musical instruments/learned Nazi songs parades/pageants
10. parades/pageants

Section 3, Context E, Red Flag: Lenin and the Russian Revolution, 1894-1921

52. *Candidates can be credited in a number of ways* **up to a maximum of 5 marks.**

Candidates must make an overall judgement about how fully the source explains the events. **1 mark** may be given for each valid point interpreted from the source or each valid point of significant omission provided.

A maximum of 2 marks may be given for answers in which no judgement has been made or which refer only to the source.

Possible points which may be identified in the source include:
1. police brutality is steadily growing
2. many workers are now imprisoned along with political prisoners
3. millions of peasants...become poorer every year
4. famine is now normal throughout the country

Possible points of significant omission may include:
5. redemption payments and high taxes meant peasants struggle
6. shortage of land/the majority of land owned by nobility
7. backward agricultural techniques led to poor output
8. poor living conditions for peasants (eg one room huts)
9. workers have poor working conditions/many accidents in factories
10. low pay/rising cost of food and fuel

11. workers have poor living conditions/many live in overcrowded conditions
12. lacked basic freedoms (eg free speech, democratic elections)
13. constant fear of arrest by Okhrana

53. *Candidates can be credited in a number of ways **up to a maximum of 5 marks.***

They may take different perspectives on the events and may describe a variety of different aspects of the events.

1 mark should be given for each accurate relevant key point of knowledge.

A second mark should be given for each point that is developed, up to a maximum of **5 marks**. Candidates may achieve full marks by providing five straightforward points, by making three developed points, or a combination of these.

Possible points of knowledge may include:
1. Stolypin Reforms introduced to improve agriculture
2. ended redemption payments
3. allowed peasant families to leave the commune or Mir
4. encouraging peasants to group their strips of land into larger fields/changed the rules of inheritance
5. created the Kulak class
6. Duma was set up/the October Manifesto introduced greater freedoms
7. Trade unions legalised
8. National insurance scheme introduced for industrial workers
9. education extended to increase literacy
10. armed forces modernised

54. *Candidates can be credited in a number of ways **up to a maximum of 5 marks.***

Candidates must show a causal relationship between events.

Up to a **maximum of 5 marks in total**, **1 mark** should be given for each accurate, relevant reason, and a **second mark** should be given for reasons that are developed. Candidates may achieve full marks by providing five straightforward reasons, three developed reasons, or a combination of these.

Possible reasons may include:
1. dual power had weakened authority of Provisional Government
2. Provisional Government losing support due to problems caused by war (eg failure to tackle inflation and shortages)
3. Provisional Government losing support due to failure to tackle the land issue
4. Provisional Government losing support for continuing the war despite military defeats
5. failure to hold quick elections to the Constituent Assembly made it unpopular
6. Provisional Government appeared weak due to Kornilov Revolt
7. Kornilov Revolt had resulted in the arming of Bolshevik Red Guards
8. Bolshevik slogan "Peace, Bread and Land" gained popular support
9. Bolsheviks had been gaining control in the Petrograd Soviet/increasingly Soviets taking charge
10. leadership of Lenin/Trotsky was decisive
11. Military Revolutionary Council set up by Bolsheviks to control army units
12. only Women's Battalion of Death and a few others still defending Government in Winter Palace/seized Winter Palace with little opposition
13. seizure of communication centres prevented help being summoned

14. blocking of transport links prevented help being summoned

55. *Candidates can be credited in a number of ways **up to a maximum of 5 marks.***

Candidates must make a judgement about the usefulness of the source and support this by making evaluative comments on identified aspects of the source.

1 mark should be given for each relevant comment made, up to a **maximum of 5 marks in total**.
- A maximum of **4 marks** can be given for evaluative comments relating to the author, type of source, purpose and timing.
- A maximum of **2 marks** may be given for comments relating to the content of the source.
- A maximum of **2 marks** may be given for comments relating to points of significant omission.

Examples of aspects of the source and relevant comments:

Aspect of the source	Possible comment
Author: Leon Trotsky	Useful as he had first-hand experience/was the commander of the Red Army and therefore well informed
Type of Source: Diary	Useful as it is an honest personal account
Purpose: To record	Less useful as may be limited to his perspective
Timing: 1921	Useful as it written at the time of the Civil War

Content	Possible comment
Formed an army out of peasants, workers and refugees	Useful as it accurately describes groups who supported Bolsheviks
What was needed were good commanders and a few experienced fighters	Useful as it accurately describes how Red Army improved leadership
The mob would fight as long as they had boots for the barefooted, a bathhouse, food, underwear, tobacco/a dozen or so Communists ready to inspire them	Useful as it accurately describes some methods used to improve morale

Possible points of significant omission may include:
1. fear of Cheka
2. Red Terror forced obedience
3. fear of Commissars/using former Tsarist officers by holding families
4. strict discipline within Red Army
5. lack of cooperation between White armies
6. Whites lacked widespread support (eg land issue)
7. Red Army controlled a compact central area/White armies were scattered
8. Reds controlled key industries/transport
9. unpopularity of foreign intervention/Bolshevik propaganda

Section 3, Context F, Mussolini and Fascist Italy, 1919–1939

56. *Candidates can be credited in a number of ways up to a maximum of 5 marks.*

Candidates must show a causal relationship between events.

Up to a **maximum of 5 marks in total**, **1 mark** should be given for each accurate, relevant reason, and a **second mark** should be given for reasons that are developed. Candidates may achieve full marks by providing five straightforward reasons, three developed reasons, or a combination of these.

Possible reasons may include:
1. Mussolini exploited weaknesses of other groups by use of his newspaper "Il Popolo D'Italia"
2. by 1921 fascism was anti-communist, anti-trade union, anti-socialist and pro-nationalism and thus became attractive to the middle and upper classes
3. fascism became pro-conservative, appealed to family values, supported church and monarchy
4. promised to work within the accepted political system (this made fascism more respectable and appealing to both the monarchy and the papacy)
5. violence showed fascism was strong and ruthless (it appealed to many ex-soldiers)
6. middle class frightened by Communism/fascists appeared to be only ones prepared to stand up to Communists
7. fascists promised strong government. This was attractive after a period of extreme instability
8. Mussolini attracted many with his powerful oratory. Mussolini manipulated his image, kept out of violence himself but exploited the violence of others
9. Parliamentary government was weak – informal "liberal" coalitions. Corruption was commonplace (transformismo)
10. the Acerbo law was used to secure a Fascist parliamentary majority
11. the King gave in to Fascist pressure during the March on Rome. He failed to call Mussolini's bluff
12. after the Aventine Secession the King was unwilling to dismiss Mussolini
13. Mussolini's political opponents were divided and this weakened them
14. Mussolini's Blackshirts terrorised the cities and provinces causing fear with tactics such as force-feeding with toads and castor oil
15. destruction of opposition press severely weakened them

57. *Candidates can be credited in a number of ways up to a maximum of 5 marks.*

They may take different perspectives on the events and may describe a variety of different aspects of the events.

1 mark should be given for each accurate relevant key point of knowledge.
A second mark should be given for each point that is developed, up to a maximum of **5 marks**. Candidates may achieve full marks by providing five straightforward points, by making three developed points, or a combination of these.

Possible points of knowledge may include:
1. from 1925 teachers with suspect political views could be dismissed
2. from 1929 all teachers were required to take an oath of loyalty to the regime
3. in 1931 a Fascist Teachers Association was set up to regulate the profession. Membership was compulsory by 1937

4. in schools, the cult of personality was heavily promoted (the Duce's portrait had to be hung alongside that of the King)
5. teachers were ordered to stress the genius and strength of Mussolini
6. children were taught the importance of obedience in the Fascist state/textbooks were altered
7. in history children were taught that Italy had been the cradle of European civilisation and that Italians had always been at the forefront of events. Italy's role in the First World War was exaggerated
8. The Fascist Youth movement, the Opera Nazionale Balliala (ONB) was set up to control young people's leisure activities
9. The Ballila and Avanguardista provided military and ideological training as well as sports and fitness training for boys
10. in the Piccole Italiane and Giovani Italiane, girls were prepared for a traditional role by being taught sewing and child care
11. at university level, the Gruppi Universitari Fascisti (GUF) provided further sporting and military training/students had to join to further careers

58. *Candidates can be credited in a number of ways up to a maximum of 5 marks.*

Candidates must make an overall judgement about how fully the source explains the events. **1 mark** may be given for each valid point interpreted from the source or each valid point of significant omission provided.

A maximum of 2 marks may be given for answers in which no judgement has been made or which refer only to the source.

Possible points which may be identified in the source include:
1. media played an important role in establishing the cult of "Il Duce"
2. the cult was intended to build popular support for the dictator and to secure support for the government
3. Benito Mussolini was shown as a man chosen by destiny to save Italy and its people from Communism and Socialism
4. he was the new Caesar/a man of genius/a man of action

Possible points of significant omission may include:
5. Mussolini started a new calendar with Year 1 beginning in 1922
6. the regime made propagandist feature films
7. the Duce was shown as a great athlete and musician
8. always uniformed to portray strength and aggression
9. the newspapers suggested that Mussolini was infallible
10. an image of youthfulness was portrayed by not referring to Mussolini's age or the fact he wore glasses
11. it was said that Mussolini worked 16 hour days. His light was left on after he had gone to bed to maintain this fiction
12. indoctrination of children into "cult" (eg school textbooks/fascist youth groups)

59. *Candidates can be credited in a number of ways up to a maximum of 5 marks.*

Candidates must make a judgement about the usefulness of the source and support this by making evaluative comments on identified aspects of the source.

1 mark should be given for each relevant comment made, up to a **maximum of 5 marks in total**.
- A maximum of 4 marks can be given for evaluative comments relating to the author, type of source, purpose and timing.
- A maximum of 2 marks may be given for comments relating to the content of the source.

- A maximum of 2 marks may be given for comments relating to points of significant omission.

Examples of aspects of the source and relevant comments:

Aspect of the source	Possible comment
Author: Mussolini	Useful as he was in charge of Fascist foreign policy/first-hand experience
Type of Source: A speech	Less useful as Mussolini might exaggerate as this is intended for public consumption.
Purpose: To persuade	Less useful as Mussolini would be keen to justify military action/offers a one-sided view
Timing: 1922	Useful as Mussolini was in power with responsibility for Fascist foreign policy

Content	Possible comment
Perfect unity in Italy cannot be spoken of until Fiume and Dalmatia and other territories have come back to us	Useful as it is accurate/Mussolini did target Fiume (which became an Italian possession in 1924)
Violence may have to be used	Useful as it is accurate/Fascist ideology did glorify the use of violence
Italy, in order to become a Mediterranean power, must have control over the Adriatic sea	Useful as it is accurate/Mussolini was obsessed with making the Mediterranean an "Italian lake"

Possible points of significant omission may include:
1. Mussolini aimed to make Italy a great power/new Roman Empire
2. he wanted to expand Italy's colonial empire in Africa
3. he wanted to increase Italian influence in the Balkans
4. in early years of power he aimed to appear as peaceful statesman (eg Locarno 1925)
5. he wanted to reverse Italy's humiliation at Versailles (eg bombardment of Corfu)
6. wanted to act to stop German expansion after 1933 (eg in Austria/Stresa Front)
7. he wanted to encourage friendly regimes abroad and discourage Socialism/Communism, eg in Spain
8. latterly he wanted to adopt a more aggressive foreign policy to distract public attention away from problems at home
9. Axis/Pact of Steel – Italian foreign policy in conjunction with Germany eg Munich Conference
10. played crucial role as mediator at Munich Conference Sept 1938/tried to appear as a moderate

Section 3, Context G, Free at Last? Civil Rights in the USA, 1918-1968

60. *Candidates can be credited in a number of ways up to a maximum of 5 marks.*

They may take different perspectives on the events and may describe a variety of different aspects of the events.

1 mark should be given for each accurate relevant key point of knowledge.

A second mark should be given for each point that is developed, up to a maximum of **5 marks**. Candidates may achieve full marks by providing five straightforward points, by making three developed points, or a combination of these.

Possible points of knowledge may include:
1. separate restaurants
2. separate schools
3. separate toilets, drinking fountains and restrooms
4. separate carriages on busses/trains
5. separate entrances and wards in hospitals
6. separate graveyards
7. separate leisure and sporting facilities
8. in some states marriage between whites and blacks was forbidden

61. *Candidates can be credited in a number of ways up to a maximum of 5 marks.*

Candidates must show a causal relationship between events.

Up to a **maximum of 5 marks in total**, **1 mark** should be given for each accurate, relevant reason, and a **second mark** should be given for reasons that are developed. Candidates may achieve full marks by providing five straightforward reasons, three developed reasons, or a combination of these.

Possible reasons may include:
1. unemployment increased after the war/immigrants were accused of taking jobs from Americans
2. concern that immigrant workers were forcing wages down by working for less
3. concern that immigrants would be used by employers to break strikes
4. WASPs feared "inferior" immigrants from south and east Europe would threaten their way of life/new immigrants had different religions
5. concern that immigrants would create pressure on scarce housing
6. feeling that new immigrants who were uneducated and illiterate had little to contribute to American life/spoke different languages
7. immigrants were often blamed for crime, disease, alcoholism and other social problems in cities
8. new immigrants often settled amongst people from their own countries leading to a perception that they were unwilling to mix with other Americans
9. fear of political unrest from communist and socialist immigrants

62. *Candidates can be credited in a number of ways up to a maximum of 5 marks.*

Candidates must make an overall judgement about how fully the source explains the events. **1 mark** may be given for each valid point interpreted from the source or each valid point of significant omission provided.

A maximum of 2 marks may be given for answers in which no judgement has been made or which refer only to the source.

Possible points which may be identified in the source include:
1. wearing white robes and pointed hats
2. during elections, the Klan would wait outside the voting place to beat up blacks if they came near
3. a divorced woman in Texas was tarred and feathered for remarrying
4. a massive march in Washington DC in 1925

Possible points of significant omission may include:
5. the Klan held elaborate ceremonies and used a coded language
6. the Klan were intimidating (eg burned large crosses on hillsides and near the homes of people they wished to frighten)
7. the Klan brutally assaulted many blacks/night raids on black households
8. the Klan lynched many blacks
9. the Klan bombed and burned churches, schools and other meeting places used by black people
10. use of propaganda/advertised to gain larger membership
11. influenced all aspects of local authority (eg courts, police departments)

63. *Candidates can be credited in a number of ways **up to a maximum of 5 marks.***

Candidates must make a judgement about the usefulness of the source and support this by making evaluative comments on identified aspects of the source.

1 mark should be given for each relevant comment made, up to a **maximum of 5 marks in total.**
- A maximum of **4 marks** can be given for evaluative comments relating to the author, type of source, purpose and timing.
- A maximum of **2 marks** may be given for comments relating to the content of the source.
- A maximum of **2 marks** may be given for comments relating to points of significant omission.

Examples of aspects of the source and relevant comments:

Aspect of the source	Possible comment
Author: A black American taxi driver	Useful as he eyewitness/first-hand experience of Malcolm X/a member of the black American community
Type of Source: Newspaper interview	Useful as it contains an honest opinion/may be less useful as possibility of bias
Purpose: To inform	Useful as the interview provides several reasons for supporting Malcolm X
Timing: 1961	Useful as it is from the time when Malcolm X was a leading figure

Content	Possible comment
I can believe in a leader who comes from the street, Malcolm is one of us	Useful as it is accurate/many black Americans did relate to a leader who had grown up in a predominantly black neighbourhood
Malcolm isn't afraid to stand up to the FBI and the cops	Useful as it is accurate/police harassment and brutality was a common complaint amongst black Americans
Those black Muslims make more sense than the NAACP and all of the rest of them put together, you don't see Malcolm tip-toeing around the whites like he's scared of them	Useful as it is accurate/many did support Malcolm X's belief that blacks had the right to defend themselves with the use of violence

Possible points of significant omission may include:
1. Malcolm X was a charismatic figure and speaker who gained support from his public speeches and his appearances on television

2. many agreed with Malcolm X that white Americans were inherently racist and blacks could only gain true equality if they separated from white society
3. Malcolm X encouraged blacks to be proud of the colour of their skin and their African American culture – this appealed to many

Section 3, Context H, Appeasement and the Road to War, 1918-1939

64. *Candidates can be credited in a number of ways **up to a maximum of 5 marks.***

They may take different perspectives on the events and may describe a variety of different aspects of the events.

1 mark should be given for each accurate relevant key point of knowledge. **A second mark** should be given for each point that is developed, up to a maximum of **5 marks.** Candidates may achieve full marks by providing five straightforward points, by making three developed points, or a combination of these.

Possible points of knowledge may include:
1. Hitler instructed industry to begin the secret production of new tanks, aircraft and other weapons
2. by 1934, Hitler had doubled the size of the German army
3. Hitler built up an air force of 2000 planes by the end of 1934
4. Hitler introduced conscription to the German army/ greatly expanded the office corps
5. by the end of 1935 the German army totalled over 500,000 men
6. the Anglo-German Naval agreement was signed giving Germany permission to build up its navy to a level that was 35% of Britain's naval strength

65. *Candidates can be credited in a number of ways **up to a maximum of 5 marks.***

Candidates must make a judgement about the usefulness of the source and support this by making evaluative comments on identified aspects of the source.

1 mark should be given for each relevant comment made, up to a **maximum of 5 marks in total.**
- A maximum of **4 marks** can be given for evaluative comments relating to the author, type of source, purpose and timing.
- A maximum of **2 marks** may be given for comments relating to the content of the source.
- A maximum of **2 marks** may be given for comments relating to points of significant omission.

Examples of aspects of the source and relevant comments:

Aspect of the source	Possible comment
Author: Historian	Useful as it is written by a well-informed expert
Type of Source: Article (from a modern history journal)	Useful as it will have been well-researched
Purpose: To inform	Useful as it gives a balanced insight in to the consequences of the Anschluss
Timing: 2008	Useful as it was written with the benefit of hindsight

Content	Possible comment
It marked the beginning of Germany's territorial expansion, starting a chain of events which continued with the occupation of the Sudetenland	Useful as it is accurate/Germany did gain control of the Sudetenland by October 1938
The lack of meaningful opposition from Britain and France underlined again for Hitler that he could do as he pleased	Useful as it is accurate/ Hitler's aggressive actions over Czechoslovakia and Poland did suggest that he did not believe Britain and France would take action against him
The persecution of Jews was greatly intensified following the Anschluss, especially in Austria	Useful as it is accurate/persecution of Jews did start immediately after German troops entered Austria

Possible points of significant omission may include:

1. Germany added 100,000 Austrian troops to the German army
2. Germany gained useful economic resources such as iron, steel and other raw materials
3. Czechoslovakia was under threat as it was now surrounded on three fronts by Germany
4. lack of action against Germany encouraged Hitler further
5. enhanced Hitler's popularity

66. *Candidates can be credited in a number of ways up to a maximum of 5 marks.*

Candidates must make an overall judgement about how fully the source explains the events. **1 mark** may be given for each valid point interpreted from the source or each valid point of significant omission provided.

A maximum of 2 marks may be given for answers in which no judgement has been made or which refer only to the source.

Possible points which may be identified in the source include:

1. a belief that given the harsh treatment of Germany at Versailles, Hitler's demands were not unreasonable
2. the British public were still haunted by memories of World War One and unwilling to back military action
3. Chiefs of the armed forces advised that that the British military was unprepared for war
4. the Treasury meanwhile warned against the financial consequences of war

Possible points of significant omission may include:

5. Germany had rearmed with a powerful army, navy and air force
6. by appeasing Hitler, Britain bought itself time to re-arm and strengthen the military
7. there was fear of war due to the likely destruction caused by bombing from the air
8. lack of allies – Empire countries unwilling, USA isolationist and France not trusted
9. Britain wanted a stronger Germany to prevent Communist expansion
10. fear of war and its impact on the British Empire

67. *Candidates can be credited in a number of ways up to a maximum of 5 marks.*

Candidates must show a causal relationship between events.

Up to a **maximum of 5 marks in total**, **1 mark** should be given for each accurate, relevant reason, and a **second mark** should be given for reasons that are developed. Candidates may achieve full marks by providing five straightforward reasons, three developed reasons, or a combination of these.

Possible reasons may include:

1. Germany had a grievance over land lost to Poland at the end of World War One
2. millions of Germans were forced to live under Polish rule
3. Danzig, a German town and free city under the League, was run to suit the Poles
4. The "Polish Corridor" divided East Prussia from the rest of Germany
5. A successful invasion of Poland would be popular/ provide land for Lebensraum
6. Hitler regarded the Poles as inferior (untermenschen)
7. The Nazi-Soviet Pact meant that Russia would not protect Poland
8. The Pact of Steel had assured Germany of Italy's support
9. Hitler did not believe that Britain would help Poland in the event of war

Section 3, Context I, World War II, 1939–1945

68. *Candidates can be credited in a number of ways up to a maximum of 5 marks.*

Candidates must show a causal relationship between events.

Up to a **maximum of 5 marks in total**, **1 mark** should be given for each accurate, relevant reason, and a **second mark** should be given for reasons that are developed. Candidates may achieve full marks by providing five straightforward reasons, three developed reasons, or a combination of these.

Possible reasons may include:

1. Hitler hated the Communist ideals of the USSR/thought Communism was a threat to Germany
2. Hitler believed in the expansion rights of the Master Race and wanted Russian land as Lebensraum (living space)/declared plans to invade in Mein Kampf
3. Hitler believed the Russian army would be easily defeated due to Russia's failure in the Finnish war/as well as by purge of Red army
4. believed USSR would be an easy target/fall in 6 to 8 weeks
5. Hitler wanted to enslave the Russian people (untermenschen) to work for the German Master Race
6. Hitler wanted valuable resources contained in Russia eg grain, oil, iron ore/Germany was running short of vital raw materials by 1940
7. Hitler believed Russia to be a threat to Germany's interests in the Balkans and Scandinavia
8. Stalin had resisted joining Germany, Italy and Japan in the Tripartite Pact of 1940
9. Nazi–Soviet Pact of 1939 was only an alliance of convenience so that Hitler could successfully invade Poland/Hitler did not trust Stalin
10. conquest of Russia would force Britain to surrender

69. *Candidates can be credited in a number of ways up to a maximum of 5 marks.*

They may take different perspectives on the events and may describe a variety of different aspects of the events.

1 mark should be given for each accurate relevant key point of knowledge.
A second mark should be given for each point that is developed, up to a maximum of **5 marks**. Candidates may achieve full marks by providing five straightforward points, by making three developed points, or a combination of these.

Possible points of knowledge may include:
1. surprise attack on the morning of December 7th 1941
2. Japanese bombers, fighter and torpedo planes were launched from six aircraft carriers in the Pacific
3. attack came in two waves and lasted around 2 hours
4. Japanese attacked US battleships and airfields
5. USS Arizona exploded when a bomb hit the ship's magazine, killing approximately 1,100 men
6. USS Oklahoma was torpedoed and listed so badly that it turned upside down
7. Japanese sent in 5 midget subs to aid the air force/Americans sunk 4 of the midget subs and captured the 5th
8. all battleships stationed at Pearl Harbour were sunk or damaged
9. over 2,400 Americans were dead/21 ships had been sunk or damaged/over 188 US aircraft destroyed
10. Japanese lost only 29 aircraft and 65 killed
11. Japanese missed main targets as American aircraft carriers at sea

70. *Candidates can be credited in a number of ways up to a maximum of 5 marks.*

Candidates must make an overall judgement about how fully the source explains the events. **1 mark** may be given for each valid point interpreted from the source or each valid point of significant omission provided.

A maximum of 2 marks may be given for answers in which no judgement has been made or which refer only to the source.

Possible points which may be identified in the source include:
1. preparations began in 1943 under the overall command of General Eisenhower of the United States
2. Normandy was chosen as the site for the landings because of its open beaches that were not as well defended as those at Calais
3. Normandy was also chosen because it had a fairly large port, Cherbourg
4. it was also opposite the main ports of southern England

Possible points of significant omission may include:
5. deception plans intended to fool Germans into believing an attack would come at Pas de Calais or Norway/Allies had decoded German messages which gave the Allies an advantage
6. imaginary army units/rubber tanks/inflatable aircraft were stationed at areas around the Kent coast (opposite Calais)
7. double agents operated to pass false information to Germans (Garbo)
8. massive drive to manufacture equipment including transport ships, landing craft, amphibious tanks, etc.
9. floating harbours constructed on Clydeside (Mulberry Harbours)
10. pipe-line laid under the channel to transport fuel (Pluto)
11. large numbers of soldiers trained in Devon and on Scottish coasts, amongst other places/mobilised in secret to Southern England

12. prior to invasion, Allied air forces targeted the railways and bridges of northern France to stop any counter-attack
13. coordination with French Resistance

71. *Candidates can be credited in a number of ways up to a maximum of 5 marks.*

Candidates must make a judgement about the usefulness of the source and support this by making evaluative comments on identified aspects of the source.

1 mark should be given for each relevant comment made, up to a **maximum of 5 marks in total.**
- A maximum of 4 marks can be given for evaluative comments relating to the author, type of source, purpose and timing.
- A maximum of 2 marks may be given for comments relating to the content of the source.
- A maximum of 2 marks may be given for comments relating to points of significant omission.

Examples of aspects of the source and relevant comments:

Aspect of the source	Possible comment
Author: US Government	Useful as it is a first-hand account
Type of Source: Leaflet	Less useful as it is a propaganda leaflet
Purpose: To persuade	Useful as it is an attempt to frighten the Japanese into surrendering
Timing: 16 August 1945	Useful as this leaflet comes from the time atomic bombs were dropped over Japan

Content	Possible comment
In possession of the most destructive explosive devised by man	Useful as it is accurate/the US were first to design the bomb
We have just begun to use this weapon against your country/ask what happened to Hiroshima	Useful as it is accurate/the first bomb had already been dropped on Hiroshima
Take steps now to surrender. Otherwise we shall use this bomb again to promptly and forcefully end the war	Useful as it is accurate/the US did threaten to drop a second bomb unless Japan surrendered

Possible points of significant omission may include:
1. US used atomic bombs to avoid losing men in an invasion of Japan
2. Hiroshima bombed using the uranium bomb "Little Boy"
3. bomb killed 70–80,000 people immediately (70,000 were to die of after effects)
4. Hiroshima chosen to be completely destroyed as an entire city/was not a military target
5. 3 days after the first bomb on Hiroshima, Nagasaki was attacked with the second bomb "Fat Man"
6. 40% of Nagasaki was destroyed, approximately 70,000 died by the end of the year
7. effects of bombing: instant vaporisation, severe burns, radiation poisoning/sickness
8. led to Japan formally surrendering

Section 3, Context J, The Cold War, 1945–1989

72. *Candidates can be credited in a number of ways up to a maximum of 5 marks.*

Candidates must make a judgement about the usefulness of the source and support this by making evaluative comments on identified aspects of the source.

1 mark should be given for each relevant comment made, up to a maximum of 5 marks in total.

- A maximum of 4 marks can be given for evaluative comments relating to the author, type of source, purpose and timing.
- A maximum of 2 marks may be given for comments relating to the content of the source.
- A maximum of 2 marks may be given for comments relating to points of significant omission.

Examples of aspects of the source and relevant comments:

Aspect of the source	Possible comment
Author: East German government	Useful as it is a first-hand account
Type of Source: Leaflet	Useful as it is an attempt to justify the building of the Berlin Wall
Purpose: To persuade	Less useful as it is a propaganda leaflet
Timing: 1962	Useful as it is from the time that the Wall was built

Content	Possible comment
We could no longer stand by and see so many of our doctors, engineers and skilled workers persuaded by corrupt methods to work in West Germany or West Berlin	Useful as it is accurate (East Germany was concerned about losing population)
These dirty tricks cost East Germany annual losses amounting to 3.5 thousand million marks	Useful as it is accurate (East Germany was concerned about economic damage)
But we prevented something much more important with the Wall – West Berlin could have become the starting point for military conflict.	Useful as it is accurate (East Germany was concerned about military escalation)

Possible points of significant omission may include:

1. West Berlin/Germany was attractive because it was more prosperous than the East
2. West Berlin/Germany was attractive because it had more democratic freedoms than the East
3. East Germans feared that open border in Berlin enabled the West to spy more easily
4. food shortages in 1960 in the East (following enforced collectivisation) added to the urge to leave
5. departures from the East made Communism look bad.
6. fear of what would happen in other East European states if exodus continued

73. *Candidates can be credited in a number of ways up to a maximum of 5 marks.*

Candidates must make an overall judgement about how fully the source explains the events. **1 mark** may be given for each valid point interpreted from the source or each valid point of significant omission provided.

A maximum of 2 marks may be given for answers in which no judgement has been made or which refer only to the source.

Possible points which may be identified in the source include:

1. crisis in Cuba because by the early 1960s the USA and the Soviet Union were bitter rivals
2. many in the United States believed that the Soviet actions in Cuba provided proof of a determination to spread Communism all around the world
3. Cuba was very close to the American mainland and this explains why Americans were so concerned by events there
4. both sides were afraid to back down in case they lost face

Possible points of significant omission may include:

5. Cuban leader Castro had formed a close alliance with the Soviet Union which alarmed the USA
6. Castro had angered American businesses by nationalising key industries
7. American spy planes revealed evidence of missile bases being constructed in Cuba
8. Soviet convoys carrying missiles to Cuba caused alarm
9. American public opinion would not accept the threat posed by Soviet missiles on the island.
10. fear in America that their country was falling behind in the Cold War
11. Kennedy was looking for an opportunity to take revenge after the failed Bay of Pigs invasion

74. *Candidates can be credited in a number of ways up to a maximum of 5 marks.*

They may take different perspectives on the events and may describe a variety of different aspects of the events.

1 mark should be given for each accurate relevant key point of knowledge.

A second mark should be given for each point that is developed, up to a maximum of **5 marks**. Candidates may achieve full marks by providing five straightforward points, by making three developed points, or a combination of these.

Possible points of knowledge may include:

1. many supported it as they believed America was defending freedom and democracy
2. many supported it as they believed it was the job of America to fight Communism
3. many supported it because of fear of the domino theory
4. many supported it as they believed it was a response to North Vietnamese aggression in the Gulf of Tonkin
5. unpopularity of the draft/the draft was disproportionate in taking poor Blacks
6. opposition to the war grew because of the media coverage of high casualties, lack of success, etc.
7. evidence of atrocities such as the My Lai massacre weakened support
8. anti-war protests and demonstrations grew
9. cost of the war led to growing opposition
10. some were concerned that the war was preventing social progress in America (eg Martin Luther King)

75. Candidates can be credited in a number of ways up to a maximum of 5 marks.

Candidates must show a causal relationship between events.

Up to a **maximum of 5 marks in total**, 1 mark should be given for each accurate, relevant reason, and a **second mark** should be given for reasons that are developed. Candidates may achieve full marks by providing five straightforward reasons, three developed reasons, or a combination of these.

Possible reasons may include:
1. in the 1960s they came to the brink of nuclear war and wanted to avoid similar crises
2. Brezhnev felt the economic burden of the nuclear arms race was too great
3. the American economy was in financial trouble as a result of the Vietnam war/growing social unrest called for a reassessment of spending priorities
4. the Soviets hoped for better relations with Western Europe, perhaps detaching them from the USA
5. the Soviet leadership was terrified of a possible Sino-American alliance
6. both sides had achieved rough parity in nuclear arms so continuing an arms race seemed pointless
7. a state of mutually assured destruction (MAD) had been reached
9. both Brezhnev and Nixon thought that it would boost their domestic popularity
10. Brezhnev was intent on using a period of détente to prepare for Soviet expansion in the 1980s

Acknowledgements

Permission has been sought from all relevant copyright holders and Hodder Gibson is grateful for the use of the following:

Source B: An extract from 'Dear Francesca' by Mary Contini, published by Ebury Press © The Random House Group Ltd. 2003 (2014 page 6);
Source A: 'The War Memoirs of David Lloyd George' 1938, published by Odhams (public domain) (2014 page 7);
Source A: An extract from 'Black Peoples of the Americas' by Nigel Smith, published by Oxford University Press, 1995 (2014 page 10);
Source A: An extract from a report on housing in Manchester, written by a doctor in 1832. Taken from 'The Report from the Poor Law Commissioners on an Inquiry into the Sanitary Conditions of the Labouring Population of Great Britain, London, 1842' by Edwin Chadwick (2014 page 11);
Source A: An extract from 'From the Cradle to the Grave: Social Welfare in Britain 1890s–1951' by Simon Wood & Claire Wood, published by Hodder Gibson 2002 (2014 page 12);
Source B: An extract from 'Leaves from an Inspector's Logbook' by John Kerr. Published by Thomas Nelson (2015 page 17);
Source A: An extract from 'Lark Rise to Candleford' by Flora Thompson, published by Oxford University Press, 1939 (2015 page 18);
Source A: An extract from 'Roads to War: The Origins of the Second World War, 1924-1941' by Josh Brooman, published by Longman, 1989 © Pearson Education (2015 page 26);
Source A: An extract from 'Scotland and the Impact of the Great War 1914–1928' by John Kerr, published by Hodder Gibson, 2010 (2016 page 7);
Source A: An extract from http://www.bbc.co.uk/history/historic_figures/charles_i_king.shtml © BBC 2014 (2016 page 10);
Source B: An extract from 'Charles I' by C.N. Trueman, taken from http://www.historylearningsite.co.ukstuart-england/charles-i/ © The History Learning Site, 17 Mar 2015 & 16 Aug 2016 (2016 page 10);
Source B: An extract from 'Black Peoples of the Americas' by Bob Rees and Marika Sherwood, published by Heinemann Educational Publishers, 1992 (2016 page 13);
Source A: An extract from 'Cannibals All! Or, Slaves Without Masters' by George Fitzhugh, published by A. Morris, 1857, Richmond V.A. (2016 page 20);
Source B: An extract from 'Trotsky's Diary in Exile, 1935' by Leon Trotsky, published by Harvard University Press, 1958 (2016 page 22);
Source A: An extract from 'Access to History: Italy: The Rise of Fascism 1915–1945' by Mark Robson (3rd edition), published by Hodder Education 2006 (2016 page 23);
Source B: An extract from an article by Professor Neil Gregor in '20th Century History Review' published by Philip Allan Updates, 2008 (2016 page 25).